D1087407

THE STRUCTURAL REVOLUTION

THE STRUCTURAL REVOLUTION

Jean-Marie Benoist

St. Martin's Press
New York

This book was first published in France
by Bernard Grasset in 1975 under the title
La Révolution Structurale

English translation © 1978 Jean-Marie Benoist

All rights reserved. For information, write:
St. Martin's Press, Inc., 175 Fifth Avenue, New York, N.Y. 10010
Printed in Great Britain
Library of Congress Catalog Card Number 78–5298
ISBN 0–312–76698–X
First published in the United States of America in 1978

Library of Congress Cataloging in Publication Data

Benoist, Jean-Marie.
    The structural revolution.

    Translation of La révolution structurale.
    Includes bibliographical references and index.
    1. Structuralism.   I.   Title.
B841.4.B4813   149′.9   78–5298
ISBN 0–312–76698–X

Contents

Acknowledgements

The author wishes to thank the editors and publishers of the following journals and book in which these essays originally appeared:

Twentieth Century Studies (the University of Kent) for 'The End of Structuralism';

Allen Lane, the Penguin Press and Jonathan Benthall, editor of the collection of essays, *The Limits of Human Nature* (1973), in which 'Classicism Revisited: Human Nature and Structure in Chomsky and Lévi-Strauss' originally appeared;

The Human Context, Chaucer Publishing Co. Ltd, London, for 'The Art of the Fugue'. This essay appeared in French and in English in volume V, no. 1, 1973 of *The Human Context*. Originally written in French, it has been translated into English by Dr Arnold Pomerans to whom I wish to express my gratitude for the remarkable translation he has achieved.

My thanks are also due to Jonathan Benthall and Dr Stephen Bann, editors respectively of *The Limits of Human Nature*, and the *Twentieth Century Studies*; not only have they offered the hospitality of their publications to my writings, but they have also provided help and advice about the formulation in English of my ideas. To the stimulating intellectual relationship I enjoy with them, I should also mention, although I cannot adequately acknowledge, the invaluable friendship they have shown to me.

And, last but not least, Robert Olorenshaw, who translated all the remaining chapters, deserves my particular thanks for his indispensable work. His patience and his knowledge of French thinking have been invaluable. Their only rival is the kindness and patience of my publishers, which is beyond praise.

1. Structuralism:
A New Frontier

Man is an invention whose recent date, and
whose approaching end, perhaps, is clearly
evident from the archaeology of our thought.

Michel Foucault, *Les mots et les choses.*

'What is structuralism?' writes Roland Barthes. 'It is not a
school of thought, or even a movement, for most of the authors
habitually associated with this word do not feel in any way
bound together by a common doctrine or cause. It is hardly a
well-defined term: *structure* is a word of long standing (derived
from anatomy and grammar) which today suffers from excessive
use.' One might indeed go so far as to say that structuralism
exists only for those who do not participate in it, and look on
from the outside; or that structuralism is analogous to Sartre's
view of consciousness – it is what it is not, and it is not what it is.
Certainly structuralism is the object of a number of curious
disclaimers. Lacan refers in the preface to *Scilicet* (the review
which he has recently founded) to the 'poubellication structur-
aliste' into which he has been in danger of being thrown.
Foucault claims that he pays no attention at all to reviews of his
work in which he is called a structuralist, since, in *Les mots et
les choses*, he does not once use the word structure.

The term structure has therefore been used and reused, and,
as if by a sort of entropy, it has been distorted and trivialized.
An attempt must therefore be made to restore it to its proper

place. A starting point might be the following remark by Barthes:

> The aim of all structuralist activity, in the fields of both thought and poetry, is to reconstitute an object, and, by this process, to make known the rules of functioning, or 'functions', of this object. The structure is therefore effectively a *simulacrum* of the object, but it is a simulation that is both purposeful and relevant, since the object derived by this process brings out something that remained invisible, or, if you like, unintelligible in the natural object . . . The simulacrum is intellect added to the object.

In this particular case, the device used consists in a kind of *mimesis*, which, by contrast with the classical *mimesis* first described by Plato, rests on an analogy not so much of substances but of functions, or homology. It therefore seems clear that, even though the concept of structure has been transferred from the particular field of linguistics opened up by Saussure and developed by Jakobson, the structuralist activity so derived, according to a rigorous process, cannot be reduced to a mere phenomenological description. On the contrary, it seems ready to integrate new methods, and entirely new patterns, always provided that they can be related to a formal possibility. 'To make known the rules of functioning' – such a programme is capable of comprising, as we shall observe, both the 'archaeology' of Foucault, as set forth in his recent book, *L'Archéologie du savoir*, and the relationship between deep structures and surface structures in language postulated by Chomsky. Indeed these are only two of the possibilities offered by a disciplined use of the notion of structure. Structuralism is a method, not a doctrine. Thus, although those who have attracted this label may be shown to have a number of methodological presuppositions in common, and even a convergent approach, we should bear it in mind that it would be more appropriate to speak of structuralism*s*, in the plural. In this way, the specific nature of the various trends would be respected, and at the same time three distinct sources for the notion of structuralism would be taken into account: philosophy, mathematics and linguistics. Even if we claim that these three focuses have remained essentially distinct, this is not to deny any sort of mutual influence or relationship. As in the field of modern music, we are entitled to speak of a *polyphony* within structuralism.

Structuralism in linguistics originated in the work of Baudouin de Courthenay and Ferdinand de Saussure. From this point of departure, one can trace a particular line of research centred around the problem of the *sign*, which has passed beyond linguistics into the field of ethnology, with Lévi-Strauss, and psychoanalysis, with Lacan. Saussure's seminal idea is that language ('la langue'), taken in isolation from the context of concrete expression, and from the historical evolution of such forms of expression, constitutes a self-regulating object of scientific inquiry and forms a system whose intrinsic arrangement lends itself to description. Within this system, the nature of the linguistic object is governed by the fact that the elements of 'la langue' can only be defined in terms of the relationship of opposition which establish its interdependence with the others. Each element is in itself colourless (to use Wittgenstein's image), and it takes its value, function and meaning from its relationship to the rest of the system as a whole.

Saussure expressed this principle of interdependence very satisfactorily through the metaphor of the chessboard: the various pieces are related not only in terms of their actual position, but also in terms of the potential moves offered to them by the rules of the game. The corollary of this principle is that a sign *signifies* only by virtue of the differential gap which associates it with other signs. What makes the sign a sign, a relevant item of meaning, cannot be discovered in its entity as a 'chunk' – a positive 'bit' of language – but in the very reverse: in the empty distance which differentiates *dawn* from *down*, for example; in an unqualifiable space that is simply an interplay of differences. Mallarmé writes: 'Je dis: *une fleur*, et, hors de l'oubli où ma voix relègue aucun contour, en tant que quelque chose d'autre que les calices sus, musicalement se lève, idée même et suave, l'absente de tous bouquets.' The absence that Mallarmé speaks of is not merely the difference between the sign and its referent ('les calices sus'), but also, by extension, the difference between one sign and another within the framework of language: a difference or absence that is the very root of meaning and relevance.

Saussure's notion of a *systematic relation of difference* has opened the way to scientific descriptions in terms of systems of opposition. In ethnology, for example, Lévi-Strauss classifies kinship systems according to rules of opposition and formal interdependence;[1] within the syntax of these rules, women circulate through marriages between clans and families, constituting a 'message' in much the same way as words circulate between members of the group. Both cases offer systems of communication which obey well-defined syntactical rules. In *La Pensée sauvage*, Lévi-Strauss develops the example of the totemic system of oppositions, which is another case of the structural correspondence of linguistics and anthropology.

A great number of structural techniques derive from Saussure's original notion. Yet it is fashionable among linguists to dismiss Saussure as insufficiently precise. While such an objection may be valid, one wonders why the linguisticians are so reluctant to admit the prime importance of Saussure's systematic approach, the first attempt to define language as a self-referring form. What is Austin's definition of the 'performative' in *How to Do Things With Words* if not an attempt to isolate structures within a self-referring field?

In a similar way, Lévi-Strauss's anthropology has incurred the reproach of being unscientific from two sides: from the literary critic who is himself perhaps not notable for rigour and coherence, and from the 'pure' linguisticain who detects a metaphorical importation of linguistic terms into a field which is alien to them. Leaving aside the former, who will continue to cultivate his 'arrière-garde' dream in all the refinement of a nebulous romantic ego, we might easily allow Lévi-Strauss himself to reply to the latter:

When studying problems of kinship, the sociologist is placed in a situation that is formally comparable to that of the phonologist. Like phonemes, the terms of kinship are elements of signification. Like them, they only acquire this signification on the condition of becoming part of a system. Systems of kinship, like phonological systems, are elaborated by the mind at the stage of unconscious thought.[2]

It is worth noting that Lévi-Strauss is well aware of the dangers of too broad a homology between different types of system, and that his syntactic parallel is very carefully drawn. Again, in his treatment of the relationships between systems of attitudes and systems of appellations, Lévi-Strauss is quick to remark:

> This reconstruction has a hypothetical character: in performing it, the anthropologist proceeds from the better-known to the less well-known: structures of kinship are familiar to him; but not those of the languages which correspond. Are the differential characteristics (enumerated above) still relevant on the linguistic level? *The answer belongs to the linguist.*[3] [My italics.]

We might also ask the linguistician *quid juris*? What is the epistemological basis for his claim against the anthropologist? Is linguistics itself an exact science? One is obliged to conclude that, as long as the linguistician has failed to clarify his methodological assumptions and establish the exact status of his approach, he is not entitled to complain of the use of linguistic concepts outside his own field.

This is all the more true in view of the fact that Lévi-Strauss himself always exercises a rigid control over his parallels. In *La Pensée sauvage*, he succeeds in disclosing systems of transformation within the particular field of totemism. And through his demonstration of the congruence between the special system of anthropology and that of grammar by means of *a posteriori* evidence (rather than the application of grammatical concepts *a priori*), he provides material that is of interest to Chomsky and the generative grammarians. In this way, he may be said to have modified the substance of Saussure's claim that linguistics was destined to be absorbed within a more general science of signs – semiology. Lévi-Strauss's approach, by contrast, implies that the relationship of each region of semiology to linguistics must be carefully defined. He confirms what Barthes has suggested in his *Elements of Semiology*: 'Semiology must perhaps be part of a translinguistics, since the semiologist, at one stage or another, is bound to come up against the spoken language.' This must naturally apply to the anthropologist as well.

However, Lévi-Strauss's modest epistemological claims are balanced by a boldness in scientific inquiry, especially when he is certain of a rigorously controlled result on a local level. Adopting Jakobson's hypothesis of the *metastructure* of a particular language, which could be specified with the help of a computer, Lévi-Strauss wonders whether it might not be possible to trace through a mathematical combinatory* all the conceivable structures of exchange by marriage:

All the empirically observable rules of marriage represent different methods of ensuring the circulation of women within a group, i.e. putting a sociological system of alliance in place of a biological system of consanguinity. From the basis of this hypothesis, we might attempt a general mathematical study of every conceivable type of exchange between *n* partners, and draw from them the rules of marriage that function in existing societies.

Here we are not far from a point of view reminiscent of Leibniz. Yet the most rewarding aspect of the exercise is that empirical observation confirms the validity of the patterns generated, in a way comparable to the validation of Mendelev's table in chemistry.

In this respect, Lévi-Strauss provides a bridge to the second field in which the notion of structure must be specified: that of mathematics. The Bourbakist mathematicians who employed notions of structure in their 'set theory' during the 1930s were entirely unaware of the work of Saussure. Yet there is a striking community of strategy and approach between their work and Saussurian linguistics: an example might be the notion that the object is to be conceived not in terms of internal properties, but as a system of relations between unspecified elements, whose

* 'Combinatory' is a Leibnizian concept for a network of relations and a matrix of structural generation.

properties derive from these relations. For the mathematicians, knowledge of a mathematical object is not directed towards the isolated qualities of an entity, but to the formal properties of a system. For instance, to state the properties of complex numbers is to state the formal properties of a *system* of objects which the mathematician sums up as the *structure* of an algebraically closed commutative set.

This parallel between the Bourbakist and the Saussurian uses of the notion of *structure* may be taken further. A recent book entitled *Hermès ou la communication*, by Michel Serres,[4] traces the relationship between the formal approach of the mathematician and the insights of Leibniz. Serres perceives in modern mathematics the final triumph of a purely formal discourse, which discards the symbolic approach as not having general enough application. According to this scheme, Gaston Bachelard is the great original genius of our age, who forms the bridge between the 'Middle Ages' of symbolism and the formal 'Renaissance' characteristic of our time. The conjunction in his works of clear reflexive epistemology and a psychoanalysis based on the elements* is seen as a modern equivalent to the miraculous combination of mathematics and mythology which typified the Greeks. Serres writes: 'Bachelard chooses his archetypes in the ultimate myth of the ultimate science (in this respect he is the last Romantic); he gathers together in an audacious combination the clarity of the form to be released and the compactness of the context to be understood (in this respect he is the first neo-classic).'

From the basis of this *Ur-symbolics* set down by Bachelard, Serres describes the development of a 'structural' age that lies in the future. Here the linguistic and mathematical senses of structure come together in a new kind of classicism founded upon pure formal models that are entirely free from any form of concrete determination of their elements, or any local empirical designation of their internal relationships:

* 'Elements' refers to the four elements: Fire, Earth, Air and Water. Bachelard provided an analysis of the way they operated in scientific discourse.

A *structure* is an operational set with an indefinite signification (as opposed to an archetype, which is a concrete set whose significance is not defined), that groups elements in any number, the content of which is not specified, *and* also relationships, in determinate numbers, the nature of which is not specified though their functions are defined, as well as their effect on the elements.

Bearing this formulation in mind, we may reassess the status of a structural approach. 'An analysis is structural if, and only if, it displays the content as a model, i.e. if it can isolate a formal set of elements and relations in terms of which it is possible to argue without entering upon the significance of the given content.' Such a profound revolution in the definition of meaning will not be confined to the self-referring field of mathematics. First of all, it proves capable of generating a new method: it becomes possible to rebuild all the models generated by a structure once that structure has been isolated as such (in terms of its elements and its abstract relations).

In the second place, at the very moment when mathematics is able to define its own epistemology in purely formal terms, and speak of itself in its own structural language, it becomes capable of achieving generality for this language. The universality of the method is achieved just at the time when mathematics and meta-mathematics withdraw into a self-referring field. Michel Serres is quite right to place this new epistemology which radically modifies the scope of the 'sciences humaines' under the aegis of Leibniz, the philosopher of formal harmony, congruency and self-regulating system. For just as mathematics, dynamics and metaphysics all converge harmoniously in Leibniz's theories, so modern mathematics can justifiably be seen as a logic applicable to 'any' object: the possibility arises of a mathematical uni-vocality and a system of continual isomorphism, as in Leibniz. In accordance with this possiblilty, Serres congratulates Michel Foucault for providing in his *Histoire de la folie* 'a geometry of the non-communicable'. This 'system of all possible variations of the negative, this structural genesis of every conceivable kind of alienation' may lead us in the direction of a general *organon* which would be of use even in scientific fields which are still at the stage of describing their objects.

Though this prospect of a formal structural classicism in the future may sound a little too optimistic, it is not entirely utopian. And Serres illustrates its possibilities in his own treatment of a number of classical French texts, such as Molière's *Dom Juan*, which he effectively analyses from a structural angle with the aid of formal patterns defined in Mauss's anthropological writings.

A third source of structural method could be found in the field of the history of philosophy, with specific reference to the approach first developed by Martial Guéroult in 1953, in his *Descartes selon l'ordre des raisons*. Later works employing this approach are Jules Vuillemin's *Kant*, Victor Goldschmidt's *Méthode et structure des dialogues de Platon*, and Guéroult's subsequent *Dynamique et Métaphysique chez Leibniz*. G. G. Granger, who is himself the author of a most interesting attempt at formalization of the field of epistemology and the social sciences,[5] has defined this method as 'an attempt to consider a work in itself as a relatively closed and self-referring system which the analyst wishes to comprehend as such'. In a sense, this amounts to a continuation of Saussure's notion of 'la langue', but there is a fundamental difference in the way in which the system is assessed:

The philosophic system under analysis is a set of thoughts which are logically linked to one another, but which are not to be compared with the rigorously abstract and closed system of a mathematical or a phonological structure. The elements of the system, whether described at the level of propositions or of concepts, are in this case open, and they are never entirely determined by their mutual relationships. Hence the impossibility of making a philosophical work axiomatic, its failure to become entirely formalized.

This third genealogy of structuralism is very interesting indeed as far as the problem of a structural method in the reading and interpretation of literary works is concerned. It opens the way for a formalization and systematic treatment of what may be considered in formal terms, but it leaves an irreducible remainder, which will resist the construction of a formal network devised with a view to exhausting the possibility of a text through combinatory means. This is a result of what might be called *semantic breadth*. In every text, we do in fact encounter a certain 'breadth' of the sign – a kind of force which challenges the possibility of complete, clear and exhaustive formalization. As Granger rightly points out, the elements of the system are 'open'. The consequence of this admission is a significant change of emphasis in the field of literary or philosophical criticism: instead of referring the works under consideration to the probable or problematic intentions of the author, the critic directs his analysis to the *text* in its various levels of meaning, open to formalization only *up to a certain point*. The question of the significance of the text in the light of Plato, Aristotle, Hegel or even Proust's view becomes secondary, and what comes to the fore is the possibility of multiple meanings, grounded upon this formalized but still open deciphering of the text. Again, what the text *means* does not coincide with what the author empirically and actually *meant*: we can, in any case, never know for sure what precisely he did mean, since this 'nucleus' of meaning is too remote from us. Every period, like every culture, has its own way of reading or interpreting works. But this fact need not lead us into a mere historical relativism. The alternative is to admit that the possibilities of interpretation remain open, and the end of critical activity is a network of *relational invariants* proceeding from the system of relationships that can be deciphered in the text or work of art: this network links the individual text to other texts produced at the same period within the same field or code. And while we may admit that such a system is open to formalization up to a certain point, we are not thereby destroying the uniqueness of the particular text as a singular utterance, or irreducible event.

We can now see why it would be inappropriate to speak of *one* structuralism, as a cohesive school of thought. The fact that there are three main sources for this characteristic notion of structure impels us, on the contrary, to make use of the metaphor suggested by Gaston Bachelard. There is a *polyphony* of structuralisms, extending over a field where various types of research can take place, as much in the area of the social sciences as in literary criticism or philosophical interpretation. This field is itself triangular, its sides being constituted by linguistics, mathematics and the history of philosophy.

It now becomes necessary to explore the new insights, methods and intellectual tools that are offered to us as a result of the opening of this new field. First of all, there is the example of the history of philosophy as undertaken by such authors as Guéroult, Goldschmidtt and Vuillemin, in which there is a convergence between the formal approach to a text and the recognition of a 'reserve' of meaning, which must be left open and liable to fresh interpretation. Here the implication is that the text, as a combination of signs set together in relation according to both 'deep' and 'surface' structures, must be considered in its own right without recourse to the 'author-generator' of traditional criticism. Proust was one of the first to emphasize this necessity of considering the work as an autonomous entity. In *Contre Sainte-Beuve* and in some famous passages of *A la recherche* (particularly when the narrator contrasts Bergotte the man with the quality of the universe of signs apparent in the reading of his books), Proust pioneers a new method of criticism, in which it is implicit that a part of the text escapes the writer's control, even at the actual time of writing. The text must be seen as a kind of challenge to its author, as a prodigal son. But this need not imply that it is treated as an object in isolation. On the contrary, it must be seen in terms of the network of relationship which links it to other texts: what Julia Kristeva calls the 'intertextuality'.

At the same time as the text is freed from the necessity of having to express *something*, an increased attention is given to the status of the 'signifiant' – the level of what signifies as opposed to what is signified. One of the presuppositions of traditional criticism was the notion that the text had to *express* a pre-established meaning. In methodological terms, this amounted to the view that the meaning existed beyond or beneath the text, as a kind of *architext* that the actual text had to *translate* or *transcribe*. Such a view appears to be rooted in a metaphysical tradition that dates back to Plato, with his distinctions between intelligible and visible, soul and body, essence and existence. It implies, as is clearly stated in the *Phaedrus*, that writing is a subsidiary activity, of secondary importance, which merely acts as a kind of *aide-mémoire* to speech. By contrast, speech is close to thought and the soul, as the word *logos* testifies. Phonetic *logos* uses writing as a mere servant, or a mere body, with all the inferior connotations linked with this status. Thus Aristotle writes in his *On Interpretation*: 'Written words are the symbols of spoken words, which are the symbols of the states of soul (or mind).' And this derivative conception of writing reaches a kind of climax in Boileau's remark:

> Ce qui se conçoit bien s'énonce clairement
> Et les mots pour le dire viennent aisément.

Traditional criticism thrives upon this metaphysical distinction, between *content* and *form*, the spirit and the letter: we can even see its influence when the critic tries to tell us *what the text is all about*.

If we reject this notion of the text as concealing within itself a substantial meaning, then we are able to admit the key concept of 'polysemy', or 'multiple meaning'. The text will not have *one* meaning, which must be discovered like a treasure: on the contrary it is a bundle of relationships between various levels of meaning or significance, which can be described in structural terms. Roland Barthes writes, in his brilliant and justifiable rejoinder to Professor Picard: 'Variety of meanings does not occur as a result of a relativist view of human taste; what it designates is not the society's tendency to error but the work's disposition to *openness*; a work carries several meanings simultaneously, by virtue of its structure, not through the deficiencies of those who read it.'[6]

Barthes goes on to say that the work is 'symbolic', in the sense that it holds a plurality of meanings. And this freedom of symbolic interpretation was, of course, fully codified in the medieval theory of the four different levels of meaning: literal, allegorical, moral and analogical. But the classical age suppressed this pattern of interpretation. Barthes rightly maintains: 'A work is "everlasting" not because it imposes a univocal meaning upon different men, but because it suggests different meanings to a unique man, who always speaks the same symbolic language, through many different stages in time: the work proposes, man disposes.'[7] Now that the classical ideal of univocality is dead, the work must be allowed to remain free of any attempt to reduce to a unilateral decipherment: it must remain 'pure ambiguity'.

It is not difficult to see that this new critical approach relates back to the Hellenistic as well as the medieval and Renaissance traditions of rigorous but fruitful interpretation. At the same time, it liberates the field of criticism from any attempt to reduce analysis to a univocal method, be it the vulgar biographical approach or the heavy-handed Marxist method which discovers in *Guermantes* little more than the product of exploitation of the masses. The field which is opened by this new approach remains in its very essence indeterminate, and so refuses to be adapted to a determinist or mechanistic schema.

If the freedom of the text is asserted against the almighty rule of the 'author-generator', and the meaning is accepted as being simply relational, the inevitable result is a challenge to the very notion of the *subject*. The subjectivity of the author becomes of minor importance in the elucidation of the text, and the supposed subject of the work – 'what it is about' – disappears when the signifying plane is brought into the foreground. This threat to subjectivity must however be seen outside the particular field of literary criticism. It relates to a widespread reaction on the philosophical level against a particular interpretation of the philosophy of Descartes. We might recognize in this modern tendency the 'end' or at least the exhaustion of the '*cogito* epoch'.

A whole range of philosophers, from the first Cartesians to the Existentialists, have interpreted the *cogito* in terms of consciousness. Whether the subject is viewed as a transcendental or a psychological ego, it is always rooted in the idea of a substance viewed as consciousness. Recently, the *cogito* has provided us with the notion of a constituting ego which offers itself as a phenomenological centre from which *free will* radiates into the world, establishing meaning. As Sartre suggests, taking account of a particular interpretation of Heidegger's *Da-sein* and *In-der-Welt-sein*, *the subject is present to itself and to the world*. It is the survival of this Cartesian free will, linked with consciousness, in Sartre's work that accounts for some of the ambiguity of his connections with Marxism. What Sartre accepts in Marxism is the idea of a man creating his own essence in the act of *praxis*, which is analogous to his own concept of the *pro-ject* (*Entwurf*). But his concept of a free *project* cannot admit the conflicting notion of historical determination by socio-cultural or economic conditions.

If attempts are made to reconcile Sartre's work and Marxism, this may be due to a misunderstanding of Marx's theories, as we shall suggest later. At this stage the most important implication of Sartre's fidelity to the Cartesian interpretation of the ego as consciousness is his inability to take account of the development of psychoanalysis. What Sartre's theory of consciousness as transparent cannot integrate is the simple notion of the *Unconscious*. In *Being and Nothingness*, he attempts to cope with the problem either through assimilating the notion of the unconscious in his theory of 'mauvaise foi', or through promoting a so-called *existential psychoanalysis* which would concern itself with disclosing the initial *pro-ject* rather than the trauma. Sartre gives a brilliant but unconvincing example of this procedure in his work on Baudelaire. Yet why fundamentally does he refuse to admit the notion of the Unconscious? The answer lies partly in the fact that it is supposed to divide the ego into two disconnected parts (ego and id), and partly in the fact that the id seems to challenge the freedom of consciousness. What Sartre wishes to preserve absolutely is the full right of the free conscience to create its own values.

Sartre's objections are made pointless and irrelevant when brought into conjunction with the new developments in psychoanalysis pioneered by Jacques Lacan and the Freudian school of Paris. Whether Lacan is properly called a structuralist or not, he has certainly brought out the major part played by linguistic phenomena in Freud's own works and in psychoanalysis as such. Instead of diverging from Freud's texts, as do the Jungians and neo-Freudians such as Erich Fromm, Lacan invites us to return to the original writings and to perceive the importance of the linguistic element in a body of work which arose at the very same period as Saussure was drawing up the first sketches for his *Cours de linguistique générale*. Free associations in the course of the cure, slips of the tongue, puns, dreams – all this kind of material had already been accepted by Freud as constituting a close relationship between language and the unconscious. But Lacan points out that this does not only take place at the empirical level: 'The whole unconscious is structured as a language.' This is particularly so in the case of dreams, where Freud's major work, *The Interpretation of Dreams*, displays a strict isomorphism between the structures through which the unconscious desire elaborates dream scenes and the rhetorical structures or *tropes*. The 'condensation process' is extremely similar to the pattern of metaphor, while the displacement process, through which the libido tries to avert censorship, is the equivalent of the pattern of metonymy. The manifest content of the dream can be identified therefore with the 'signifiant' of a text, and what Freud alludes to in terms of latent meaning can be considered as its 'signifié', on condition that we do not see the two levels as essentially separate, but as a network of possible interpretations linked by syntactic structures, through which desire *insists* on the level of the 'signifiant'.

Dreams can thus be compared to cryptic texts, or palimpsests, whose *polysemy* must be deciphered by the psychoanalyst. And the romantic conception of the unconscious as a kind of deep layer or mysterious cave where occult forces are at work can be dismissed entirely. Following Freud, Lacan has demonstrated the *syntactical status* of the unconscious, its network of deep structural patterns within the framework of which our clear thinking and discourse is caught up, in just the same way as the act of speech is conditioned by the underlying deep structures, comparable to the rules of a game. And the process by which dreams are generated resembles that of the displacement of meaning which occurs in the field of written language and literature under the category of tropes: metaphor, metonymy, zeugma, hypallage, etc.

The dividend of this approach lies in the possibility it offers of universalizing the teaching of Freud, in spite of the effects of cultural diversity. When the Oedipus complex is seen not from the point of view of its content but from that of its form, it becomes a universal syntactic pattern or structure, and can be linked to the general prohibition on incest which the anthropologist recognizes as universal. The dual error of certain interpreters of Freud and Lévi-Strauss has been to foster a romantic idea of the relationship between nature and culture which these two thinkers have discovered, whereas this relationship should in fact be seen as a formal pattern, a structural articulation in terms of which the deep structures and rules of communication in fields as far apart as kinship and economics can be found to arise. The incest taboo is a synthetic inflexion which establishes the network of a relationship that we encounter in a particular case in the Oedipus myth. Desire (nature) meets its first obstacle (guilt) by coming up against the forbidden and the forbidding (father image, or chief's image). And the Oedipus myth is simply one instance of a universal pattern within the framework of which each libido determines its own course.

What Freud brings to light is the possibility of articulating each particular *idiolect* of the patient or dreamer within a system composed of universal deep structures and rules. And Lacan brings out this potentiality very forcibly in his *Ecrits*, in two major articles, 'Fonction et champ de la parole et du langage', and 'L'instance de la lettre dans l'inconscient'.

Of course the corollary of this approach is a challenge to the self-sufficiency of the individual *subject*. In another fundamental article, 'Le stade du miroir comme formateur de la fonction du Je', Lacan utilizes the structure of the mirror image in early childhood as a model to illuminate the relationship of the ego to the self as one of division and non-coincidence. He draws his conclusion from the discovery that the child feels at the same time a deadly anguish and an intense rapture when confronted with his own image at the age of eight months or so: it follows that this dual split (separation from himself and ambivalence of feelings) determines the future structure of the ego as one of division. Such a principle, which involves the notion of a 'gap' or *Spaltung* within the ego, is in fact fatal to the interpretation of the *cogito* as fulfilment and presence. When we combine it with the principle that the unconscious is structured as a language, through its syntactic patterns, that it is not the 'I' which speaks exclusively but the 'id' also, we can appreciate Lacan's joke about a new *cogito*, which splits the subject: 'I think where I am not, therefore I am where I do not think.'

There is a clear comparison between the status of the mirror image and that of the proper name of the child caught up in the code of the speaking adults around him. A similarly ambivalent feeling occurs when, *in-fans* (not speaking), he listens to his name being spoken in the linguistic chain, and yet cannot assume this name proper to him because he has not yet formed himself as a speaking ego. Proper name and mirror-image are at the same time present and remote, and the state of simultaneous anguish and jubilation generated by such a structure of coincidence and division can be compared to the pre-logical Eros/Thanatos relationship in Freud's psychoanalysis. What matters principally in this theory is the point that the ego is already split in two, divided against itself, before encountering others. And Lacan is quite aware that here he is challenging Sartre's theory of the *Other* as agent of division within the self, a theory demonstrated in *Being and Nothingness* and succinctly conveyed in the phrase from *Huis clos*: 'L'enfer, c'est les autres.' He is also impelled to reassess the status of mental illness in terms of a kind of irony: 'Its function is irony. When one has gained practical knowledge of the schizophrenic, one comes to recognize the irony with which he is armed, which strikes at the roots of all social relations.'

Lacan's theory of the 'radical eccentricity of the subject to himself' thus strikes at forms of humanism relying upon the proximity and presence of man. Both the notion of man as a specific *object* of knowledge, and as *subjectivity* – the clear and lucid source of all the meanings arrayed around him – are challenged at their very foundations. What in France were once called the 'sciences humaines' took as their goal man as a whole, man as an object. But the object of knowledge which now comes into view is not man at all: it is the unconscious as a bundle of deep syntactic patterns; it is the deep structures of kinship and the systems of transformation which generate such and such a classification of concrete data within a totemic system; it is the relationship between deep structures and surface structures in linguistics. Man, in other words, is the great absence. What emerges in every field is a network of relationships, of general and local laws, and a set of operations whose functions are to enforce a certain type of communication between various levels of meaning.

In this context, we can appreciate the force of Foucault's assertion placed at the head of this study. Man's 'approaching end' has been greeted with fear and anger, as was the case with Nietzsche's 'God is dead'. Yet it is undeniable that what Foucault has unearthed in that excavation of Western knowledge which he calls the 'archaeology' of our thought[8] is not man himself, but the systems of rules and systematic distinctions which account for the transition from one *episteme** to another, i.e. which explain how our culture has changed from one code to another, how certain formal conditions of possible scientific and non-scientific discourses have been replaced gradually by others. In the footsteps of Bachelard, who promoted the idea of a succession of *epistemological configurations*, Foucault provides us with an epistemology of discontinuity, revealing the hidden rules and patterns which underlie different types of discourse at a certain period, and the new system of rules which ushers in a

* *Episteme* is a concept developed by Michel Foucault in *The Order of Things* to describe the epistemological foundations held in common by different areas of scientific discourse.

new 'order'. Foucault demonstrates that these deep structures which form the hidden *a prioris* of culture can be formalized to a certain extent, just as the patterns of the unconscious and the classifications of totemism can be said to form a kind of logic. He also shows that the notion of man as a subject present to himself, an everlasting conscience, is a very recent creation. Neither the thinkers of Port Royal nor the Encyclopedists were in search of man as a whole, as object or subject. The 'end' of man which he refers to is therefore the end of the comparatively short-lived metaphysical era of *consciousness*, and the future belongs to the era of *concept* and *symbolism*.

This dismissal of the transcendental ego is linked with the necessity to abandon a unulinear conception of history. If man is no longer a relevant category, the univocal causalist scheme of history that we see at work in Marxism is not adequate either, since it is rooted in the most degraded by-product of the transcendental ego, *the praxis of man as a producer*. We have mentioned the necessity for an acceptance of *polysemy*, or multiple meaning, in the critical investigation of texts. The same principle holds true for history. Every enterprise that reduces the analysis of a fact, or system of facts, to the level of a univocal approach is neglecting the polysemy or plurivocality of the event. What is too narrow in Lukacs's theory of the novel, for example, is the reduction of criticism to an operation which characterizes the text as the result of economico-social trends. The reproach can be extended to the entire method of Marxism, which has not yet bid farewell to the positivism of the nineteenth century. Indeed at a time when mathematics and even physics have become increasingly axiomatic, the pretensions of Marxism to be called a science is simply grotesque.[9]

Fortunately the Marxist historians have themselves realized the necessity of abandoning the original delusion. What is in doubt now is the possibility of describing the production of the superstructure by the infrastructure in terms of a univocal causal relationship. But, on a more radical level, one may question whether the concept of history as a diachronic sequence of facts is a sufficiently illuminating one, at a stage when the most relevant insights seem to come from a synchronic approach. An analogy is provided by the game of chess, in which the diachronic succession of the move does not explain anything, while the situation may be deciphered on a much more basic level through examination of the synchronic state of the system. Lévi-Strauss quite justifiably raises this point in the last chapter of *La Pensée sauvage*, entitled 'History and dialectics', in which he writes that it is sufficient to recognize that history is a method to which no distinct object corresponds, and consequently to reject the equivalence between the notion of history and that of mankind, which certain people attempt to impose on us with the concealed purpose of making historicity the ultimate refuge of a transcendental humanism: as if, on the condition that they gave up their ego with its inconsistencies, men were able to encounter the illusion of freedom once again, on the level of the collective *We*. History and diachrony are produced by the development of a system which is legible only in terms of synchrony: even if the moves are actually engendered in the field of diachrony, it is only in the field of synchrony that we can decipher their effects and consequences as modifications or alterations of the system.

Exhaustion of the traditional *cogito* and genesis of a new *cogito* in the tradition of Leibniz; curtailment of the unilinear view of history as a field of causal relations; fertilization of literary criticism as a result of new decoding methods borrowed from psychoanalysis, linguistics and even anthropology – all these developments can be associated under the title of 'structuralism'. And the balance sheet is clearly in credit. Yet a current reproach against the originators of this new approach is that their work rests upon obsolete linguistic concepts, in particular the binary approach developed, among others, by Jakobson. In Edmund Leach's recent book on Lévi-Strauss we find, apart from the usual complaint that certain empirical 'facts' are contrary to Lévi-Strauss's system,[10] the suggestion that Lévi-Strauss is basing his work upon this obsolete binary system. The argument is less frequent than the empirical one, but rather more interesting. It is supported by the belief that Chomsky's generative grammar constitutes a refutation of

Jakobson's theories, which consequently have become old-fashioned. However, this argument cannot be maintained for very long. As Chomsky himself puts it,[11] his aim is not to refute Jakobson's thesis as if it were wrong or false, but to extend and integrate Jakobson's work in a new, more complex apparatus, designed to take account of deep structures and to explain the laws according to which the surface structures studied by linguistic structuralism are built up. His relation to Jakobson is therefore not one of opposition and contradiction, but of integration: a relevant analogy would be the corpuscular theory of light which integrates but does not invalidate the wave theory.

Thus we can say that even if Lévi-Strauss were adhering to Jakobson's patterns in his anthropological work, he would not be 'wrong' in so doing. But in effect he does not do so. In the third chapter of *La Pensée sauvage*, entitled 'Systems of trans-formations', we discover that the surface structures perceptible in totemism and kinship are rooted in a far wider system which generates them as in the field of grammar. As with Chomsky, we are invited to observe the finite set of deep structures which underlie the infinite set of surface structures. The parallel is obvious, and it leads to the conclusion that Lévi-Strauss is in no way the prisoner of a single method, but finds himself able to elaborate new devices when this is required by the materials under review.

What is true for Lévi-Strauss is also true for the other practi-tioners of structuralist analysis. They are not bound to utilize one particular model from the area of linguistics – that of Saussure, Jakobson or Hjelmslev according to choice. On the contrary, they feel able to draw on new intellectual tools when the material offered by the field which they are studying demands it. This confutes the rather naive idea put about in some circles that Chomsky's generative grammar represents a kind of liberation from the monster structuralism, which is coldly determined to choke human creativity in the coils of its systems and structures. According to this argument, the idea of generation developed by Chomsky appeared to introduce the possibility of a return to the creativity of the free ego. But this is clearly seen to be nonsense if we reflect that Chomsky is very far from abandoning the Saussurian distinction between 'langue' and 'parole': indeed the linguistics of the act of speech which he builds up on the basis of this distinction lends itself particularly to formalization and is totally at variance with Sartre's free, unpredictable *pro-ject*.

It is valuable to recall Chomsky's major work in linguistics, especially with regard to the behaviourist presuppositions concealed in many formal approaches to logic, linguistic analysis and linguistics. In direct opposition to these tendencies, Chomsky pledges himself to a return to the grammar of Port Royal, and the theories of language of Leibniz and Géraud de Cordemoy, which he sees as the ancestors of transformational grammar. In his revival of the idea of innate knowledge or innate structures, we might have anticipated a resurrection of the Cartesian ego in its metaphysical implications. But the formalized Leibnizian way in which Chomsky considers these innate ideas prevents any confusion. By using innate ideas in a seventeenth-century sense, yet devoid of metaphysical content, he not only acquires a weapon against the reductionist attitudes of the behaviourists, but also provides new insights within the field of the Saussurian distinction between 'langue' and 'parole'. By his use of the terms of surface structure and deep structure on the one hand and the notions performance/competence on the other, Chomsky has succeeded in establishing an articulated network, within the matrix of which the creative forces of speech can be analysed. This has nothing in common with a linguistics of speech ('parole') as individual act, pure contingency or happening. It is an approach which accurately accounts for the formal conditions under which such acts of speech are possible, and it brings into focus a system of differentiation in their syntagmatic production which was not clearly demonstrated in the previous forms of structural analysis.

The question of innate ideas still raises a problem, since although Chomsky makes it clear that his conception of the subject is not in any way a substantialist one, his innatism could still be associated with the claims of a universal, transcendental ego that overrides the differences between the codes (a risk also incurred by Lévi-Strauss when he more or less postulates the existence of universal recurrent mental patterns). Of course this element of innatism is necessary in order to combat Behaviourism, with its internal contradiction of trying to conceive an 'externally observed' behaviour by reference to terms whose connotation is 'internal'. It is this very metaphysical residue that Chomsky tries to eliminate from linguistics, while at the same time attacking the empirical methods whose lack of formal pattern and model is all too evident. Yet Chomsky is right to accept a minimal definition of Behaviourism as a part of his system: 'conjectures must eventually be made sense of in terms of external observation', he writes. 'This is, to be sure, a sense of "behaviourism" that would cover all reasonable men.'[12] The dual effect of such a definition of Behaviourism is to dismiss at the same time the excesses of empiricism and the transcendentalism of the Husserlian ego. Chomsky could therefore justifiably be compared to Kant in his combined attack on empiricism and dogmatic metaphysics.

It is worth dwelling briefly on the new concept that Chomsky invokes to demonstrate the relationship between competence and performance: this is the concept of *knowledge*. In effect, this is the critical point where, despite Chomsky's precautions, we might expect the return of the question of subjectivity with its metaphysical implications. A controversy has been set on foot by Julia Kristeva and Philippe Sollers of the *Tel Quel* group which suggests the possibility that Chomsky may have reverted to a psychological, or metaphysical, conception of the introspective ego in a Cartesian tradition. And indeed this notion of 'knowledge' as a possible substitute for the narrowly determined notion of *competence* is somewhat disturbing, since it raises the question of the *subject who knows*. Perhaps the best solution is to let Chomsky explain himself on this particular point:

Suppose one is willing to accept the characterization of knowledge of a language in terms of possession . . . of a generative grammar . . .

Suppose one is prepared to apply the notion 'knowledge' in this case including cases that lie beyond awareness. Suppose that further investigation leads us to the conclusion that this knowledge is acquired on the basis of certain innate principles of 'universal grammar' . . . would we want to say that the child *knows* the principles of universal grammar? It seems to me that very little turns on the answer given to this question. It is also unclear whether the concept 'knowledge' is sufficiently clear to guide us in making a decision.[13]

Certainly the concept of 'knowledge' is the source of many a confusion in this context, because its usage is likely to oscillate constantly between the pole of conscious possession of clear rules and that of the unconscious situation within the field of deep structures of which the subject is not aware. When Chomsky says that 'very little turns on the answer given to this question', he simply denies the real problem of the status of this particular kind of knowledge. The question remaining unsolved might be expressed in the following way. Clearly all the rules and principles of this grammar are not accessible to consciousness in general: at the same time some undoubtedly are. Chomsky's solution is to invoke the possibility of a concept 'X', in terms of which we could say that a subject 'Xs' a language. But even if we admit this novel concept in the place of 'knowledge', we are still confronted with the problem of the impact of 'performance' in the field of 'competence'; and this question raises the issue of the unconscious whether in Freudian or in Leibnizian terms. There is therefore a need for accurate definition of the concept X, so that generative grammar may avoid the recurrence of the substantialist view of a Cartesian ego endowed with free will on a metaphysical level.

Chomsky's system may run the risk of inconsistency precisely because of his humanist beliefs, which lead him to emphasize the difference, for example, between the animal code and the human code. The humanism which he avows in his conception of a discourse free from causalist and behaviourist pressures cannot be divorced from the humanism which he so courageously embodies in his liberal attitude to violence, either on the campus or in Vietnam. And these two convergent aspects of humanism

would benefit greatly if Chomsky were to avoid terms too close
to the substantialist fall-out of the late Cartesian ego and incline
towards a 'metastructuralism' in the tradition of Leibniz. Too
great a reliance on Géraud de Cordemoy, for instance, would be
unwise: for this author too often assimilates the 'signifié' to the
soul of the word, while the 'signifiant', the perceptible part of
the sign, is equated with the *body*. Not only metaphysical but
also theological traps are very near.

If Chomsky were to assess the status of his new concept of
knowledge, we might have the opportunity of observing a
striking convergence between certain formalized approaches to
linguistic analysis, the unconscious, mathematics and logic.
How this would relate to the work of Lévi-Strauss is a matter
which must depend radically upon the extent to which we admit
the existence of transformational techniques in his work. And
on this subject Edmund Leach has recently given two somewhat
conflicting views. He writes in his study of Lévi-Strauss:

> The influence of Jakobson's style of phonemic analysis on the work
> of Lévi-Strauss has been very marked; it is therefore relevant that
> although certain aspects of Jakobson's work have lately been sub-
> jected to criticism, Noam Chomsky specifically recognizes the
> fundamental importance of Jakobson's main theory and phonetic
> universals, which is all that matters so far as Lévi-Strauss is con-
> cerned. . . . On the other hand, the rigidly binary form of Jakobson's
> distinctive feature analysis (which reappears in Lévi-Strauss's
> Structuralism) is now rejected by many leading linguists.[14]

One realizes, of course, that this account of Chomsky's
relation to Jakobson is far from being a condemnation of Lévi-
Strauss: Leach is certainly not making a hard and fast distinction between *good* transformationalism based on generative
grammar, and *bad* structuralism. At the same time, it is a pity
that Leach reserves for a concluding footnote what is perhaps
the most important aspect of his fair account of Lévi-Strauss's
thought. Here he shows that, however irritated he may be by
Lévi-Strauss's cavalier attitude to empirical or accidental facts
that are sacred to an Englishman, he remains quite genuinely

an admirer of Lévi-Strauss's genius for building systems: Bacon encountering Leibniz (despite the anachronism). Leach's footnote reads as follows:

In the view of many professional linguists the publication of Noam Chomsky's *Syntactic structures* (1957) had a significance for linguistics comparable to that of Einstein's early papers on relativity theory for physics, and it has sometimes been argued, to Lévi-Strauss's discredit, that he relies on a Jakobson-style linguistic model that is no longer viable. Two points need to be made on the other side. Firstly, even if Chomsky's work is an advance on that of Jakobson, it does not invalidate the genuine merits of the latter; secondly, the characteristics of Chomsky's linguistics, which are subsumed under the titles Generative and Transformational Grammars, have many points in common with the generative and transformational rules for myth analysis which Lévi-Strauss has developed on his own quite independently.[15]

The reason why I consider this the most important idea in Leach's book is because it demonstrates in an illuminating way that, far from being the *end* of structuralism, the generative grammar of Chomsky and the systems of transformation in Lévi-Strauss are opening up new frontiers for the method.

If Dr Leach's book is the most interesting piece of homage paid by his country to the theories of Lévi-Strauss and the field roughly labelled 'structuralism' – a homage made all the more challenging by its store of empirical objections – this book also leads us to further thought on the possible connections between the approaches of Lévi-Strauss and Chomsky. Our conviction that the structuralist field still offers many exciting vistas is linked with the assumption that these two thinkers will venture further in the direction of particular goals: that Chomsky, on the one hand, will clarify the relationship between 'knowledge' and Cartesian subjectivity, and between 'knowledge' and unconscious patterns; and that Lévi-Strauss, on the other hand, will provide us with more material on his concept of universal formal patterns, thus dissipating confusion as to whether he allows them substantialist connotations or simply conceives them as mobile structural patterns devoid of content, which are thus capable of subsuming the diversity of human codes on a worldwide scale. On this particular matter, Leach's reproach of universalism would be relevant, if Lévi-Strauss had not begun to provide a convincing solution in his studies of the structures of kinship. This solution will have to be applied to other fields, such as that of totemism, if Lévi-Strauss is to refute the accusation of integrating only part of the relevant data in the interests of the coherence of his system.

Quite recently a new, most rewarding, approach has been developed which overrides the artificial opposition between phenomenology and structuralism, yet links them together only under the common accusation of being still caught up in the matrix of Western metaphysics: this accusation would hold despite their claim to constitute a critique of metaphysics, leading in the direction of epistemology in the latter case and mere science in the former. The author of this approach is Jacques Derrida, and he has developed his position in three books published simultaneously in 1967: *De la grammatologie*, *L'Ecriture et la différence* and *La Voix et le phénomène*. The argument rests upon the suggestion that metaphysics has always given pride of place to Logos (oral speech) at the expense of writing. For the category in which metaphysics has established its base is that of *presence*, that is to say proximity to oneself and proprietary control by the ego. As I suggested previously, this tendency began when Plato condemned writing, in the *Phaedrus*, as something that eliminated this presence or proximity, by exposing it to the hazards of interpretation.

Writing has thus been regarded from the metaphysical point of view as a body, an external part or clothing, as opposed to the pure interiority of the soul and meaning, which is preserved in the proximity of the voice. As a consequence, all metaphysical discourse throughout history can be regarded as a perpetual effort to restore this presence, which is constantly threatened by language and, more specifically, by writing. The privileged status granted to logos, in its dual meaning of thought and voice – this phonocentrism or logocentrism – is not only the product of metaphysical discourse, but of all the types of discourse which have their roots in metaphysics.

It is at this point that Derrida attacks the Husserlian and Sartrian phenomenology of consciousness, which retains the proximity to itself of a subjectivity existing within the metaphysical field of free will. In *La Voix et le phénomène*, he establishes that any transcendental ego remains the prisoner of a metaphysics of the present. Yet his objections stretch beyond this stage into the field of 'structuralism' itself. In *De la grammatologie*, he challenges the validity of the phonological patterns developed by Trubeckoj and Jakobson, and applied as models by Lévi-Strauss. These also he would see as related to a metaphysics of the present. And it is certainly one of the basic questions which the structuralists must attempt to answer: whether they have in fact naively settled upon the field of linguistics without considering whether the epistemological possibility of a linguistic discourse may not be rooted in this metaphysics. Saussure can certainly be regarded as being indebted to this matrix of presence, not only through the primacy which he grants to spoken speech, but also through his distinction between 'signifiant' and 'signifié'.

The main strength of Derrida's position lies in that fact that he does not destroy anything – or even refute – but simply offers a diagnosis. He scrutinizes and, in the process, *deconstructs* the foundations of culture. But if he provides no alternative apparatus of concepts to replace the metaphysical ones, and ultimately demonstrates how difficult it is to step outside this metaphysical matrix, at least he draws notable conclusions from the effects of the inhibition on writing. He suggests that such thinkers as Nietzsche, Freud and Heidegger have made us aware of the closure, so to speak, of metaphysical discourse. And he invites us to a new reading of the crucial texts of our culture, which would lay stress precisely on the element of *writing*. In *L'Ecriture et la différence*, Artaud, Bataille, Jabès and Freud are shown to be impatient to emerge from a metaphysic of the spoken word, from the field which Derrida himself qualifies as *phonocentrism*.

Derrida suggests that, for these writers, writing becomes the ground of a *logic of supplementarity*, which goes beyond the traditional logic of identity and contradiction. He derives this new concept ultimately from Rousseau who, though he remained firmly within the boundaries of traditional metaphysics, at the same time examined the problems of language in a most radical way in his *Essai sur l'origine des langues*. Rousseau used the term 'suppléer' in this context to convey the relationship between 'signifiant' and 'signifié' as a perpetual oscillation between what is *added* and what is *substituted* (both being implicit in the French word). In so doing, he raised the whole question of the *figurative* sense of words (the *tropes*) in relation to their *proper* sense.

Which is the original sense, the *proper* or the *figurative*? Derrida allows this question to remain unanswered. The *logic of supplementarity* in effect enables him to break free from the confines of a traditional logic, based on the metaphysical presence of an ontological *signified*, and to withdraw writing (the *signifier*) from the field where it is merely a *substitute*, so that it genuinely acts as a *supplement*. Derrida's aim is therefore to revise the Saussurian notion of the sign as a secondary element, which represents the present in its absence. In place of this conception, he introduces the idea of a 'différence originaire': in other words, an original state of deferment, which would imply that the sign should no longer be thought of '*from the basis of* the presence which it defers and *in view of* the deferred presence which we seek to reappropriate'.

This new view of writing allows us to take a fresh look at the central texts of Western culture. Equally, it enables us to draw closer to the non-oral, non-linear writing used in science, and to the non-logocentric cultures (China, Japan) which enshrine meaning in the written form of the text. Derrida is particularly attentive to the emergence in our modernist culture of non-logocentric signs, which are still to a great extent entangled with logocentric ones. A relevant example would be Mallarmé, who combines the traditional metaphysical conception of the book, as a totality or circle enclosing the sense, with hints of a type of poetry that would no longer be legible orally (*Un Coup de dés*), and of a type of book that would not involve the presence of the sense to the sign, but prolong and *defer* the significance indefinitely.

This approach is certainly a demanding one, which casts suspicion not only upon Western metaphysics but on the forms of discourse effectively based upon it. We might indeed envisage Derrida's work as a step further in the direction already taken by Nietzsche, Freud and Heidegger. Yet the fact that both phenomenology and structuralism are vulnerable to his analysis need not lead us to a negative conclusion. We have already suggested that the direction of research carried out by Chomsky and Lévi-Strauss leads not to the *end* of structuralism, but precisely to the development of new *ends* and new objectives. Derrida's diagnosis puts even more radically the need for Chomsky to clarify his concept of 'knowledge' and free it from the contagion of the substantial ego: at the same time, it casts doubt on Lévi-Strauss's use of phonological, and therefore phonocentric, patterns. Yet, despite the force of Derrida's critique, his work holds the promise of a new frontier for structuralism: a frontier defined by the development of a new, open mathematics, on the one hand, and, on the other, by a closer attention to the sign as it is used in Oriental civilizations. Derrida has already signified the existence of this area of inquiry by the term grammatology, a science of the written sign.

2. New Adventures
of the Dialectic

It was once thought that Marxism provided the only possible approach whereby one might conceive of and deal with the end of ideology because it proposed a demystifying reading of it. If ideology is indeed that shimmering effect of the surface, that nebulous infinity of cultural signs, then it is necessary to uncover what it hides, what it removes from our gaze, what it masks. It was believed that Marxism afforded the most reliable instrument that would enable one to locate and question the ideological lineaments whose outlines we have just drawn, and that this deciphering grid was to be rooted in one's reading of the relationship between infrastructure and superstructure. In the name of a new science, historical materialism, it was thought possible to arrive at that decisive position that we ourselves have been trying to reach; not only that of exposing ideology but also of producing its *truth*, as its latent meaning.

Scientific materialism has aspired to become the science of ideology, thereby announcing the latter's *truth*. Sometimes this has taken place in the shape of a simple identification of a predicative nature, such as: 'Consciousness can never be anything else but conscious being and the being of men is their real life process', and sometimes in the more subtle metaphor of the 'camera obscura'. Against 'German philosophy' that descends 'from heaven to earth' and which starts from the thoughts of men to arrive at 'flesh and blood creatures', Marx and Engels claimed to proceed 'from earth up to heaven', from the 'real activity' of men to its 'ideological echoes'. 'If in all ideology men and their relationships appear to us to be upside down as in a "camera obscura", then this phenomenon arises out of their historical life process, exactly as the inversion of objects on the retina arises from the directly physical life process.'[1] We will have to question the relevance of this metaphor that introduces the schema of an optical inversion and which thus indicates perhaps the inevitable imprisonment of Marx in the theoretical and optical space of Western metaphysics. The urgency of this question can be seen in the publication of a remarkable essay on *La Camera obscura de l'idéologie* by Sarah Kofman.[2] However, for the moment let us not forget that Marxism, as historical materialism, has established itself as the science of ideology defined as an inverted reflection, which means in essence that once its truth has been put right the way up it will coincide with the *being* of social relationships and with that of the relations of production.

The boldest and most courageous venture in Marxism has been that of Althusser and his friends. Bold because it has claimed to lay the foundations of historical materialism as a science and courageous because it has not flinched from denouncing all that has remained ideological in Marx and in Marxism generally. As is well known, Althusser has mapped out in his reading of Marx an 'epistemological break' (a concept borrowed from Gaston Bachelard) which separates the texts of the young Marx from the supposedly scientific ones of his maturity. It would be wrong to say that the young Marx of the '1844 Manuscripts' is still a Hegelian in his historical outlook. He is rather a product of that Feuerbachian space from which he was to break away in *The German Ideology*. Here, however, the various concepts of alienation, the still confused notion of the role between infrastructure and superstructure, have all been shown by Althusser to belong to *ideology*.

This has been a venture whose political stakes were and remain considerable, at a time when so many self-styled Marxist utterances provide us with a true festival of ideology. From Marcuse to the various leftist movements there exists a whole current that was seen surfacing in May 1968 but which was deep at work for a long time before, with its roots, often in divergent ways, in the texts of the young Marx – and at a time when one despairs of this Marx, too. In addition to the theme of alienation, the vision of the revolution, the problem of achieving consciousness, the messianic view of the proletariat, the profound conviction that subjectivity is the motor of history, all this is articulated in a space whose eponymous hero is the young Marx. This particular brand of Marxism, even if the carrier of large hopes, remains a derivative of a humanism of the human essence, of an historicist line of thought in the sense that we have seen denounced by Foucault. And it is easy to work out how it has now managed to smile its broadest grin, in the most complete confusion, at an historicist and almost immanentist Christianity of the Tilehardian variety.

Now Althusser and his group have had the courage to purge the reading of Marx of any mindless leftism, of any Teilhardian-cum-Marxist pseudo-Christianity, of all those concepts of the subject, of human essence, of consciousness and of history which belong to the addled metaphysics of the nineteenth century. In his reading of *Capital*, the only text that he considers as having a scientific value, Althusser claims to have subordinated ideology to science, and this science is called historical materialism. It remains for us to examine the scientific value of *Capital*, to question it and above all to ask ourselves if this supremacy accorded to science is not one of the last avatars of a logos which would peremptorily shut off any alterity and operate a denegation upon the resourcefulness of discourse in all its liberty. Let us simply give Althusser the credit for having delivered Marxism from the mechanistic conception of the relationship between infrastructure and superstructure, for having been able to recognize that they act reciprocally upon one another, for having shown that the reflection that links a culture to its 'material conditions' is neither simple nor univocal but possesses all the richness that overdetermination bestows upon it and, consequently, for having liberated Marx's texts from a causalist scientism whose disastrous effects are felt in domains as different as political practice (economism or Stalinism) and literary criticism (*Phèdre* reduced to a 'product' of the lesser 'noblesse de robe'). These are all dogmatic aberrations and the offspring of that refusal, identified and denounced by Althusser, actually to read *Capital*, to look the texts straight in the face, to know how, if the need arises, to apply linguistic structures or psycho-analytic concepts, which, though proceeding from different quarters, have none the less given proof of their fecundity.

But before returning to the gains of this epistemological liberation let us note provisionally that this movement which, in fact, frees the study of Marx's texts from any ideological nostalgia, with its stale reek of idealism, should perhaps have been pursued to the end. It would then be seen that the scientific-ness with which Althusser credits Marx is one derived from the positivist bleakness of the nineteenth century, and that it has been superseded. The theory of surplus value, in spite of the play of the unconscious and the gap in the signifying process that it presupposes, though both naive and subtle, is, in its very evanescence, still trapped in the metaphysical circuit of the oscillation between absence and presence, as I have tried to show elsewhere.[3]

Since the late nineteenth century science has managed to rid itself of the ontology of presence and to cross the ideological Rubicon. The extraordinary emancipation of mathematics represented by the conquest of axiomatics in all its plurality, in contrast to Euclidean space, and the subsequent relativization of any logic or dialectic of contradiction, the discovery by physics of a non-Newtonian science and by chemistry of a non-Lavoisian one, all these epistemological breaks have opened up for scientific discourse a new space where its fecundity, its inventive and – why not? – figurative rigour may unfold. Not that there is any question of denying or destroying the old regions; they have simply been relativized, combined with other, multiple data where they become 'possible instances'. Now, I doubt whether one can do as much with the alleged science of Marxism, which drags the old dialectical arsenal behind it even in *Capital*, condemning it in its formal simplicity as a hopeless archaism, in spite of the Althusserian dusting job. And the famous *in the last instance*, for all the airing given to the classical schema by the theory of the efficacy of the super-structure, remains perhaps the last fetish of positivist 'science' that has to be contested.

But to go back to the gains of what we shall call, without a shadow of irony, and in the most positive way, *the lesson of Althusser*. First of all, it is the theme of *contradiction* which has been remarkably enriched by the courage that Althusser has displayed in pluralizing and breaking up, to the point of rupture, the Hegelian *Aufhebung*, instead of letting it and its Others labour metaphysically in the text of Marx and the vulgate of his epigones. This was the price that had to be paid for wresting Marx from Hegelianism – something that did not escape Mao Tse-tung's attention either. A corollary of the pluralization of contradiction, this rescue of Marx from the ideological space of Hegel spelt a crisis for the dialectic. There is nothing left to say about this extraction process by which Althusser shows that the dialectical inversion of Hegel to arrive at Marx is not just an optical inversion, one whose terms merely repeat themselves, but is the bringing to light, from a mystical husk, of a kernel of rationality. But at the same time, everything remains to be said, for as we shall see, the possibility of either considering the dialectic as an outmoded logic, a captive of metaphysics, or on the contrary of observing its pluralization driven to such a point that the principle of negativity that structures it is placed in doubt, depends on the retention of this kernel within a positivist space. Thus it will be timely to examine that polemical gesture of Bataille which takes the Hegelian-Marxist notion of the dialectic to task and through which is realized a trans-gression of the metaphysical and undeclared notions of Marxism. Bataille's notion of expense ('dépense') introduces the chink of a non-mediatizable* negativity, it cracks the kernel of positivity that constitutes the dialectic, which as far as it is concerned,

---

* 'Non-mediatizable' – a common concept in dialectical philosophy meaning that a moment in a dialectical process cannot be transcended or sublated into a synthesis.

always subjects the negativity of contradiction to some eventual unification by means of the funds, the *reserves* of positivity upon which it is built.

That silent, underlying notion that Bataille brings to light is the unexceedable limit that grips the dialectical logos in the vice of a principle of identity, and which the various guises of negation have never really disturbed.

The cost of enrichment

In order to pose this basic problem that will entail disturbing the theatre or stage on which the 'play' of the dialectic is produced, it would be best to measure the enrichment given by Althusser to the cardinal notion of contradiction, by placing it in its relationship to overdetermination, a concept of structuralist and Freudian parentage. It is a perilous enrichment, if ever there was one. But first of all let us list the diverse gains with which the dialectic, perhaps against its will or at any case at a heavy cost, has found itself enriched. First, *overdetermination*, of which Althusser, reading Freud and Lacan, is the eponymous interpreter; secondly, *the efficacy of the superstructure on the infrastructure*, elaborated by Gramsci, re-reader of Marx and of the famous letter to Bloch, quoted by Althusser in a footnote; third, *determination in the last instance*, emptied of its economist substantialism by Maurice Godelier to reveal that it functioned according to several variables; and finally, the *hierarchy between principle contradiction and secondary contradiction, plus diverse aspects connected with this*. It is to the essay 'On Contradiction' by Mao Tse-tung that we owe the introduction of this fertile conceptuality, as Philippe Sollers has pointed out in an article that has also become famous.[4]

It is from such points that the question arises as to whether these *enrichments* lead to a relativization of the dialectic, either in favour of a structural network of the Leibnizian type, a multi-dimensional organon where it would only appear in the form of a singularly impoverished instance, clinging to its little territory of contradiction, or, on the other hand, of a progression, à la Beckett, in the direction of an all-encompassing, non-mediatizable and consequently non-metaphysical negativity, such as that which Bataille in *La Part maudite* or *La Notion de dépense* has pointed to. But let us first remember the originality of the contribution made by Althusser to the scientific status of historical materialism. It resides in the recognition of a relationship of fertile asymmetry between the Hegelian and the Marxist dialectic. Against the idealist use of the dialectic proposed by Hegel and his followers, Marx enabled an articulation to emerge between theory and practice, one that assumes the paradoxical form of both unity and struggle, which seems at first glance to indicate an Heraclitean ancestry for Marx. Whereas the unification produced by the Hegelian dialectic in the movement of *Aufhebung* dissolves the antagonistic and polemical character of the instrument of the dialectic, which finds itself absorbed back into a metaphysical synthesis and reconciliation, the pluralization of contradiction in Marx, its passage from a singular to a multiple principle, seems to keep it within the framework of the Heraclitean structure of conflict where antagonism is not doomed to become reconciliation.

The articulation of theory and practice assumes a place for the class struggle in the theory. For Althusser, the struggle of materialism against idealism and of science against ideology finds its correlative in the struggle of the proletariat for its liberation. Or better still: one expresses the other in a reversible isomorphism.

To proceed from there and recognize in historical materialism the validity of a science and to declare it the substratum of a philosophy separate from itself, namely dialectical materialism, is the second distinctive feature of the originality of Althusser's ambition.

Marxist 'science'

It would be legitimate, in the light of what we know today of developments in the sciences and of transformations of the scientific ideal, to question this claim of having founded the scientificness of historical materialism. Does it imply an eternal, immutable and superhistorical conception of science, or, does Marxism on the contrary have the wherewithal for transcending, like psychoanalysis, the habitual concept of Science in general? In this case the same applies to Marx as to Hume and Kant, and the critical approach that he proposes would provide the opportunity for contesting the dogmatic and positivistic determinations of scientificness. The risk run by Marxism would then arise from this immersion of materialism's critical scientificness in the flux of history and thus of its own admission of membership in the superstructure. Recognizing like all science that it is bound to the future of human culture, this new science would henceforth have to accept the modifications that the series of epistemological conditions prevailing at its birth and its own subsequent pronouncements would make it undergo. It would be impossible at this point to escape from the following alternative: either historical materialism remains a science in the sense that this concept was understood by Marx and after him, i.e. as a form of positivism, or else it is a science with the meaning that our modernity has given to this word. In the latter case, we are confronted with a pluralization of the notion of scientific discourse, with the necessity of accepting the test that the intercommunications between various fields of knowledge submit it to, and with no possibility of subsuming these, as in the good old days of Auguste Comte, under one homogenous concept of the scientific in general. Science has become a bountiful and wide-meshed network where it is accepted that the barriers between disciplines are precarious and constantly shifting, where no region, no continent can be sure of its own independence or plenitude. And it is by measuring the contribution of other discourses and theoretical practices to the field of historical materialism, especially of psychoanalysis, that we will be able to test the validity of Marxism's ambition to establish itself as a science.

Psychoanalysis edges its way into Marxism

In the tension between historical materialism and dialectical materialism, in that gap between the One science and the Other philosophy, appears the first occurrence of that conceptual ensemble imported by Althusser from psychoanalysis into the field of Marxism, in accordance with the laws of an epistemological necessity. Their relationship assumes in effect the form of a denial whose scope Althusser purports to uncover for us. There are several possible notions implied in the combinatory between science and philosophy, including two noteworthy borderline cases. If one grants too high a supremacy of the scientific aspect of Marxism over its philosophical aspect, then one will founder on the reef of economism, that is, on the reduction of the political superstructure to those factors present in the economic infrastructure. The reverse position of leaving the dominant position to philosophy, so that science becomes its mere vassal, gives rise to leftist subjectivism or opportunism, the mirrior-image of mechanism and causalism. Now it is upon the equilibrium between historical materialism and dialectical materialism that the theoretical vigour of Marxism may sustain itself, but to the extent that it will have to first of all give historical materialism all its attention, accepting that dialectical materialism, Marxist *philosophy*, lags far behind *science*. Philosophy always arrives late – 'the owl of Minerva rises at dusk'. An immense denegation has operated upon this displacement, due to the bourgeois ideology that has marked our era. The displacement recognized by Althusserian theory between historical and dialectical materialism is transitive and irreversible and alone enables one to avoid those regressions towards the 'infantile disorders' of economism and subjectivism. It is thus not only a chronological displacement but also one upon which weighs the failure to recognize a denegation, in the Freudian sense. In relation to the science of history, dialectical materialism or Marxist philosophy has been occluded or suppressed, in accordance with the misapprehension that the 'scientificness' of historical materialism has been subject to, for the terrain on which the battle was to be fought was occupied by the alleged human sciences whose ideological status Marxism was going to denounce. *Liberating itself through its accession to scientific status, historical materialism not only shakes off the chains of a denegation that was weighing upon it, but also frees other branches of knowledge from their ideological status and* PRODUCES *dialectical materialism as philosophy to come.*

In its action it takes its cue from the proletariat which, freeing itself from its chains, liberates in one and the same movement the other social classes and the whole of humanity, and *produces* in this revolutionary gesture the classless society, the parallel here of a liberated Marxist philosophy for the denial whose victims were Marxist science and then philosophy is homologous to the class oppression from which the proletariat suffers. And it is in this unprecedented status of the proletariat which, at one and the same time, *is and is not a class* that the rich potential of its salutary historical mission resides, just as it is in the unprecedented and unresolvable status of historical materialism which *is and is not a science* that the leverage enabling it to cast aside the denials that were weighing upon it as well as around Marxist philosophy is to be found.

It is in such a way that Althusser maintains the coherence of his proposals about the isomorphism he had proclaimed between class struggle in practice and the struggle for theoretical liberation; and what enables him to confirm the relevance of this isomorphism is his *productive* reading of the relationship of denial. But we must now ask ourselves if the price paid for these displacements is not, epistemologically speaking, burdensome to the point of repatriating his proposals back into the field of a precritical metaphysics.[5]

The reading of the history of science as the uneven frontal moraine of a glacial advance that unsuspectedly brings forth ideological concretions and survivals is very close to the analysis made, since Koyré, by historians of science of the forward or retarded emergence of the conditions in which a given object may become known. The emergence into knowledge of such an element depends in fact on the lifting of occultations whose relationship with the logic of denial as Althusser practises it in the field of materialist knowledge should not escape attention. This denial, tracked down by Althusser as the equivalent of the socio-economic exploitation that weighs upon the proletariat, and the hope of reaching the truth that it masks, constitute the first formal borrowing from the conceptual apparatus of psychoanalysis. Now this loan is to have a quite peculiar destiny in Althusser's hands, for whereas the concept of denial only functions in Freudianism in the structural and operational form of a circulation and a connection, and no peremptory judgement is made of its themes or contents, the use which Althusserian Marxism makes of it, through its very novelty, unquestionably subjects it to a certain logic of truth that psychoanalysis had been able to go beyond. The scientific truth of historical materialism is in effect opposed to the ideologies that purport to refute it as what is true is opposed to what is false. This freezing up of the functioning of denial in a division between truth and falsehood arises from the fact that Althusser hierarchizes the Freudian metaphor of denial beneath a more powerful regulatory metaphor, namely, that of production as factor of the truth. Whereas in Freud the functioning of denial in relation to the lacunae and blank spots of the unconscious is tied to the operation of a *translation*, the Althusserian use of denial subordinates it to the positive, creative operation of *production*. Here once again lies the isomorphy between social reality and the struggle of materialism against idealism: the metaphor retains a referent in social practice. To produce is, in both cases, not only to bring into existence what was not but to make an object appear in the fabric of a partition that separates the displayed from the concealed; and it is to this that the scope of denial is reduced when Althusser interprets it.

It can thus be said that the fundamental borrowing by Althusser from psychoanalytic theory at this first level manages to transform the instrument of denial but, deprived of its customary status, this concept finds itself subject to a logic of truth commanding a division between clarity and mystification. Thus Althusser repeats Marx's gesture in the opposite direction, importing the Hegelian dialectic into the human sciences. Marx managed to transform the dialectical instrument at the very moment when he let it accomplish its work of productive trans-formation: a transformation of the instrument of production through the action of transformation that it itself makes possible.[6] The upper hand gained by the epistemology of pro-duction therefore confirms the *control* that historical materialism exercises over the concepts imported from its neighbour, psychoanalysis. The potential corrosive action of the Freudian *Verneinung* upon Marxist 'science' is therefore here circum-vented, exorcised and allayed: the decisive clarity of a binary opposition between scientific truth and the chiaroscuro of mystification is substituted for the perilous drifts of the Freudian concept.

The discourse of historical materialism, thus assured of its scientificness, can then well allow itself, without running the danger of harbouring a formidable challenge at its very centre, to undergo the Freudian grafts. The irony of the movement by which this is accomplished is that the acclimatization of the concept of denial brings into play phenomena of conversion and plasticity that are directly related to the metamorphoses that this gesture undergoes in relation to its 'own' object, namely *symbolic* phenomena. The transformation of the Hegelian dialectic into the materialist dialectic and the transplantation of the concept of denial mean not only that the nature of epistemological schema are modified but also their structure; that the concept of denial which functioned for Freud as the economy of a division with no referent is here regulated by an epistemology of truth indicates that one is faced with a kind of function comparable to the one which, in the Freudian economy, ensures the act of repression. It is noticeable, at another level of its relationship with Freudianism, that Althusser's work joins up with one of the functions of psychoanalysis, i.e. that which consists in trying to guarantee a *liberating* repression in the service of a reality principle. But what is even more extraordinary is that this liberating repression is exerted against the under-mining, corrosive scope of these Freudian imports themselves.

This transaction, which might be likened to the raising of some sort of immense rampart to preserve some sort of presence, is successfully brought off by Althusser under the guise of Freudian appearances, but only through sending back the gains of Marxism to the metaphysical land of a logic of truth. How-ever we shall now have to ask ourselves if the transaction can succeed as well when Althusser performs the transplant with the most ominous consequences – that of the concept of over-determination.

Overdetermination

Althusser certainly states that he handles this notion of over-determination with care, given the absence of any other satis-factory term, and that it should be seen as an index and as a problem, as well as the criterion of the emergence of the Marxist in relation to the Hegelian dialectic. And although this concept only appears marginally, as a substitute or occasional supple-ment (like the problematic of the political sphere in Plato's *Republic* when one tires of trying to decode in the individual soul the small writing in which the question of justice is posed), it will be seen that the concept of overdetermination (like the problematic of the city in Plato) will assume a crucial import-ance. In fact it not only points to a gap in the theory which it will try and cover up, but it also cuts through the dialectic to a point of no return as regards the very notion of contradiction. Its impetus is to be found in its challenge to the Hegelian dialectic which is denounced in its status of *explanation by means of the simple*, a dialectic that forecloses and unifies contradictions and that brings about conciliation in the interests of that unity. Now simplicity is the fundamental feature of idealism and of the ideological status of the Hegelian dialectic. The touchstone of the radicalism of the challenge addressed by Marx to Hegel will therefore reside in this 'supplementary' concept of overdetermination. But as we shall see it has the momentum to go much further than this, and constitutes, literally, a *dangerous supplement*.

Overdetermination is defined as 'the reflection, within itself, of the conditions of existence of contradiction', an articulation of its unevenness and fundamental dissymmetry.

In addition to overdetermination are found two other concepts with Freudian origins, those of condensation and displacement, which make their entry on to the stage of the Marxist dialectic. These three concepts refer back to the nodal character of contradiction, that is to the assertion that the intelligibility of one element in a structure is to be derived from its simultaneous membership in other structures. This filling in of a gap in the Marxist schemata through the introduction of conceptual supplements borrowed from Freud's *Interpretation of Dreams* exposes the inadequacy of the general contradiction between forces of production and relations of production, essentially embodied in the contradiction between two antagonistic classes. It corresponds to the necessity of describing the way in which a contradiction becomes *active*. The problem could be put in Kantian terms as one of *active* or *dynamic subsumption*, resembling the articulation of the categories and of intuition. There is in fact a general contradiction between the forms and the relations of production. If revolution is not on the agenda, there remains the riddle of how it emerges into historical reality. But let us note in passing that it is the emergence of a 'superstructural' political problem which obliges Althusser to ask an epistemological question. 'If this contradiction is to become 'active' in the strongest sense, to become a ruptural principle, there must be an accumulation of "circumstances" and "currents" so that whatever their origin and sense (and many of them will *necessarily* be paradoxically foreign to the revolution in origin and sense, or even its "direct opposite"), they "fuse" into a "ruptural unity".'[7]

This introduction of a conceptual join between revolution as burning actuality and revolutionary situation poses the problem of what permits the Kantian 'in depth' connection or articulation between intuition and the pure categories or concepts of the understanding. As we shall see, the solution to this problem lies in that 'metaxu' or intermediary status of the 'schema'. For Althusser the equivalent of the Kantian schema would be the introduction of the concept of the overdetermination of contradiction as a palliative to the inadequacy of the theoretical tools represented by the Leninist notions of the weakest link and of the paradox of contradiction, making Russia the most backward and the most advanced country in relation to the imperialist world. 'Lenin was correct to see in this exceptional situation that was "insoluble" (for the ruling classes) the *objective conditions* of a Russian revolution and to forge in its subjective conditions the means of a decisive assault on this weak link in the imperialist chain, in a Communist Party that was without weak links.'[8]

The poverty of the theory is such that in order to retrospectively explain the Russian Revolution, the concept of overdetermination has to be imported, and this constitutes more than a confession. Not only does it bring with it the necessity of thinking of the efficacity of the superstructure as being to react in an essential way upon the infrastructure – and that is the implication of all those poliorcetic and demiurgic metaphors such as the weakest link – but, what is more, overdetermination undermines, in its very foundations, the notion of contradiction to the extent that it extracts the dialectic from the very field of contradiction, which is of a syntactical nature, in order to launch against it the flow of a semantic corruption. Overdetermination, through the ambiguity that it carries, introduces a process of signification, a subversive genotext which constitutes the text of history as oniric, or rather which makes the dialectic admit to its status of dreamlike text.

Overdetermination produces a *hernia* in the dialectical tissue, because it makes a mockery of contradiction. Sollers saw this point when he wrote: 'Althusser's gesture none the less inaugurates the dissolution of an idealist conception of contradiction.' Struggle is in fact rehabilitated by him back into theory, a struggle in which we would also like to see Heraclitean

Discord embedded. But 'having the momentum to go much further' the concept of overdetermination does more than lay waste an idealist conception of contradiction. We would even go as far as to say that any conception of contradiction is idealist in so far as it represents the repressive work of a *logos* upon the heterogeneous and the dissymmetrical. Now, to mark the impact of overdetermination upon contradiction is to open the sack of Aeolus, and Althusser, by accepting to compensate the theoretical poverty of Marxism through the introduction of the Freudian concepts of overdetermination, condensation, displacement etc., has brought with them a logic of the signifier which, by means of the unparalleled relationship that it establishes between semantics and syntax, unsettles the comfortable arrangements of the logos of contradiction. The heterogeneity and dissymmetry of what Lacan names the symbolic here penetrate together and thus propose a new logic, which as Freud tells us in the *Interpretation of Dreams*:

ignores the non-logical . . . the way in which the dream expresses the categories of opposition and of contradiction is particularly striking: it does not really express them as it appears to ignore the 'no'. It excels in uniting contraries and in representing them in one object alone. A dream may also represent any element whatsoever by the desire of its contrary, in such a way that one cannot know if a dream element, liable to contradiction, betrays a positive or negative content in dream thoughts.

Such is the web of overdetermination and the graft that it inflicts upon the dialectic as well as upon the form of contradiction; it is a lethal graft for the logos of identity but also for that of the dialectic.

Such a (non-)logic as we have written elsewhere[9] is directly transplanted into a deep structure of *Verneinung* or denial in which the dynamic of the unprecedented and unpredictable relationship between Eros and Thanatos, as something inherent, is revealed and becomes active; and the antagonism that binds and separates them exceeds through its hybris any possibility of coagulating into a mere contradiction, even if it were mediatized by the divisions put forward by Mao Tse-tung between the principal/secondary aspects of principal or secondary contradictions. The logic to which we are introduced by Freud's awareness of the death wish, the support of over-determination, when it edges its way into the problematic of contradiction and the dialectic is utterly fatal to the latter, for not only does it relativize them upon a decentred and un-manageable topology where the question of an open polysemy as challenge to the dialectic is constantly posed, but it also and most importantly points to the fact that ever since Heraclitus we have been party to a gravely mistaken philosophical tradi-tion. The whole of Western knowledge, up to and including Marx, has chosen Parmenides, whereas the truth alone per-ceived by Freud in the gap of the Eros/Thanatos relationship which structures the unconscious as a decentred symbolic field is this: that the thought of Heraclitus, the thought of an original Discord and Separation, is not a dialectical thought – of contradiction – but one whose contraries both struggle against and equal each other at the same time. It is the thought of the overdetermination of the psychotically symbolic, and it was an error to have believed that Heraclitus' thought was the ancestor of the dialectic, whether in its Hegelian or Marxist form. It is time we travelled upstream, and only Freud, as we shall see in a later chapter, can lead us there. In order to forge the dialectical tool, whose most subtle and elaborate avatar is Mao Tse-tung's essay with all its cross-connections, the dialectic had to be con-nected into the Platonic logic, itself rooted in Parmenidean logic, the logic of being. This whole gesture has suppressed the sophisticated break represented by Heraclitus, namely that the heterogeneous cannot be dialecticized. The Other that Freud, Lacan and in a certain way Bataille have glimpsed like a buried Heraclitean gem that has lost nothing of its brilliance, *this Other has nothing to do with alienations, alterations, antitheses and contradictions even if they have reached the arachnean stage that Mao Tse-tung in his genius took them to.*

It is through this Freudian excess that only Althusser has had the courage to introduce into the Marxist dialectic that the

Heraclitean poetic may resurface intact in its wish to speak to us with its still unexploited novelty. 'Cold things burn; hot, they freeze; moist, they dry; arid, they flow.' Such would be the lesson of overdetermination introduced to fill a gap, to provide for an inadequacy in the dialectic. Such would be the opening and the blossoming out that would force one to return to that enigmatic place where, as the generators of overdetermination through the warfare and struggle they engage in (*Polemos pater panton*), the Freudian Eros and Thanatos suddenly make obsolete the notion of contradiction and force the dialectic to admit that even in its inclusion of negativity, even at its Maoist peak, it began with Plato, and that it would be incapable of going back beyond its source and of putting new possibilities into play. However, the effect of introducing the Freudian notion of overdetermination has nevertheless been to pluralize contradiction, to unhinge it from its fastidious binarism to a point beyond which Althusser would not have wished it to go. The emergence of the notion of ruptural unity required by the need to explain history and the emergence of an element that is deviant as regards theory – and that element is nothing less than the Russian Revolution of 1917 – has made possible the integration of diverse parameters and contradictions, some of which were completely heterogeneous, as well as their regrouping along the lines of a parallelogram of forces which form a scalene and multidimensional network, a structural one. This diffraction thus jeopardizes the chances of preserving the general concept of contradiction as the general *modus operandi* or invariable of the dialectic. But it is upon the universality of this notion that Lenin and after him Mao Tse-tung continue to lean, with no concern for the heterogeneous whose awesome powers Althusser, partly without his knowledge, has liberated.

Partly without his knowledge: in fact, if we recaptiulate the three original contributions which Althusser thanks to his psychoanalytic grafts has enabled Marxism to integrate, it will be seen that their fortunes differ.

First, the essential introduction of *denial* as the symptomatic structure that presides over the decentred, unsynchronic relationship between Marxist philosophy or dialectical materialism and Marxist science or historical materialism. The corrupting effects of the introduction of Freudian logic lose their edge and are conjured away by a radical transformation in their nature. In Althusser's thematic importation, denial functions as a transitional operator between mystification and truth. It is linearized and loses sight of its symbolic origins. The object of Althusser's second flirtation with psychoanalysis is the operational and no longer thematic introduction of a *repression* that would conserve the reality principle, and this operational expropriation also succeeds beyond all hope, as it is against the subversive effects of Freudian (non-)logic that this repression takes its stand.

It is at the third level of Althusser's consortation with psychoanalysis that things begin to deteriorate and where Marxism, with no way out of the problem of articulating historical events at odds with theory other than recourse to the semantic virtues of overdetermination, finds itself caught in the trap of the heterogeneous that it has triggered off inside itself. Far from being able this time to englobe or reterritorialize the Freudian and structural conceptuality, as had been the case with the concept of denial, here the dialectic is circumscribed and regionalized by a *logic of the heterogeneous* in which it would no longer play a leading role. Althusser and Marxism were to attempt a final intellectual manoeuvre to vanquish the structuralist danger on its own terrain. They would consent to accord the relations of production the status of a term among many others of the complex contradiction, but their unconsciously causalist desires forced them to proclaim once more that these relations of production are 'contradiction's conditions of existence'. The stop-gap introduction of a non-symbolic *pseudo-unconscious* in the shape of an *absence of the last instance* is the pathetic attempt by which Althusserianism tries to imitate the workings of the heterogeneous. It will thus be with all the affection of a clinical and symptomatic attention that we will welcome those pronouncements of Althusser where, caught in the difficulties that his epistemological courage has led him to, he completely denies the contributions of structuralism:

Structuralism, born of the theoretical problems encountered by scientists in their practice (in linguistics since Saussure, in ethnology since Boas and Lévi-Strauss, in psychoanalysis etc), is not a 'philosopher's philosophy' but a 'philosophy' or a 'philosophical ideology for scientists'. That its themes are diffuse and unstable and their limits poorly defined does not prevent one, however, from characterizing its *general tendency* as rationalist, mechanical, but above all as formalist. At its limit (and this can be read in certain texts by Lévi-Strauss as well as by linguists or other logicians prone to philosophize), structuralism (or better, certain structuralists) is attracted by the ideal of the *production of the real under the effect* of a *combinatory of any elements whatsoever*.[10]

In this incomplete and oversimplified description that reduces structuralism to a formal combinatory, and whose gross inadequacy we intend to prove, we see the evidence of the terror that the structuralist Althusser experiences vis-à-vis the contribution of concepts which he has been forced to bring into the field of materialism and of their noxious effects for the theory whose gaps they fill in with a destructive generosity: *dangerous supplements*. The only way of averting this danger is to pretend to take structuralism lightly, for he knows only too well that if it were confronted head-on he would be forced to admit that the dialectic as he thinks and is trying to preserve it could hardly survive. And we have to give a last description of the underlying motives for this denial in so far as the job of bringing to light the effectivity of the superstructure is also affected by the mark of overdetermination.

Effectivity of the superstructure and the last instance

The other major concession made by Althusser is then the recognition of the superstructure's peculiar effectivity. The problematic has been changed and there is no more risk of confusing the effectivity that can be legitimately accorded to the superstructure with the disturbing seductions of the wiles of reason, the last snare of Hegelian idealism disguised as History's unconscious. Once safely within the bounds of materialism one can afford not to fetishize the function of the socio-economic infrastructure, to the extent that it does not finally explain very much. The role that will be allotted to international conjuncture, for example, is a part of that explanation by the superstructure that militates against it. The contribution of Althusser, following Gramsci, has been to free the superstructure from any *immediate* determination by the infrastructure and in particular from that murky theory of the reflection which for a long time has been one of the dogmatic articles of faith in the French Marxist vulgate. The importance given to the superstructure comes in two stages. First, it is recognized that the superstructure has a specific and *autonomous* existence which can no longer be reduced to the simple 'phenomenality' in the Hegelian sense of the infrastructure or of the structural principle of contradiction. Then it is accepted that conditions of the structure's existence can be seen in the superstructure; the latter is thereby granted its own effectivity.

It is legitimate to call this effectivity of the superstructure reciprocal or return action. In any case, what is gained by pluralizing the dialectic through the forced recognition of the importance of the superstructure is compensated by the emphasis placed on the role of determination *in the last instance* by the economic. At this first stage then we have to thank Althusser for having been able to draw from his reading of Engels the glittering theory of the effectivity of the superstructure: far from being pure phenomena of the economy (in the inverse Hegelian sense), those factors writes Engels: '... preponderantly determine the form of historical struggles.' But at the same time the movement is exposed by which Althusser tries to blunt their impact thanks to the fixed point of the last instance. The question which is then posed,' writes Althusser, 'is the following: how, in those conditions, can the unity of the real but relative effectivity of the superstructures be thought – and of the determinant role "in the last instance" of the economy? How can the relationship between these distinct effectivities be thought? How, in this unity can the role of the 'last instance' of the economic be founded?' And Engels's reply is: 'All these factors [i.e. the superstructures] act and react and in their midst the movement of the economic finally forces its way through the infinite throng of chance events (that is, of things and events whose innermost connections with each other are so far removed or so difficult to demonstrate that we may consider them as nonexistent and not worthy of our attention).' Therefore it is *in order to put a stop to the infinity of the effects* of the elements of the Superstructure, a sort of pleasure principle in the Freudian sense, that Engels and then Althusser judge it necessary to bestow a regulatory principle upon it, namely the last instance.

But where Althusser distinguishes himself from Engels's superficial reading is when he makes the remark that this last instance is far from recreating the conditions of economism, a materialist position whose demon Althusser has already exorcised. On the contrary, by introducing the notions of mediation and of overdetermination on the one hand and of the unconscious on the other, he shows that the effectivity in the last instance of the economy is no longer 'exterior to the chance events through which it makes its way but is the interior essence of those events'. The concepts are taken from a perceptive reading of Engels by means of which Althusser manages to produce in the former's text the importance and relevance of a model which in the apparent haphazardness of the infinite effects of the superstructure introduces a sort of profound but nevertheless accessible 'nemesis' for the scientific investigation of historical materialism: the model of a parallelogram of compound forces whose resultant transcends the forces that compose it. It is the immediate corollary of the determination of the last instance as the unconscious at work in the parallelogram of compound forces producing a resultant that transcends these forces; and the necessity arises of thinking this unconscious as one that evicts the subject – 'unequal to the consciousness of each separate will and at the same time a force without a subject' Althusser writes.

Aware of seeing Engels being engulfed in spite of this by a

epistemological vacuum, the correlative of a space *fully occupied* by philosophy where a desubjectivized Sartrian existentialism would find its comfort, Althusser is forced to oppose the 'specifically Marxist' concept of *overdetermination* to the metaphysical theory of the last instance such as Engels frames it. The mediations introduced by Engels into the model of the parallelogram of compound forces are certainly effective, and Althusser aligns himself with them to attack the economism and subjectivism which are, like idealism and empiricism for the Kantian critique, his two main enemies. But when Engels sets out to find a 'foundation' for his model (in the letter to Bloch of 21/9/1890), his epistemological ambitions make him resemble the Kantian dove that would like to keep itself on the wing when it no longer has the resistance of the air to support its flight. In claiming to think the last instance as the *interior essence* of chance events and especially in conceiving the genesis of individual wills upon the infinity of circumstances, and that of the final result upon the infinity of parallelograms, Engels wishes to salvage the whole cargo; a causalism of a Spinozist *conatus* variety present in its effects as well as the production of a resultant that transcends the forces that compose it, and finally, a naturalist philosophy upon which are grafted the mechanisms of the economic instance – a sort of omnicombinatory structuralism. From this model, Althusser retains only the cutting edge of its criticisms against the ideological and positivistic dangers of economism and subjectivism, but he denounces its empty and abstract character:

Such is the level of Marx's historical theory: the level of the concepts of structure, superstructure and all their specifications. But if the same scientific discipline should set out from another level than its own, from a level which is not the object of any scientific knowledge ... to produce the possibility of its own objects and of the concepts corresponding to it, then it will fall into an epistemological void, or, and this is what gives it its vertigo, into a philosophical fullness.[11]

The most silent hour

In this letter to Bloch, Engels basically commits the same idealist mistake as does the Hegelian dialectic. Believing in the universality of his schema, he only manages to produce an absurd, abstract and empty effect. Through a movement that is related to Marx's transformation-through-inversion of the Hegelian dialectic, Althusser puts Engels's parallelogram back on its feet, and this inversion is no longer a simple optical one but a transformation through extraction, producing the regulated autonomy of the superstructure and its specifications as well as the overdetermination of contradiction, the only condition by which one may take into account the historically concrete and particular without falling into vague generalities. Althusser's epistemological courage has thus consisted in extracting from the mystical husk of Engels's instrument the rational kernel which enables him to accord the superstructure its full scope, that is to conceive of the concrete in the unfolding of all its specifications:

It is sufficient to retain from him what should be called the accumulation of effective determinations (deriving from the superstructures and from special national and international circumstances) on the determination in the last instance by the economic. It seems to me that this clarifies the expression overdetermined contradiction, which I have put forward, this specifically because the existence of overdetermination is no longer a fact pure and simple, for in its essentials we have related it to its bases, even if our exposition has so far been merely gestural. This overdetermination is inevitable and thinkable as soon as the real existence of the forms of the superstructure and of the national and international conjuncture has been recognized – an existence largely specific and autonomous, and therefore irreducible to a pure phenomenon. We must carry this through to its conclusion and say that this overdetermination does not refer to apparently unique and aberrant historical situations (Germany, for example), but is universal; the economic dialectic is never active in the pure state; in History, these instances, the superstructures, etc., are never seen to step respectfully aside when their work is done or, when the Time comes, as his pure phenomena, to scatter before His Majesty the Economy as he strides along the royal road of the Dialectic. From the first moment to the last, the lonely hour of the 'last instance' never comes.[12]

The structural Shirt of Nessus

It was necessary to quote this passage in its entirety in order to fully appreciate how Althusser has managed, in unambiguously revealing his epistemological hostility towards all forms of positivism, to pluralize and dislocate the dialectic by inseminating it with this revolutionary instrument of overdetermination, one of the offspring of Freud. The mode of presence of the last instance whose hour, like that of the unconscious, never comes, is also Freudian. In such a way the debt that Althusser can admit to vis-à-vis psychoanalytic structuralism may be measured. This debt, as we have said, to the extent that it exhausts the dialectic by dragging it to the shores of modernity where a suppressed Heraclitus may re-emerge, is so costly to the dialectic and its logos that one has to seriously question the use of the term.

The end of the dialectic?

In the same way, although along the lines of the combinatory traits of a more static or at any rate more rigid network, the enrichment to which Mao subjects the notion of contradiction strains the dialectical process to such a point that it hardly seems useful to recognize any necessity in the further employment of this concept which was tied, as we have seen, to a certain use of the logos. And from within this same dialectical logos, the effect of these innovations has been to stretch and pulverize contradiction to the point where it becomes unrecognizable. The added leeway that is thus produced is one which deconstructs from within the dialectical sign and the intellectual instrument that it denotes. And so Althusser's strange refusal, tucked away in a footnote, to travel further with Mao's notion of contradiction in an exploration of a kinship of approaches can be better understood. Althusser, feeling that with the fatal instrument of overdetermination (which we maintain introduces the structural play of the unconscious into the fabric of the dialectic) he places the binary determinations that are subject to the logos of identity and which compose the dialectic in danger, dreads confronting them with the Maoist dislocations between principal and secondary aspect, principal/secondary contradiction and antagonistic and non-antagonistic contradiction. For this system that is more rigid with Mao would shatter on contact with them and would not survive the shock of overdetermination that ushers in a semantic and signifying dimension, whereas with Mao one remains at the level of a purely syntactic and combinatory vision. Mao's key contribution consists in this difference of antagonism/non-antagonism, but his system can no longer be wedded to the conception of dialectical over-determination introduced by Althusser. These two cases represent restricted regions and local aspects of a structural network whose unpredicable wealth must, it seems, no longer be subsumed under the common term of dialectic.

The threat looming over the dialectic is thus that of its fracturing and exploding into too many sites and logical areas, to such an extent that the coherent process of a logos may no longer be placed under this label. When Godelier announces for example that the function of the last instance can be exercised by elements disclosed by anthropology, such as royalty or the political and religious spheres, he manages to credit these elements with an effectivity that even the recognition of the backlash action of the superstructure could not have accorded. For this effectivity, the 'open' Marxism of the Althusserians, could only be admitted on condition that it was reaffirmed that the last instance in the interplay of an absence-presence was nevertheless the dominance of the economy.

Here structure becomes plural and centrifugal with no vectorial orientation, and to such a degree that the very possibility of recognizing as specific an infra- and a super-structure seems to have withered away. The enrichment of the dialectic here seems to be lethal to it and to belong to the pluralization which may be posited in accordance with Foucault's conception of history: the economy no longer has any power, but symbolic elements elsewhere can, according to the epistemes, receive a peculiar effectivity.

This pluralization of the dialectic therefore deprives historical materialism of its hold and leads us to a recognition of the heterogeneous that exceeds the notions of contradiction and mediation. Even the concept of causality is worked upon by an action of the symbolic that liberates it from the metaphysical and realist taints of the dialectic; the most penetrating advance of this process of deconstruction of the dialectical fabric, achieved by Mao, is produced inside the supposedly scientific field posited by Althusser at the moment when the 'science' of historical materialism admits the notion of overdetermination, which brings with it a problematic of the unpredictable and unparalleled relationship between Eros and the death wish, and makes any re-absorption into a logos of simple contradiction impossible. The difficulties and denials with which Althusser in his *Eléments d'autocritique* reproves, with a certain affectionate scorn, his youthful sins and his 'flirtation' (*kokettieren*, like Marx with Hegel) with structuralism can thus be better understood. He is driven to this position in effect, and it is even vital for him if he wants to keep on calling himself a Marxist and to ward off the untolerable contribution of structuralism, that opening which lacerates the dialectic and tears the gap of a relationship *other* than that of a logos of truth/contradiction into its very fabric.

The thought of Heraclitus that places the logos and the dialectic in peril shows itself to be far more faithful to that hidden face of Apollonianism whose herald was Hölderlin than to any Dionysiac force rediscovered by Nietzsche. What our epoch has to contend with now, encamped on the debris of its exhausted dialectical logos, is the lesson of Heraclitus, repressed for too long and whose immanence only structuralism, because it pluralizes all logic of identity and contradiction to the point of open warfare, has been able to foresee.

3. The Limits of Human Nature in Chomsky and Lévi-Strauss

Plato's dialogue the *Cratylus* is based on an essential debate between two characters, Cratylus and Hermogenes, whose theses are completely antagonistic to each other. The question at issue is the adequacy of nouns and names. Hermogenes, who speaks first, considers that names and nouns are the consequence of a convention, a treaty, a contract or a covenant, that they are artificial and arbitrary. Cratylus, on the contrary, holds the view that nouns and names are proper, that is to say they are modelled on the nature of things which they imitate, or to which they are linked according to a binding of causality. In any case, a natural relationship.

Hermogenes versus Cratylus, law versus nature, *nomos* versus *physis*, or culture versus natural necessity. Socrates is invited to take part in the debate. He declares himself incompetent but ready to study the question with them. Against Hermogenes he will establish that nouns, words and names represent the essence of things; against Cratylus he shows that the relationship between names and things is anything but stable and that there is a mixture of motion and rest in the act of designation. Unable to admit Cratylus' thesis that a God might have attributed names to things, he instead proposes the more modest image of a self-contradictory or intoxicated legislator.

This is one of the most exciting dialogues, for it is one which does not end in certainty but in aporia. And this aporia, this inconclusive outcome, this lack of ascertained answer, con-

tinues all along the twenty-five centuries of Western metaphysics and Western knowledge. Philosophy first, and then
linguistics and the so-called human sciences, have given no
satisfactory reply whatsoever. The whole history of Western
knowledge unwinds between the two poles set by Plato in the
opposition between Hermogenes and Cratylus, caught up in the
matrix of the opposition between nature and its antonyms,
between *physis* and *nomos, physis* and *techne*, nature and culture.
No wonder if we rediscover this pattern in the claim made by
Saussure according to which *the sign is arbitrary* and no wonder
if Peirce replies in a definitive paper: *the sign is not arbitrary*. To
the eyes of a grammarian who wishes to study language as a
self-regulating set of forms or structures, the sign is arbitrary,
it is unmotivated, the words and the code do not bear any
relation of likeness or necessity with the things they stand for.
In that case, the whole of a language can be compared with a
contract which was never signed but whose provisions would
explain the relative status of signs towards one another.

But for the users of language, for those who speak, those who
are within the limits of the contract, who denote and communicate, there must be some sort of link between the sign and
its referent, or at least with its signified; there must be a minimal
propriety of nouns, on which the users of the code agree and
rely – otherwise language would be nothing but a subset of
Lewis Carroll's 'Jabberwocky', or a tale told by an idiot.

On the one hand, linguistic or cultural *signs* are seen as self-
regulated *symbols*; on the other hand they are *icons*, i.e. rooted
in the thing they represent.

Hermogenes versus Cratylus, Saussure versus Peirce: Western
knowledge since the Greeks has always put, and tried to solve,
the question of the relationship between culture and nature. Is
culture rooted in nature, imitating it or emanating direct from
it? Or, on the contrary, is culture at variance with nature,
absolutely cut off from it since the origin and involved in the
process of always transforming, changing nature? The matrix
of this opposition between culture and nature is the very matrix
of Western metaphysics. Metaphysics constitutes it, or, in

virtue of a circular argument, whose name is history, is constituted by it.

Are we still bound to reply as Socrates was tempted to do, that the legislator when he instituted language and culture must have been self-contradictory and even drunk, drunk to the point of playing sometimes the game of aping the world, and sometimes the more luxurious game of creating with words a world of his own, both at the same time?

But this myth of a drunken legislator threatens to blur another question. Whether one considers that there is a split, a discontinuity between culture and nature, or on the contrary that they are linked by a relationship of continuity, one cannot avoid the problem: how is man and how is human nature related to culture and to nature? Is there a human nature that one has to consider as integrated with the nature of things, or has this concept of human nature a role to play as a connector, mediator or shifter between culture and nature? The position at stake here is that of man as a centre of the universe, as interpreting the world and ruling over it, as an absolute source of codes, languages, practices and meaning as a whole. Man, the meaning-giver? Or on the contrary is not this concept of human nature a hindrance, a nuisance that epistemological purity would have to dismiss?

The works of Lévi-Strauss and Chomsky will help us to raise these points. Because they are not philosophers but specialists engaged in a research connected with mankind without being obscured in their quest by humanist ideology, they both meet the question of the relationships between nature and culture at the very root: language and code. Not only do they touch this question technically, in the process of their researches as ethnographer and linguist respectively; but also the philosophical question of their concept of human nature can be raised at the level of the epistemological claims they make. And there we shall notice a certain kinship with classical formulations, as if the breakthrough they had made in the field of their techniques were redeemed or compensated by their belonging to a classical universe of concepts.

The epistemological question that one is entitled to ask these two scientists runs as follows: is the concept of *human nature* as a stable essence the necessary corollary of their exploration of the borderline between nature and culture, and are they right to situate it where they do? Lévi-Strauss will indeed postulate under the name of *nature* a universal combinatory matrix whose local and particular cultures are only empirical products ever destroyed and ever rebuilt by the motion we call history. Chomsky in his fight against empiricism and behaviourism will revert to a concept of innate structures which characterize the human mind and make it capable of building language.

Are these two concepts of human nature that we shall scrutinize the inevitable and necessary results of their approaches or on the contrary do they bear arbitrary ideological connotations which will have to be examined and contested? In other terms, assuming that, in spite of the novelty of these thinkers, we have remained on a Platonic stage with the same scenery where Cratylus, Hermogenes and Socrates are performing the same hackneyed play, one may ask the following question. Is the only escape from the spectre of a drunken legislator to be found in an anthropocentric conception of the *gnothi seauton*, know thyself, prescribed by Socrates?

Let us first consider how Lévi-Strauss fights against traditional metaphysical concepts of human nature; in this he will remind us of Rousseau and the difficulties Rousseau had with the thinkers of the Enlightenment. Then we shall be entitled to ask: with what relationship between culture and nature does Lévi-Strauss provide us?

Lévi-Strauss's approach to anthropology has now become common knowledge. It assumes that customs, myths, attitudes, behaviours that an external observer of a culture collects at random, are not the accidental or fortuitous products of haphazard circumstances but the performances of an underlying logic which generates them from below, and that this logic can be deciphered and formalized far beyond the awareness to which the performers caught within a code have access.

This system of rules which articulates partial and isolated

phenomena constitutes a logical network which allows the building of a 'model' of how the social system works both at the level of denominations and at the level of attitudes. We shall take three examples of this structuralist method concerned with formal relationships between elements more than with the individual elements themselves, and see how they militate against traditional substantialist notions of human nature conceived in terms of individual subjectivity. These three instances are: structures of kinship, myths and totemisms.

Lévi-Strauss's structuralist method has been built under the influence of Saussure and Jakobson's linguistics, which deal with systems of formal oppositions that are, at the same time, tables of possible permutations between terms. An empirical phenomenon – for instance, the actual observable structure of kinship in a given group – will be only one example among all the possible combinatory permutations for that group. Moreover the marriage systems of different societies are treated as paradigmatic transformations of an underlying common logical structure. In his book *Anthropologie structurale*, in the chapter 'Langage et parenté' (language and kinship), Lévi-Strauss produces a comprehensive table which shows how various communities, completely isolated from one another, in fact embody each in its turn a possible transformation of the whole combinatory system: the terms combined here are patrilineal/matrilineal filiations, relations of brother and sister, father and son, and relations governing the extent of affection or hostility, reserve or intimacy. If the question is 'What does the avuncular relationship consist of?' one can easily see from this diagram that the uncle's relationship, to be understood, must be treated as a relation within a system. The first consequence of this structure is to produce a shift from an existentialist, or phenomenological, concept of human nature and human relations. One replaces the image of each individual as an independent subject or source of meaning, by that of a term, an element interdependent with the others in a formal pattern. Within each structure, the type of kinship behaviour is prescribed to each of the performers by the rule of the code, which means he does not choose it, even in a primordial choice that existentialists would have called a project. And the performers are not necessarily aware of these forces by which the kinship behaviour is programmed, although they are sometimes able to formulate them consciously: Lévi-Strauss resorts to a social *unconscious* which is at variance with the phenomenological concept of human nature as subjectivity and consciousness. Simple as this structure is (Lévi-Strauss calls it the unit of kinship), and given the fact that it is still at the level of field observation, it still allows us to measure how remote is Lévi-Strauss's approach to culture through kinship behaviours from any existentialist concept of conscious free subjectivity, and especially from Sartre's in *Critique de la raison dialectique*. It even helps us to show this treatise as part of an ethnocentric pattern restricted in its relevance to Western societies.

An important consequence of this is that Lévi-Strauss repudiates the idea that culture merely imitates nature: he writes: 'the system of kinship is a language'. And we can imagine that here he ranks with those who, after Saussure, have proclaimed the non-motivation of the symbolic function. The fact that the avuncular relationship, which has no procreative foundation, is a key feature of the elementary structure, indicates that Lévi-Strauss does not map his basic kinship structure on *biological* relations. He is at variance with Radcliffe-Brown, who had written: 'The unit of structure from which a kinship is built up is the group which I call an "elementary family" consisting of a man and his wife and their child or children.'

Lévi-Strauss replies: 'The idea according to which the biological family constitutes the point of departure from which every society builds up its system of kinship does not belong only to R. Brown; but there is no more dangerous idea.'

A system of kinship does not consist of objective links of filiation or consanguinity given among individuals: it exists only in man's consciousness; it is an arbitrary system of representations, not the spontaneous development of a factual situation. In a sort of Copernican revolution, comparable to that achieved by Kant in knowledge, Lévi-Strauss shows that biological filiation instead of being the basis of kinship structures is only a parameter which has a limited and defined location in a wider unmotivated network. 'In order for a kinship structure to exist, three types of family relations must always be present: a relation of consanguinity, a relation of affinity and a relation of descent.' Hermogenes has evidently won the first round. Culture is different from nature and cut off from it. Lévi-Strauss indeed still speaks in this early quotation in terms of *conscious representations*; but later in his work he shows that conscious representations are only surface layers produced by a set of deep structures which can be deciphered through the combinatory process. 'Linguistics presents us with a totalizing dialectic external to or below the level of consciousness and will power. As a non-reflective totalization, language is a human reason which has its reasons that man does not know.' This universal logic is only implicit in the confrontation between the five patterns set up by Lévi-Strauss: Trobriand, Sivai, Cherkess, Tonga, Kutubu; taken together they lead to the claim that there is a general matrix whose combinatory power, agent of all possible permutations, is the law of these empirical arrangements. We shall see later that this leads Lévi-Strauss, as in the example of totemism, which I shall discuss later, to conceive of a deep source of these operations and combinations and that this deep structure might be called *nature*, because it roots culture back into natural laws.

But before we are invited by Lévi-Strauss to accomplish this *Vaterländische Umkehr* (as Hölderlin says in his Remarks on Antigone), before we are led to postulate a structural nature which would be the source and the substratum of these deep combinatory structures, we must note that Lévi-Strauss uses these confrontations and convergences between various patterns isolated from each other as heuristic instruments, i.e. he claims only that they build a network of probability for the finding of other family structures: like the Mendeleev table of elements in chemistry. But the limit to formalization must here be carefully set: even though the avuncular relationship is seen as part of a structure, first of all it is difficult to universalize the system in spite of the striking congruences between these isolated groups; and second, these surface structures do not exhaust the family reality and one can easily find other types of relationship which are omitted by this pattern. For instance, an exchange between husband and wife can be compounded of affection and reserve together; and this is but one example of the complexity of relations which Lévi-Strauss admits he has tactically simplified. As in the field of dreams and unconscious analysed by Freud, we are in the field of overdetermination: that is to say a symptom or a sign is the junction of several threads of significance. And this articulation of overdetermined symptoms on the features of a combinatory matrix, far from being a repudiation of culture as a formalizable language, might be related to the pre-established harmony which in Leibniz's writings prevails between the formal network of the monads and the semantico-syntactic display of a universal characteristic or theory of writing.

This is the first shift brought about by Lévi-Strauss: human nature no longer rests in the field of consciousness, or of the universal substratum or subjectivity of man as centre of the world. Various cultures have to be considered as decipherable overdetermined patterns produced by a deep set of structures which, according to his argument, altogether constitutes a great combinatory power. Might we call such a power nature in a new key? Human mind is not consciousness but concept. But the syntactic law of this linguistic pattern is the incest taboo, as we shall see later on.

This assimilation of culture to a language is not new: Marcel Mauss in his remarkable essays on *gift-giving* and on *magics* had already emphasized how the associations brought about in the universe of so-called primitive societies are comparable in their structure to a rhetorical *corpus*: the system of give and take, the sacrificial exchange of goods which characterizes potlatch, and the associations between signs and symbols operated by magics, have been analysed by Mauss as a world where *tropes*, that is symbolic and rhetorical structures, were at work. But Lévi-Strauss's approach represents a step further, in the sense that he succeeds in formalizing the field, ridding the structures of their semantic remainder in favour of paradigmatic networks which lead to the fecundity of harmonic Leibnizian isomorphism:

> Marriage rules and kinship systems are a sort of language, that is to say a set of operations designed to ensure, between individuals and groups, a certain type of communication. The fact that the message would here be constituted by the women of the group who circulate between clans, lineages or families and not, as in the case of language itself, by the words of the group circulating between individuals, in no way alters the fact that the phenomenon considered in the two cases is identically the same [*Structural Anthropology*, 1].

This does not mean that the performance or utterance is in both cases similar. There is a similarity inasmuch as both sets of performances, the linguistic and the social, are regulated by codes or laws which underlie them without the performers being aware of them; and in the fact that they are regulated by a syntactical matrix. The main difference lies in the fact that, as we shall see in the discussion of Chomsky later on, the structures of kinship are a limited set which generate a limited number of performances, i.e. a closed system; whereas the linguistic exchange allows an infinite and unpredictable number of utterances. The case is not simple, because the patterns of kinship attitudes are intermingled with a pattern of appellations, i.e. a linguistic pattern; and at both levels there is a return of the symbolic or semantic problem through the occurrence of overdetermination or polysemy.

But the basic novelty lies in a displacement of humanism which could be formulated in this critique of Sartre's man-centred philosophy, by Lévi-Strauss: 'In a century when man is bent on the destruction of innumerable forces of life, it is necessary to insist that a properly equipped humanism cannot begin of its own accord but must place the world before life, life before man, and the respect of others before self-interest.' In this statement there is an echo of Rousseau's thesis, in particular of this difference or shift which made Rousseau's quest so much at variance with the traditional humanistic claims of the

Enlightenment: claims which were concerned with light, progress and reason. What one finds here is the difference stated by Rousseau between 'amour propre' and 'amour de soi': 'amour propre' – or love of self – being a corruption of 'amour de soi', and subsequent to it, whereas 'amour de soi', which is equated with pity, can be translated into English by 'love of the human species' as opposed to 'love of self'. In this opposition one finds an anticipation of the key opposition between the general interest and self-interest which will be the core of the political state in the doctrine of the general will.

In his second *Discours sur l'origine de l'inégalité* Rousseau proposes *pity* as a basic passion from which all affective and intellectual movements of the mind will be deduced and derived, after a succession of stages which will be generated from each other not in a continuous pattern, but through a succession of discontinuities or splits or hiatuses. But this pity or natural goodness or 'amour de soi' does not exist actually in what Rousseau calls the state of pure nature or pure state of nature. It is only a virtuality, a potentiality. What distinguishes his approach from all the others is that he does not assume that there is a natural law which is of mutual love (as in the case of Locke). Rousseau breaks the circular discourse in which jurists and philosophers used to enclose the formation of political laws, which were held to be mapped on a concept of natural law; whereas in fact the natural law was deduced from these social laws themselves. Rousseau goes back to a pure state of nature which is neither altruistic nor a state of war as in Hobbes, but a theoretical construction, a sort of degree zero of the state of nature, an absence of essence which cannot at its origin bear any predicate: man then, is null and dull; he does not even assess his own existence in terms of time. As Alan Ryan has put it: in Rousseau's state of pure nature, 'men are mere isolated animals, isolated in space and time. For Rousseau natural man is not the noble savage nor is he Hobbes's rational egoist. Both these conditions are social conditions and in an important sense non-natural. As an animal man is neither moral nor immoral, but amoral.'

The consequence of this strategic move towards a degree zero will be to allow Rousseau to deduce another type of history than the one which has led to alienation, inequality and injustice. By breaking this circle he avoids giving an undue legitimacy to existing laws in actual society.

A superficial reader of both Rousseau and Lévi-Strauss would have been struck by the similarity that the legend of the *noble savage* in Rousseau bears to some allusions made by Lévi-Strauss to the tenderness, innocence and gentleness of the Nambikwara tribe whose life is described in *Tristes tropiques*. This is one of the misleading analogies that have been drawn: to label Lévi-Strauss as the romantic and Rousseau as the pre-romantic. But there is no such thing as the noble savage in Rousseau, only this degree zero of nature. The gap between the two concepts is important because it allows Rousseau not only to invalidate the circular generation of unjust political laws, but also to fight the myth that there was a real evolution in time from primitive to civilized, from nature to culture. Genesis in the history of mankind as described in the second *Discours* must be interpreted as an epistemology of discontinuity, an analogue of which appears in Lévi-Strauss. First of all Rousseau warns us against a possible misinterpretation of this genesis: it is not an anthropological chronicle but a theoretical problem embodied in the figure of a parable.

The fictional generation of the concept of culture through various rhythmic, discontinuous cycles ('Commençons par écarter tous les faits') is Rousseau's methodological claim. Let us begin by discarding all factual data. We may see the same methodological recommendation made by Lévi-Strauss when he generates formally and theoretically some kinship structure or totemism relationships, and there he distinguishes himself from the culturalists or the empiricists as much as Rousseau did from the conventional Enlightenment philosophers.

But a parallel which is more striking is the one which is drawn between the two battles that both Rousseau and Lévi-Strauss fight against a continuous evolutionary myth of history. By refuting the anthropological circle and breaking his way towards the degree zero of culture and of nature Rousseau shows that faculties like imagination or industry, and later the political state obtained through the contract, were born in *discontinuous hiatuses*. Culture emerges through discontinuity, and all at once. One cannot but quote here the famous passage of the *Introduction à l'oeuvre de M. Mauss* when Lévi-Strauss writes:

Language was born all at once. Whatever the moment and the circumstances of its appearing in the range of animal life, language necessarily appeared all at once. Things cannot have begun to signify gradually. After a transformation the study of which has no relevance in the field of social sciences, but only in biology or psychology, a change has taken place, from a stage where nothing had meaning to a stage where everything had.

But the strangest impact of this fight against evolution is to be found in the denunciation of the concept of history as an ethnocentric product of Western knowledge. The introduction of hiatuses and discontinuity patterns into the theoretical account of genesis had allowed Rousseau to refute a certain ideology of natural law. Similarly, the use of discontinuity will allow Lévi-Strauss to refute the linear evolutionist pattern according to which so-called primitive societies were conceived as earlier stages of a development of mankind whose Western culture would have represented the latest stage. Such a myth, which Lévi-Strauss denounces in *Race et histoire*, is a consequence of this subtle Western ethnocentrism, a sort of intellectual colonialism in the process of which we try to annex the cultures of *other* peoples and consider their evolution as subordinated to the goal of reaching our own stage. Against this ideology, Lévi-Strauss provides a pattern of discontinuity and differences: he shows as well in *La Pensée sauvage* as in *Race et histoire* that cultures are various strategic moves in which mankind approaches and transforms nature according to the theory of games with different formal codes or deals, simultaneously. This helps to shatter the ideology of primitive as opposed to civilized cultures; it challenges the axiological hierarchies between savage, barbaric and civilized and it preserves at this stage ethnographic relativity. What Rousseau achieved at the level of time, introducing discontinuity in genesis, Lévi-Strauss does in cultural space, introducing discontinuity between cultural codes and destroying the ethnocentric illusion of a common history of mankind: 'The equivalence between the notion of history and that of humanity which is imposed upon us with the hidden aim of making historicity the lost shelter of transcendental humanism' is finally denounced by Lévi-Strauss, which allows us to see how opposed his views are to those of Sartre and of certain Marxists. His views have helped us to realize that history, and the difference between peoples within a history and those without a history, were ideologies rooted in a culture which would be wrong to take itself as an absolute. As a consequence, history will only be seen as a factor of degeneration of formal systems. For instance, those corpuses of myths which are built in cultures by networks of structural patterns are similar to musical scores which can be deciphered vertically as well as horizontally. Musical genres of the classical age and myths are mutually isomorphic, because they both provide a deciphering grid, a matrix of relationships which filter and process experience, substitute themselves for it, and give the illusion that contradictions can be overcome and difficulties surmounted. This formal equilibrium is threatened by the erosion of history, that is lived by men, built by historians, and dreamt by philosophers.

In a beautiful passage of *La Pensée sauvage* in the chapter called 'Histoire et dialectique', Lévi-Strauss denounces the ethnocentric reductionism practised by Sartre when he continues to postulate history and dialectics as universal cultural predicates: Sartre is accused of overlooking the prodigious richness and diversity of fashions, beliefs and cultures; 'it is too often forgotten', Lévi-Strauss alleges, 'that in their own eyes each of the tens of hundreds of thousands of societies which have coexisted on earth, or which have succeeded each other since the advent of man, has prided itself on a moral certitude – similar to that we invoke for our own sake – proclaiming that in itself – reduced though it might have been to the dimension of a little group or a village lost in the darkest forest – in that society were condensed all the meaning and dignity of which human life is capable. But whether it is in them or in us, much egocentrism and naivety are necessary to make us believe that the whole of human nature is lodged in only one of the historical or geographical modes of his being, whereas the truth of man resides in the system of their differences and of their common properties.' So Lévi-Strauss not only refutes the ideology of a unified human nature in history in favour of a cultural polyphony, but he challenges the hierarchy between science and so-called primitive thinking when, at the beginning of *La Pensée sauvage*, he writes: 'Two distinct modes of scientific thought exist, which are functions not of unequal stages of the development of the human mind, but of the two strategic levels at which nature lets itself be attacked by scientific knowledge.'

Therefore the corpuses of myths which are the result of these deep combinatory logics are formal sets whose synchronic equilibrium is threatened by history: history is not, as in Hegelian, Marxist or Sartrian theories, a positive orientated force which would gradually generate meaning; it is only a destructive power which brings disorder and entropy into the formal equilibrium of these networks of signs. And there is a striking similarity with Book VIII of Plato's *Republic*, where history and the succession of regimes is seen only as a degrading process damaging a synchronic purity. One could also notice that, once more, Lévi-Strauss is faithful to Rousseau's distrust of *history*. In Book III, Chapter VIII of the *Contrat Social*: 'Even the best Constitution will one day have an end, but it will live longer than one less good, provided no unforeseen accident bring it to an untimely death.' Both Rousseau and Lévi-Strauss see time and history as eroding factors which the frail balance of structures and culture try desperately to arrest: we are far from the ideology of progress in history endorsed by Marxists, Sartre and the philosophers of the Enlightenment.

The way in which Lévi-Strauss revisits classicism is a very anti-conformist way: it leads him back to a complicity with the most anti-conformist of all the philosophers, Rousseau, the one who fights against a substantialist or empiricist determination of human nature and who demystifies the myth of history as orientated progress.

We are now able to frame a new paradox which finds Rousseau and Lévi-Strauss akin in the same violation of the difference between nature and culture, although they have formally proclaimed the methodological necessity of this split.

Prohibition of incest as human nature

Once the relationship between nature and culture has been purified by Lévi-Strauss of all its substantialist and metaphysical elements, once the illusion of a common substratum – which would in theory be exposed after the shedding or stripping away of all particular or specific features – has been discarded, the only formal feature which remains universal is the *prohibition of incest*. The prohibition of incest, or exogamic imperative, is in Lévi-Strauss's view 'a fact or a whole set of facts' and, against Malinowski and siding with Geza Roheim, he claims it is universably observable. But it is also a rule, and, as such, it is a methodological scandal:

> For [Lévi-Strauss writes] prohibition of incest presents, without the least equivocity, and indissolubly united together, the two characters where we have recognized the contradictory attributes of two mutually exclusive orders: it constitutes a rule, but a rule which, alone among all social rules, possesses at the same time a character of universality.

The scandal is that in this rule/fact or fact/rule the two domains of nature and culture meet, whereas they had been recognized as opposed to each other: then, as in *Cratylus*, the legislator must have been self-contradictory. And not only do they meet, but their meeting is fecund: prohibition of incest constitutes the archetype of all rules, the degree zero of syntax, the paradoxical place whence all rules can be considered as formal patterns, and above all, as a language, because by the transport towards an outside world, by the circulation between the *identical* and the *other*, the possibility of considering culture as a field of communication and transport occurs for the first time. Prohibition of incest as the degree zero of the rules or laws is a space where the field of the identical first escapes the monotony of a tautological repetition of itself and where the question of relationship with *another* begins. 'Je est un autre.' But it remains an epistemological scandal, which defies the barrier erected between nature and culture by an Aristotelian logic of identity; Lévi-Strauss's concept of human nature, if assimilated to prohibition of incest – and it seems to be so – produces a logic which defies logical imperatives: *une logique qui se moque de la logique.*

Prohibition of incest belongs to the field of culture, and even constitutes the possibility of culture, because, from it, an element (clan, ethnos, tribe, etc.) begins to communicate with another according to some rules and on a formal network. But it is also and at the same time *natural*, for it is universal. Lévi-Strauss, in fact, writes, in *Structures élémentaires de la parenté:* 'Let us first suppose that all that is universal in man corresponds to the field of nature and is characterized by spontaneity, and all that is submitted to a norm belongs to culture and presents all the predicates of relativity and particularity'. Now, prohibition of incest, or exogamy, in which one could find a manifestation of Lévi-Strauss's conceptions of human nature, remains a scandal because it presents these two aspects indubitably united together. Its universality remains in Lévi-Strauss's view a theoretical as well as a factual piece of evidence.

However, its privileged position as an archetype does not prevent us asking the following question: Is this meeting point that we name prohibition of incest a strange exception that one encounters as a challenge in the pure system of difference between nature and culture? Or, on the contrary, is not this system of difference between nature and culture to be conceived as a consequence of prohibition of incest? In that case this prohibition of incest would be outside the system, or prior to the system; and to think of it as a scandal would be an absurdity. It would mean assimilating it into a system whose very condition it is. This paradoxical situation is related to what Lévi-Strauss said in an interview published by *Le Monde*: 'Structuralist thinking tries to reconcile the perceptible level and the level of the intelligible', or to his view of myth as a shifter between concrete and intellectual levels: neither a concept nor an image.

At this point there is again a striking similarity with Rousseau's point of view, for, at the end of *Emile* the goal of the hero's education is assessed as the purpose of 'making' the pupil 'un sauvage fait pour habiter les villes', a savage able to live in cities. Such a formation of compromise, such a definition which overrides the logical imperative of non-contradiction, can be seen as an analogue of Lévi-Strauss's definition of the prohibition of incest as a source of rules and exchanges and a scandal at the same time.

And Rousseau is indeed acknowledged by Lévi-Strauss as the founder of ethnology: in *L'Essai sur l'origine des langues* as well as in second *Discours sur l'origine de l'inégalité*, Rousseau provides 'the first treatise of general anthropology in French literature'. Lévi-Strauss credits Rousseau with having distinguished the object of the ethnologist from that of the psychologist or the historian. 'One needs to look near at hand if one wants to study men; but to study man one must learn to look from afar; one must first observe differences in order to discover attributes.' For Lévi-Strauss, ethnological work achieves a fictional variation which is in search of the essential invariant, beyond empirical diversity. And that justifies Rousseau's epistemological claim: 'commençons par écarter tous les faits' and refutes the objections made to Lévi-Strauss about his so-called contempt for field ethnology and empiricism.

No wonder we see in the 'sauvage fait pour habiter les villes' as well as in the scandal of prohibition of incest, the paradoxical result of this quest for the invariant. At this level the absolute split between nature and culture is challenged and contested. Lévi-Strauss writes: 'The opposition between nature and culture, on which we had insisted in the past, seems to us to offer now nothing more than a methodological value'.

The dream of Lévi-Strauss as an ethnologist is now to reinsert culture into nature, but nature in a new key conceived in terms of a deep combinatory power. Yet this concept of nature is modified by the reductive detour accomplished: 'The idea of general mankind to which ethnographical induction leads, has no relationship with the one which was held about it before. And the day when one is able to understand life as a function of inert matter will mean the discovery that it possesses properties which are very different from those which were previously ascribed to it.' This day has come, and modern biology had now started explaining life in terms of a combinatory process. For Lévi-Strauss it has become legitimate to combine the study of, on the one hand, the deep structures and logic of myths, of totemic operations, of kinship and commercial exchanges, which constitute culture, with life and nature, on the other hand, provided that life and nature are no longer opaque and dull, but that life is also seen as the great combinatory power which the modern studies of Watson, Wilkins, Crick, Monod, Lwoff, Jacob and others have now revealed it to be.

Moreover, Lévi-Strauss is not so naïve as to expect to discover the formal invariants which underlie myths or totemism in the form of empirical evidence; a system of rules is not a fact. As with Rousseau's theory of a social contract which is not an historical event nor an empirical event but gives sense to historical or political realities which are conceived in its limits, Lévi-Strauss's invariant is not likely to be unveiled by the ethnologist in its complete and exhaustive clarity: in *La Pensée sauvage*, in the logic of totemic classifications, Lévi-Strauss writes that an underlying system can sometimes be postulated *de jure* but it might be impossible to reconstitute it *de facto*.

Lévi-Strauss has been right to denounce the ideologies of traditional humanism, which triumphs in Sartre's fetishism of history and in certain types of Marxism which I have myself attacked elsewhere: he has shown that ethnocentrism and a recourse to a transcendental Ego were hidden there. But in postulating a new type of formal congruency between culture and nature as both decipherable with the help of a theory of codes and models, he has not completely avoided the risk of falling back into a regressive metaphysical attitude. Derrida has shown elsewhere, in *De la Grammatologie*, how Rousseau and Lévi-Strauss by a privilege granted to the voice and spoken word as well as to phonological patterns and by their common dismissal of writing, were prisoners of Western metaphysics.

One can also wonder whether in postulating a certain structural inherence of culture in nature Lévi-Strauss has not come back to the substantializing of a nature conceived in Spinozist terms as a *natura naturans*, whose congruency with itself and generalizing power is somewhat alarming. In that case, all the shifts operated by Lévi-Strauss away from the rural self-deluding humanistic and anthropocentric concepts would have been only an incestuous journey within metaphysical boundaries. The question deserves to be asked when we meet such affirmations by Lévi-Strauss as this: 'It would not be sufficient to have absorbed particular mankinds into a general mankind; this first undertaking leaves the way open to others which Rousseau would not have admitted as easily and which fall to the exact and natural sciences: to reintegrate culture into nature, and eventually life into the whole set of its physico-chemical conditions'. It seems that his criticism against history has led Lévi-Strauss to a curious fixist point of view where, formal though it is, this general network of patterns is at risk of solidifying into an essence.

The limits of human nature: classicism revisited

It is against such a view that Chomsky has reacted; he has proclaimed the specific difference between human language and nature by affirming its main attribute: creativity. This concept is ambiguous and bears romantic connotations: we must resituate its scope in the very context of the revolution that Chomsky accomplished in the field of linguistics when he challenged conventional, empirical and behaviourist approaches and licensed a new theoretical field for the investigation of language.

Behaviourists and empiricists held the view that the acquisition of language only comes from experience and that there is no linguistic mechanism, however complex, which has not been acquired through a process of learning from the outside world or environment.

A corollary of this view was that grammar was only concerned with the study of data which were directly observable or physically measurable. The epistemological presupposition of this scientific school – 'scientific' in a restricted sense – came directly from Watson's behaviourism, that is a school of psychology which acknowledged no need to postulate the existence of anything which was not observable and measurable: mind, etc.

Against this view, Chomsky's major contribution to linguistic theory consists in asserting the rights of grammar, i.e. of 'a device of some sort for producing the sentences of the language under analysis' (*Syntactic Structures*). A grammar thus is a machine, in the cybernetic sense of the term, whose models are not only to be conceived from the point of view of the speaker but of the listener too. This model or device is not to be limited to the aspects which can be externally described: what accounts for the *creative* aspect of language is, on the contrary, that a grammar is to be conceived in terms of a system of transformations which is autonomous and generated from a certain number of patterns and structures which constitute the innate framework of the human mind.

Chomsky writes in *Cartesian Linguistics*:

A central topic of much current research is what we call the creative aspect of language use; that is its unboundedness and freedom from stimulus control. The speaker–hearer whose normal use of language is 'creative' in this sense must have internalized a system of rules that determines the semantic interpretations of an unbounded set of sentences; he must, in other words, be in control of what is now called a *generative grammar* of his language.

And in his first Russell Lecture: 'Furthermore, all known formal operations in the grammar of English or of any other language, are structure dependent. This is a very simple example of an invariant principle of language, what might be called a formal linguistic universal or a principle of universal grammar.'*

The main idea is that surface structures in language are derived through a set of transformations from deep structures. It is true that the surface structures of various utterances are different from one language to another. But Chomsky hypothesizes that at the level of deep structure, all languages involve the same type of construction. This could lead to the idea of linguistic *universals*. Transformational grammar also refers to the idea of *innatism*: the linguistic ability would be innate to the child and would allow him the acquisition of his mother tongue. Given the fact that the child gets his information only from the utterances he hears around himself, and that these utterances appear to him in their surface structures, the question that behaviourism does not solve is: how does the child reconstruct their deep structure, i.e. how does he operate the transformations which are the reverse of those operated by the linguist? How for instance does he build *he will come* out of *I guarantee his coming*, if he does not have, *a priori*, built in his mind before any empirical datum, the innate patterns of deep structures? An *a priori* pattern of deep structure seems to be the condition of possibility for acquiring a language. Deep structures are thus not discovered by the child, but rediscovered, just as, in Plato, the argument of Reminiscence shows that to know is to recall to oneself (*Meno*).

We shall have to examine these claims later on. The novelty remains the postulate that the acquisition of language and knowledge, far from owing its result to the information gathered from the outside world or to a stimulus response system, is facilitated by the presence in the subject's mind of a set of rules which is at variance with the vulgar empiricist position that remains the core of the behaviourists' thesis in spite of their claims of scientific sophistication.

The second important feature consists in proclaiming the

* Russell Lectures given in Cambridge in 1970 and first published in this country by courtesy of Noam Chomsky in *Cambridge Review*.

autonomy of grammar. Grammar had been too often mixed up with literature or anthropology. Even Boas and Bloomfield's approaches are not completely devoid of all interference from anthropology. Chomsky, by contrast, was to proclaim the formal and epistemological purity of grammar: if, in the course of his studies, he resorts to psychology or biology, it is after having assessed the limits of their use and articulation as a result of a formal decision.

The scope of such a revolution in knowledge is comparable to that of Kant's achievement in the epistemology of physics in the eighteenth century. Fighting at the same time against rational and substantialist dogmatism and against empiricism, Kant in the famous 'Copernican revolution' claims the right of a rational subject who is conceived of in terms of formal conditions of possibility of knowledge: this subject is constituted by a certain set of categories or *a priori* concepts which build human understanding and are not a result of information gathered in the empirical world, or a construct brought about by stimuli.

Knowledge, before this Copernican revolution, used to be subordinated to objects and turned around them, as in Ptolemaic astronomy the stars turn round the earth; Copernicus's model on the contrary shows the earth turning round the stars, and that provides an epistemological model to explain how the object of knowledge must turn round or be subordinated to the categories of a reason which builds *a priori* concepts. The question runs as follows: what must reason be to be able to know the world? Which implies that this *a priori* and trans-cendental formal construction is a set of conditions of possibility for properly knowing the outside world: scientific experimenta-tion is substituted for the random experience of the empiricists.

This implies that external observation is not discarded but intervenes at the end of the rational process in a calculated way, and it answers properly the questions asked by the *a priori* inferences supported by the set of *a priori* concepts which are independent of empirical data.

In a similar fashion, Chomsky allots a place to behaviourist description of language, as a description of performances. But this place is limited and has to be accounted for in terms of formalist *a priori* models. The deep structures are inaccessible to behaviourist observation, and yet they make it possible. The similarity to Kant is striking, because both Kant and Chomsky fight against the dogmatism and ontology of the absolute and against sheer empiricism: they show that these two systems of thought were accomplices of each other and both denounce their hidden links. They both preserve the formal purity of the fields of physics and linguistics respectively.

Chomsky is the author of a Copernican revolution as important as that achieved by Kant in epistemology of the exact sciences. Both have produced models of scientificness which do not dismiss perception, but allocate it a predetermined scope in a theoretical system. Moreover, by recognizing that all rules of a grammar possessed by a subject are structure-dependent and only structure-dependent, Chomsky poses a sort of *requisitum* to the acquisition of a language which is confirmed by factual evidence; otherwise it would be impossible for human children to learn in the normal way, though perhaps other systems might be learned as a kind of puzzle or intellectual exercise.

And Chomsky makes a definitely clear contribution to the debate between Cratylus and Hermogenes: 'The rules in question are not laws of nature nor, of course, are they legislated or laid down by any authority. They are, if our theorizing is correct, rules that are constructed by the mind in the course of acquisition of knowledge. They can be violated and in fact departure from them can often be an effective literary device.'

This kinship with a Kantian way of posing problems can also be recognized at the level of the formulation of Chomsky's questions. It is not only a quest which would concern the aspects of grammar as it is *de facto*, but the formal conditions of possibility of a grammar *de jure*. In the same fashion as Kant, he asks: 'What formal properties must a grammar have if we want it capable of automatically enumerating the grammatical sentences of a language and of assigning to these phrases in the same fashion structural description which could be represented in the form of a tree? More specifically, what form must the rules of such a generative grammar take?'

This concern for rules, and rules of the rules, which is common to Kant and Chomsky, leads to the recognition of a transcendental philosophy at the root of their approaches. Transcendental, not in the Husserlian sense of substantialist ego, but in the sense of a *formale quid sub lumine quo*, i.e. a formal set of rules or structures which permit the question *quid juris?* to be asked.

In the first of his Russell Lectures, Chomsky reverted to this very clearly: 'Knowledge of language results from the interplay of innate structures of mind, maturational processes and interaction with the environment.' This statement is very congruent with Kant's affirmation about the complementary articulation between *a priori* structures and *a posteriori* data in experimental physics. The following statement by Chomsky might even be mapped on a Kantian proposition: 'It is natural to postulate that the idea of "structure-dependent operations" is part of the innate schematism applied by the mind to the data of experience.'

And this Kantian feature is accentuated by the homage paid by Chomsky to Russell and Hume together for being, in spite of their myths, the introducers of a certain scope for innatism. Russell, quoted by Chomsky, writes: 'Part of empiricist theory appears to be true without any qualification.' And Chomsky goes on:

However, Russell writes: 'We need certain principles of inference that cannot be logically deduced from facts of experience. Either, therefore, we know something independently of experience or science is moonshine.' And Hume, in spite of his reputation as an empiricist had written too: 'Though animals learn many parts of their knowledge from observation, there are also many parts of it which they derive from the original hand of nature.'

It is not my intention here to discuss the validity of such a quotation by Chomsky: it may prove a difficult task to reconcile Hume's theory of knowledge with the Cartesian recourse to innatism. But, after all, Kant himself credited Hume for having opened the way to his own *Critiques*. Let us observe also that Chomsky's use of these quotations is polemical and rightly contests the claim made by some contemporary movements – behaviourism and empiricism – that Russell and Hume are their ancestors.

One must however ask a question which remains unsolved or not completely answered by Chomsky. What is, in Chomsky's view, the articulation between deep structures in language and deep structures at the level of the subject (the speaker-hearer)? One can accept the idea that to possess a grammar is to be able to perform a certain number of operations and transformations according to an innate set or bundle of structures. But how does this set of structures that a subject possesses (or *has*, or *is*) relate to the deep structures of a language? In other words, what is the area of impact of the subject on the deep structures of his code, given the fact that he has not internalized all of them?

Chomsky uses the word competence or knowledge. But this word does not so far provide a satisfactory answer. Chomsky has not completely anticipated objections of this kind. When in his first Russell Lecture he tries to preserve a certain relativity of the invariant, he does not show completely clearly the relationship, if any, between the invariant properties of human language as an *impersonal* code and the invariant that one discovers in the human subject in the form of these innate structures which underlie the knowledge and performance of a language for an *individual*. One cannot avoid thinking that Chomsky has generalized an idea from the field of Western culture to an ethnocentric concept of a universal human nature. And there he is liable to be criticized by anthropologists who could rightly invoke ethnological relativity and the diversity of cultures and codes.

There we could invoke Lévi-Strauss against Chomsky. However, that could not be done without our having first assessed the similarity and convergence between the two researches. The term *transformation* used by both can however be very misleading. When Lévi-Strauss in *La Pensée sauvage* uses the word transformation ('les systèmes de transformation'), he alludes to the world of totemism and the combinatory processes which underlie it as a deep set of structures: but this logic is a logic of classification, a taxonomic network, whereas the system of transformations used by Chomsky concerns the *unpredictability* and *creativity* of speech. To assess the difference provisionally, one could say that Lévi-Strauss deals with performances or utterances which constitute a limited set generated from a finite set of deep structures (called the totemic operator, all of whose combinatory possibilities are systematically explored), where the individual subjects are only marks or signs combined in the general system. On the other hand, Chomsky deals with an infinite set of performances generated from a limited set of deep structures. Chomsky draws a careful line between structure-dependent utterances and structure-independent utterances, which preserves the uniqueness or singularity of utterances and shows the limits of creativity and innovation in human language.

Moreover, whereas Lévi-Strauss is concerned with systematic combinatory powers (e.g. the totemic operator), Chomsky provides a linguistics of the sentence, i.e. of the *syntagm*. In this he is revolutionary because he challenges the dichotomy drawn by early linguists who were only concerned with 'la langue', at the expense of 'la parole' or speech. Deep structures control the production of syntagms, and the recognition of phrase-markers allows a structural description of all and any utterances. This does not reduce the structural inquiry to a combinatory account of the governing code, limited in its possibilities as in the Lévi-Straussian analysis of the totemic operator.

But the two major objections one feels entitled to address to Chomsky still hold.

First, he provides a quest for the invariant which overrides cultural diversities of codes, and he is there at risk of confining his search within the ethnocentric limit of human nature defined in a Western way, and generalized by extrapolation to the dimension of universality. The great merit of Chomsky is, of course, to describe the sentence in syntactic terms: speech, 'la parole', is no longer the unwanted jungle of random and haphazard elements which Saussure had left to run wild when he decided to study 'la langue' only. Chomsky conceives the generation of the terminal or concrete sentence on the model of a tree-like derivation from general grammatical categories; and in order to make it more accurate, he hypothesizes a subtle system of transformations which will authorize or exclude a certain number of structural changes leading to the actual sentence, as it is. From this point, Chomsky concludes that under the surface structure of the sentence as it is pronounced or written there is a deep structure constituted by the whole of the derivation and of the transformations which have produced it. He has thus fulfilled his intention of providing a logic of the actual utterance, and he has been able to formalize 'la parole', which in itself is a revolution. The speech act, the relationship between *signifier* and *signified*, can no longer be satisfactorily described in empirical terms.

However, when, in the process of describing deep structures, Chomsky comes to the point of postulating a system of grammatical rules which would bind the phonological and the semantic utterances, and when he equates this system to a *universal* of language, it may be that this move leads him back to psychology, or to dogmatic metaphysics.

One of his disciples and major European exponents, Nicolas Ruwet, goes even as far as wondering whether there are not *substantial universals*, given the fact that the deep structure of the sentence is less diversified from one language to another than the surface structure would induce one to imagine? Hence the claim that syntactic categories are common to all languages.

One can see easily where this leads. Through the question of the acquisition of language, and because linguistic competence is dependent on deep innate structures in the subject, there is a risk of reimporting here a substantialist concept of subjectivity. What would be the use of Chomsky's fight against descriptive psychology and behaviourism if it were to reimport a Cartesian psychology of the faculties of the mind? This would indeed be a regression from a Kantian formalist *cogito* to a substantialist one, which recurs here and there in *Cartesian Linguistics*.

Thus the second question, that of innatism, is a key question. If one looks carefully into Chomsky's approach to innatism one notices that the question of the insertion of a competence, or an individual grammar or knowledge of a language, into a code and into language in general is still unsolved. Chomsky writes in his first Russell Lecture, in a strictly Kantian manner:

It is natural to postulate that the idea of structure-dependent operations is part of the innate schematism applied by the mind to the data of experience. The idea is innate to the mind in the sense in which Descartes argued that 'the idea of a true triangle is innate' because we already possess within us the idea of a true triangle and it can be more easily conceived by our mind than the more complex figure of the triangle drawn on paper; we therefore, when we see the composite figure, apprehend not it itself but rather the authentic triangle.

This sentence starts indeed with a Kantian connotation, and ends up in a Cartesian style. The rediscovery of this classical Cartesian problem of the insertion of these seeds of truth, or clear and distinct ideas, on to the mind of a subject seems to me to be a regression from the Kantian promises and the Leibnizian relevance of Chomsky's epistemology.

Leibniz can rightly be invoked when one poses the question which Chomsky's work implies: is it true that among all languages and among all the possible deep structures, only a few are actualized? Such a question would find elements of an answer in Leibniz's *Monadology*. And this is a very legitimate question. But when Chomsky describes innatism with reference to the Cartesian idea of the triangle, one is disappointed, for a reference to Kant's categories would have been more welcome. Categories, or *a priori* concepts of the faculty of understanding, regulated by the transcendental activity of human reason, are not substantial but constitute a formal set of conditions of possibility of statements and knowledge. They remain forms, and they are in the field of law and rules. Chomsky seems to prefer innate schemas conceived in rigid terms which risk being mistaken for essences, and which reinstate the obsolete problem of interiority as opposed to exteriority. He is threatened there by the pitfalls of naturalism when he postulates human nature as an immutable concept in his paper 'Changing the World' (second Russell Lecture). He does not take enough account of the changes that history has brought into the codes and the systems of culture. However, the polemical use of such a concept remains valid against empiricism and behaviourist reductionism.

Chomsky, by apparently dwelling in the field of normative psychology ('What must our thinking faculty be for its products to have such logical properties? What must our linguistic faculty be to allow such and such a transformation?'), reduces rationalist theory to the level of naturalism, or a hidden empirical trap, which is the ally of dogmatic metaphysics of a Cartesian kind. Similarly the notion of creativity – which has a technical sense as a result of the precise analysis of sentences treated as systems of operations and transformations – risks being somewhat arbitrarily projected into the field of metaphysical or ideological freedom conceived in Cartesian terms, linked with a concept of the subject as substance and substratum. Both creativity and competence, as well as the question 'Where to locate deep structures?', seem to send Chomsky back into an empirico-dogmatic situation that his linguistics and his criticism of behaviourism once avoided. (See *Cartesian Linguistics*).

The notion of an unconscious conceived in Leibnizian as well as in Freudian terms, i.e. specified in terms of a structural network, is never touched by Chomsky. He provides a clear and effective criticism of Descartes' introspection (see *Cartesian Linguistics*, p. 58), but the notion of the unconscious status of deep structures is not elaborated. A relating of this unconscious to the Freudian formal unconscious determined as a language and a syntax by Lacan would be useful for Chomskian research for it would have spared the determination of subjectivity as substance. Through the discovery that the Freudian unconscious remains structural while disobeying the Aristotelian principle of non-contradiction, Lacan and Freud provide a *split* in subjectivity which forbids any regression to idealist or substantialist concepts of the *cogito*.

Human nature and biology

However, these innate principles of mind that on the one hand make the acquisition of knowledge and belief possible, and on the other determine and limit its scope, are related to biology and the new frontier opened by the neurophysiology of the brain. A temporary solution to the objections that one can put to Chomsky may be found in the relationship that Chomsky builds between his innate set of deep structures and Jacques Monod's approach to biology in terms of linguistic codes: 'These modern discoveries,' Monod alleges, 'give support in a new sense to Descartes and Kant, contrary to the radical empiricism that has dominated science for two centuries, throwing suspicion on any hypothesis that postulates the "innateness" of forms of knowledge.'

Chomsky quoting Monod, and Monod quoting Chomsky, together assert a mutual fertilization of biology and linguistics:

It is likely that the evolution of human cortical structure was influenced by the acquisition of a linguistic capacity so that articulated language not only has permitted the evolution of culture, but has contributed in a decisive fashion to the physical 'evolution of man'; and there is no paradox in supposing that the linguistic capacity which reveals itself in the course of the epigenetic development of the brain is now part of *human nature* itself intimately associated with other aspects of cognitive functions which may in fact have evolved in a specific way by virtue of the early use of articulated language. (Monod, *Le Hasard et la nécessité*)

But one realizes here that as Chomsky's theory of innatism suffers from the risk of reinstating a substantialist view of nature through hazardous inductions, gradually building an invariant substratum and an innatism psychologically determined, Monod's work bears anthropocentric connotations which are not clearly elucidated and leave the way open to a positivist ideology which poses science as being able to provide an ethics of its own. These two moves entertain a certain similarity in their essentialist approaches.

A new classical age seems to offer itself as an opportunity of our century. Knowledge has been purified from metaphysical and substantialist imports or remainders; and, at the same time, it has not lost touch with the concrete data of experience, and has accepted the challenge of formal and structural theorization. A new Leibnizian harmony is at hand, exempt from any metaphysical pre-establishment. Departing from the dogmas of empiricism and narrow-minded behaviourism, science in our age allows an epistemological reflection which has many things in common with the Enlightenment, but freed from any illusion of a unilinear and always progressing history. Lévi-Strauss and Chomsky are among the artisans of this new approach to a demythified classicism. That is the reason why their approaches have to be all the more carefully scrutinized in order to prevent any regression to a metaphysical, substantialist view.

Against regressions of this kind towards a naïve view of human nature as invariant and of the subject as a substance, modern biology and Freudian formal and structural psychoanalysis are able to consolidate the results obtained by linguistics and anthropology. The new concepts of human nature must keep the formal purity of structural mobile networks able both to vary in their displays and to avoid the pitfalls of essentialism without neglecting the duty of dealing with diversity and otherness.

4. A Presocratic Poem?

The title of Jacques Monod's work *Chance and Necessity* ('Le Hasard et la nécessité') has the simplicity of those great inaugural poems of the dawn of Science and Philosophy, the works of Empedocles, Democritus or Epicurus. At a time when the power of experimental investigations and the wealth of theoretical elaboration reach unparalleled proportions there is a sort of audacity and challenge in reviving these concepts blunted by a long and heavy history, these terms that haunt and deposit themselves in and around all the old systems, and in thus launching them free of any metaphorical alluvium, simple and pure, as if in a state of wonderment before a new-born presocratic clarity.

And it is indeed a birth or rather a Rebirth that Monod talks to us about. Like the Lucretius of *De rerum natura* he tells the story, in the form of brief 'chants', of the redistribution of notions in the space of contemporary knowledge that biological discourse has brought about and that the absence of sufficient scientific information had frozen in illusory and ideological figurations.

Brought under the cutting edge of that new Occam's razor that molecular biology introduces to the contemporary epistemological field, the old problematics of animism and vitalism, of emergence and reduction, of the determination of 'Life' in its specificity, as well as the narcissistic obsession by which man has for metaphysical reasons always wanted to consider himself the central point of reference for biology – all these debates on which the history of philosophy has fed ever since there has been a scientific discourse taking the living for its object – now find themselves placed under a searching light where their theological and metaphysical elements are to be denounced as outdated scholastic quarrels. They are seen to be incapable of integrating into the framework of their disputes or their efforts at intelligibility this new discovery of molecular biology, namely the informational and linguistic role of DNA and of protein clusters in the cell organized around the transcriptive action of enzymes. *The living – and no longer, as it used to be said until recently, life – is bound together and can be decoded in terms of language and more particularly of scriptural language.* Hence the necessity of substituting a new conceptual apparatus for the old procession of signs, one which displays its fertility and the wealth of the operational properties that it bears. Once the lures of teleology and the demons of finalism have been exorcised, the cellular code can for Monod be expressed simply in terms of an autonomous morphology, of reproductive invariables and of teleonomy. The concept of teleonomy which Monod presents and develops in the course of his work is a key concept that, in spite of the finalist appearances of its equivocal prefix, is articulated around the two fields of structural causality and of a revisited Cartesian mechanism. On one side it thus communicates with reproductive invariables, enabling Monod to propose the following theorem:

As it is a question of the capacity to reproduce a structure of a high degree of order and given that this degree of order of a structure can be defined in units of information, we maintain that the 'content of the invariables' of a given species equals the quantity of information which, transmitted from one generation to the next, ensures the preservation of the specific structural norm.[1]

But on the other side a *project* is at issue:

To be more precise we shall arbitrarily choose to define the essential teleonomic project as consisting in the transmission, from one generation to another, of the content of the invariables characteristic of the species ... the 'teleonomic level' of a given species corresponds to the quantity of information which must be transferred on average, per individual, to ensure the transmission to the following generation of the specific content of reproductive invariables.[2]

It seems that a reference could be made here to the structural definition given by F. Jacob in *La Logique du vivant*: 'Every cell *dreams* of becoming two cells.'

However it is here perhaps that we will have to question, in spite of the infinite precautions taken by Monod to ensure the rigour and logical coherence of his proposals, this recourse to a hidden finality. Even if this project is certainly not born of a Subject (divine or human) and even if it is limited to the description of the mechanisms of microcellular production whose action does not go beyond the linguistic arrangements of simple chemical elements, there remains the question of the status of these secret finalist implications which Monod does not manage to shed. And it is strange that these implications are not necessarily revealed at the level of the manifest epistemological functioning of the new concepts whose scope can be measured in the redistribution of ideological problematics. It is, on the contrary, in a somewhat displaced and deferred way that they enable the risk of a return to ideology to resurface, at that perilous moment of philosophical 'feedback' that is realized *in fine*, after the insistent step-by-step approach in the rest of the work.

But first let us be generous in our recognition of the purifying work of these concepts. Their essential fertility consists precisely in the fact that they are elaborated at the level of the cell and that from there, through a transfer of virtually flawless rigour, they then operate upon the stages of what had until now been considered as the discourse of biology, or more generally the science of the living.

The most noteworthy modifications are the corollary of teleonomy, conceived as the end product of all the individual systems that constitute the organism; it is at this level that the interplay between chance and necessity is produced. Chance comes first, or rather every beginning is a chance event, but from the outset what chance produces is taken in hand by a process of repetition whose physico-chemical necessity is a law. The book's title comes from this proposition, which opens the chapter on evolution:

The initial elementary events that enable these intensely conservative systems of living beings to evolve are microscopic and fortuitous with no relation to the effects that they might entail in the teleonomic operations. But once it is embedded in the structure of DNA the singular and as such essentially unforeseeable accident will be mechanically and faithfully reproduced and translated, that is, it will be both multiplied and transposed millions and millions of times over. From the reign of pure chance, it enters into that of necessity, of the most implacable of certitudes.[3]

Monod's 'stroke of genius' consists in not confining this redistribution of the role of chance and necessity to the level of the most elementary organisms where it had been located, but in extending it to the whole of the biosphere, which brings about a rigorous and indefinite circulation of the structure from the microcosmic to the macrocosmic levels. The possibility emerges therefore of formulating a modified evolutionist theory, a neo-Darwinism, whose principles of natural selection, far from being realized in virtue of a divine project or final cause whose action would only be grasped retrospectively, by a sort of backward illusion of knowledge, are on the contrary only the product of the necessary reproduction of structures whose source is accidental. The modifications in the genome are due to chance and can be thought of in terms of physico-chemical instability. The operative choice then, that has hitherto been called *natural selection*, would no longer be the consequence of a design but of the good or bad performance of structures that fortuitously sprang up when they came into experimental contact with the physico-biological environment. 'Selection has its effects on the products of chance and cannot sustain itself elsewhere, but it functions in a domain of strict exigencies from which chance is banished. It is to these exigencies and not to chance that evolution owes its generally progressive movement, its successive conquests and that ordered fulfilment whose image it seems to give.'[4]

Integrating the contributions of molecular biology into the theory of evolution, Monod's neo-Darwinism enables one to conceive of evolution's direction no longer in terms of a normative orientation (an idea that gives shape to all those philosophical evolutionisms from Teilhard de Chardin to Bergson that deified progress) but as a simple *orientation in time* whose irreversibility cannot be deduced *a priori* as teleological (given that a simple, point-like mutation such as the substitution of one letter of the code for another in the DNA is indeed reversible), but which is the product of a large number of independent mutations in the original species that are then recombined, always at random thanks to the genetic flux produced by sexuality.

The corollary of this new perspective for evolution would therefore be the displacement of an anthropocentric point of reference, the decentring of man, who would no longer think himself as the hierarchized and teleological conclusion to the evolutionary process, as its *end*, but who would have to consider the emergence of that admirable machine, the brain, as the product of that game of roulette set in motion by chance alone.

In a gesture that lends his thought a Pascalian vertigo, but a vertigo of immanence, Monod then produces the biosphere as that space which has been and is always caught between the two circles of language: on the one hand the cellular code of the DNA script, and on the other human language, which Monod shows is not only the ultimate product of evolution, but the decisive factor in the physical evolution of man.

It is therefore impossible to consider language as a simple superstructure: 'It has to be admitted that in man there is a strict symbiosis between the cognitive functions and the symbolic language that they summon forth, and through which they become explicit, a symbiosis that can only be the product of a long and commonly shared evolution.'[5]

Now it is here, precisely, that a problem is posed and a

suspicion begins to emerge. Jacques Monod has been able to admirably renew the biological problematic in its entirety, through proposing the shifts of understanding that may be operated due to molecular biology and to its readability as a theory of information. He asks us to consider the emergence of the biosphere as a massive 'arbitrariness of the sign' whose product would be articulable in terms of a repetitive necessity, a structure where Hermogenes, the theoretician of the arbitrariness of signs, and Cratylus, the theoretician of their natural necessity, would both be right, but in a displaced way as in the Platonic dialogue. Operating these displacements, Monod manages to shake and undermine the foundations of the old scholastic questions.

But the philosophy that he arrives at in his book is caught in that very circle whose pattern we have just uncoded, of mutual causality between language and evolution. This circularity by which Monod's proposals closely ally themselves with humanism and anthropocentrism, at the very moment when he thought he was furthest from them, is crystallized in the declaration of the innateness of the system of human rationality, which is not thought of in structural terms but which is hypostatized at the expense of the diversity of linguistic codes and cultures. It is a circularity that fixes itself in the 'naive' recognition of a *human nature*. What is the use, from then on, of maintaining that language and writing are partly bound to chance and necessity if it is only to restore, beneath a different mask, the eternal anthropotheology which, under the name of humanism, weighed upon all the problematics of the nineteenth century and constituted *the* major epistemological obstacle? Perhaps this anthropotheology is not openly admitted or declared, but it nevertheless functions as an ineradicable residue in the wake of Monod's thought. The metaphor of the 'project' that underlies the definition of teleonomy ('one of the fundamental properties which characterize all living beings without exception: that of being objects *endowed with a project* which they both represent in their structure and accomplish through their performances');[6] 'the realization of the fundamental teleonomic project, that of invariant reproduction . . .'[7] – this term, which does not allow the cybernetic one of *program* to be substituted for it, is the result of a latent anthropomorphism, even if the epistemological displacements brought about by Monod are made at the expense of the privileged position that man occupied at the centre of the universe in nineteenth-century ideology. The notion of adaptation that extends that of project – 'This apparatus is entirely logical and marvellously adapted to its project of conserving and reproducing the structural norm'[8] – in its turn taints with a pragmatic finalism of latent anthropocentric implications the magnificent analysis of the relation between teleonomy and thermodynamic loss, regulating it in favour of the principle of the highest return.

Stage by stage, step by step, Monod's 'inevitable' use of certain metaphors or inverted commas gradually uncovers the fact that his thought belongs to the humanist domain in the traditional sense, of which it remains a prisoner. It is in vain that he denounces the anthropocentric illusion, for his thought does not succeed in eradicating its last traces, which indeed function at the very core of his ideas, even in the correlation made between *teleonomy* and *objectivity*. As for the first concept we have already said that it bears the imprint of a project 'for-itself' that is metaphorically conveyed from man to the cell in the form of a language but regrettably maintains its anthropocentric co-ordinates. Seen from this point of view Jacques Monod is a direct descendant of those *naturalist* philosophers of the eighteenth century who, having attacked the theological arguments of revelation or the *a priori* proofs for the existence of God, stopped short along the right road to proclaim the omnipotence of *design* in the universe, in both senses of the word, of a scheme and a pattern. Hume in his admirable little work *Dialogues concerning Natural Religion* was able to spoil their game in making the character of Cleanthus their mouthpiece. The latter, who supposedly refutes theology (which is what Monod does, p. 55 and *passim*), reintroduces the elements of a natural theology where the notion of human nature plays a central role just as it does in this 'essay on the natural philosophy of modern biology'. Furthermore, at the very moment when he claims to be denouncing anthropocentrism, Jacques Monod constantly uses as latent, operative concepts, references which postulate the existence of attributes *peculiar* to mankind.

An ambiguous employment of the notion of *objectivity*, the second cardinal term after teleonomy, is the upshot of all this. Monod's thought never stops oscillating between a 'scientific' notion of objectivity where a certain *Dasein* of the thing-in-itself functions (i.e. in this spellbinding sentence on p. 33: 'Objectivity forces us to recognize the teleonomic character of living beings, to admit that in their structures and performances they realize and pursue a project.') and the axiological notion where objectivity is seen as a value-laden fulfilment. This oscillation, which could have given rise to a sort of Kantian articulation between the critique of speculative reason and that of pure reason, highlighting the question of the transcendental, finally settles down in the values of *objective truth*, unfortunately conceived of as the extension of an ontologically privileged reality. Hence the value of *authenticity* (p. 190), in which the two notions of objectivity sewn together 'by the head' are telescoped together: 'The notion of authenticity, thus defined, becomes the common domain where ethics and knowledge meet, where values and truth, associated but not confused, reveal their full meaning to the attentive man who experiences their resonance.' All this of course gives rise to the backlash effect of the most traditional humanist discourse of a lay Mounierist kind. Man in fact is none other than that privileged form of life in whom alone scientific objectivity as both ontological reality and absence of bias can be articulated. From their pairing emerges what Monod then calls 'the ethics of knowledge', inspired by a somewhat surprising reading of Descartes' *Discourse on Method*,[9] seen as the 'ethical choice of a primitive value that founds knowledge'. There seems to be a confusion here between axiological foundations and axiomatic formalism, a singular confusion that doubtless could have been avoided by critical scrutiny of a Bachelardian kind. It is here, in any case, that the circle that we have pointed to as being on the debit side of

Monod's normative epistemology comes forward once again. triumphant, in such propositions as this: 'The ethics of knowledge do not impose themselves upon man; on the contrary it is he who imposes them on himself through axiomatically making them the condition of authenticity of all discourse and action.'[10] Instead of deriving these ethics from the knowledge of a transcendental critical epistemology without a subject/substance that would bestow meaning, Monod presents them as an ethical and ontological wager realized by a kind of phenomenological subject. Having skidded off the Kantian and Bachelardian road where the sagacity of his scientific analysis should have assured him a rightful place, the ethical philosophy of Jacques Monod swells the ranks of all those personalisms and phenomenologies that tirelessly continue to fuel the old anthroponarcissistic dream whose last somersault one had hoped momentarily was Sartrian existentialism.

This theology of man is both the prisoner and the accomplice of an ethnocentric rationality which takes the historical product known as Western reason with its technico-metaphysical scientificness for an absolute. But it also omits, and this is more serious, one of the most fruitful lessons we owe to Bachelard and Marx, namely that scientific knowledge is a practice, a theoretical practice whose relationship with the practice known as *labour* should always be examined according to the historical determinations that condition it.

If Monod had not omitted this aspect then not only would he not have had to search for the values of truth and authenticity in an axiological neo-Platonic heaven, serenely floating above history, but he would also have certainly found it more difficult to dispose of Marxism so facilely as he does from pages 46 to 52. We are in full agreement with him when he denounces historical materialism's usurpation of the title of science, and we would even be tempted to go further than he when it comes to showing that dialectical logic, even as enriched by the complexities and overdeterminations that Mao Tse-tung is pleased to recognize in contradiction, is only a meagre and linear example of all the logical and formal possibilities accessible to thought upon the multipolar and multidimensional network of scientific discourse's possible combinations. But all this should be the object of the most careful study, and the glib caricature that Monod gives of Marxism through 'resuming' its basic propositions turn out to be so many windmills that he can easily tilt at. But what is even more serious is his detaching scientific discourse from the historical conditions that made it possible, whether these conditions be socio-economic or linguistic. *Science* is privileged to find itself at the centre of the code, but with no real reasons offered for this choice. In thus eluding the problem of scientific discourse as theoretical practice, it was inevitable that Monod's 'philosophy' would yet again fall into the traps of existentialism and the theological humanism of man. It looks as if there are then two Monods, one, the invincible man of science, whose genius lies in having been able to treat the living world as a language through combining in the most fertile and rigorous way the gains of information theory and the discoveries of molecular biology. It is this side of the man that exhales the presocratic freshness of a reinvented chance and necessity.

But the philosopher has not been able to profit from the scientist's victory, for his propositions make an odd switch towards a natural philosophy that the ideologues of the eighteenth century would not have disowned, the very ones who in the person of Cleanthus are forced to confess their internal contradictions, mercilessly unmasked by Hume, whose tactical scepticism reveals the anthropocentric idealism of their discourse. Can the subsequent discourse of Jacques Monod itself become that Humean interrogation, that purifying demystification by which the great scientist might purge his own discourse of its hidden metaphysical complacencies? Or should it be hoped that this critical labour will come from other quarters, from the field of a Foucauldian discourse for example? If the consequence of Monod's brilliant discoveries in the domain of biology is only to make us abandon Teilhardian elucubrations so we can reach the shores of Albert Camus's anthropotheology (he is quoted as a chapter heading), then it is perhaps time for contemporary epistemology to derive its theoretical practice

rom these lines of Foucault on Nietzsche which, at the end of
L'Archéologie du savoir, form an ineluctable warning:

Discourse is not life; its time is not your time in it; you will not
reconcile yourself with death; it may well be that you have killed God
under the weight of all that you have said but do not think that you
will from all that you say make a man who will live longer than He.[11]

5. The Age of Leibniz or the Return of the Repressed: Oedipus

1 The axiomatic breakthrough

With Descartes something emerged which had not previously existed in Western philosophy, namely the question of subjectivity, a notion which, as we have said, is fundamentally contested by psychoanalysis. What form does this contestation take, appearing at the end of the nineteenth century at a time when other forms of knowledge in the exact sciences were destined to undergo profound modifications, thereby introducing us to modernity such as we know it? The signs of this break could be found in many domains but it is in the fields of the sciences and of philosophy that its presence and impact were most deeply felt. In science and in mathematics the break is that of the axiomatic revolution. Ceasing to develop on the basis of an unprovable assumption, the postulate, mathematical reason accomplished a liberating leap, enabling it to cast aside its servitude to undemonstrable postulates so that it could freely choose them among many other initial possibilities. Through the conquest of axiomatic choice, reason immediately placed itself in a position of primacy in relation to the undemonstrable. In physics new theories arose, new schemata for explaining the world, having this assumption in common; that it was no longer possible, by fetishizing 'things' and facts, to believe in a positive, objective that is, definitive truth of the phenomena studied.

Mathematical axiomatics gave a new impetus to logic as well

which resulted in the rediscovery of formal logic, foreshadowed by Aristotle and the scholastics. But whereas with them it remained tied to a philosophy of being, the formal logic that emerged once more at the end of the last century attacked descriptive or transcendental logic with its presupposition of an ontological foundation or substratum of subjectivity, and in so doing it revealed, in distinction to its predecessors, a complete freedom in its enterprise of formalization.

In *Le Nouvel esprit scientifique* and *La Philosophie du non*, Gaston Bachelard described the characteristics of these epistemological upheavals while denouncing the possibility of any linear interpretation of them. When the field of Euclidean postulates was left for that of axiomatics, the former, far from being declared false in the way that it had been declared to be true before, was circumscribed and enclosed in other possible axiomatic fields, and each one of these fields including the Euclidean one, remained stamped not so much by a relative truth but by a truth that could be described as *relational*, that is, relative in its rigour, the fecundity of its theoretical field and its coherence or regional consistency, *to the initial possibilities* that reason has freely chosen for itself. The Euclidean field is thus flanked by non-Euclidean ones that are neither truer nor more erroneous than it, but which are all, in their axiomatic areas, accorded a theoretical validity than can be accounted for *with complete freedom of reason*. The ideology of an absolute, monolithic and permanent truth is thus here contested, dogmatic *alethocentrism* reaches its limits, and even its end.

We are therefore a long way here from any refutation of one field by another. Far from there being negativity and contradiction, there is englobement. That is why the linear conception of a knowledge that would gradually establish itself in sudden leaps and bounds of truth, later to be recognized as errors and refuted, is here rejected. The history of science does not progress along an axis guided by the prospective and finalist light of an eternal truth to be gradually approached through a succession of groping stages. Similar to the epistemological break which the structural event of the Copernican revolution spelt for each of the sciences, the epistemological revolution at the end of the nineteenth century proposed a radical reshuffle in the field of knowledge; but instead of substituting a space of critical rationality for a field of empirical and unmanageable judgements, the outcome of this break was the *centrifugal multiplication* of 'non'-Euclidean fields for mathematics, 'non'-Newtonian ones for physics, 'non'-Lavoisian ones for chemistry and 'non'-Aristotelian or Kantian ones for logic.

The levels of meaning of this 'non-' still have to be carefully explored. Does it only point to the relativization of the former field taken at first as the absolute centre of reference, and then disturbed by the luxuriant flourishing of these new fields that, through the very discontinuity that separates them from it, outflank it in an ironical procession without however refuting it? Or does this 'non-' signify, in spite of the absence of linear succession, a negative dialectic, an *Aufhebung*, a *relief* from duty, the basic feature of which would consist in going beyond the primitive field while preserving it in a different form?

The dialectic and philosophy of 'non-'

In that case, Euclidean geometry, Newtonian physics, Lavoisian chemistry and Aristotelian logic would constitute *ideology* while on the other hand the scientific moment would occur when all these new axiomatic field are unfolded in a state of co-existence, with the multitude of Others outflanking the Same in a spirit of derision. In other terms, is the Bachelardian 'non-' reducible to the Marxist-type opposition between ideology and science such as that which *The German Ideology* and the followers of Marx have put forward?

First let Bachelard explain himself on this point:

The philosophy of 'non' is not the will to *negate*. It does not proceed from a spirit of contradiction that contradicts without proof, that gives rise to vague quibblings. It does not systematically flee from all rules. On the contrary, it abides by rules within a system of rules. It does not accept internal contradiction. It does not deny anything, anywhere, anyhow. It is upon well defined articulations that it brings about its characteristic inductive movement, determining a reorganization of knowledge on widened foundations.

The philosophy of 'non' has nothing to do with an *a priori* dialectic either and *in particular it cannot be allied to Hegelian dialectics.* (Author's italics.)[1]

This close and infinitely distant relationship of Bachelardian 'super-rationalism' with dialectical thought will have to be examined. In particular we will have to ask ourselves what critical relationship Bachelardian epistemology manages to enter into with a dialectic liberated from both Hegelian ideology and from the procedures of a return to unity and simplicity, after the perhaps insufficiently dangerous adventures of alienation and antithesis. The supporters of the materialist dialectic, even those who have with Althusser attempted to map out in Marx's text an epistemological break of a Bachelardian nature, have perhaps taken too easy a way out. We have already formulated this suspicion elsewhere,[2] and it will have to be taken up again and developed, but by centring it this time not upon the works of Marx but upon those of Bachelard. With this in mind we could read the following lines of Bachelard as a pointer, for he announces how singularly impoverished and inadequate dialectical logic is, inasmuch as it depends upon contradiction, when what has to be analysed is the development, the polyphonic and polycentric proliferation of new scientific fields on the flanks of the old, secure and monolithic spaces:

If the dialectical theses of Octave Hamelin are still far removed from the operative foundations of the philosophy of contemporary sciences, it is none the less true to say that with them, the philosophical dialectic comes close to the scientific one. As an indication of this rapprochement we may cite the works of Stéphane Lupasco. . . . He has developed his dualistic philosophy by referring it to the results of contemporary physics. . . . However we will not go as far as he. He does not hesitate to integrate the principle of contradiction into the intimate workings of knowledge, given that for him the mind is for ever splitting things up. For us however its function is to set a kind of logical kaleidoscope into motion that suddenly overthrows old relationships, but which always maintains its form. Our super-rationalism is therefore composed of rational systems that are simply juxtaposed. The dialectic only helps us to handle a rational organization through a very precise super-rational one. It only helps us to gravitate from one system to another.[3]

For Bachelard then, the dialectic has a servile instrumental function, yet it is not quite a prisoner of the rational contents that the super-rational and polycentric explosion of the end of the last century suddenly relativized without making obsolete. The dialectic then is not exactly the poverty-stricken instance of an archaic scholasticism frozen in the closed space of metaphysics. But it also looks as if there is little chance of seeing it assume the important role of an open, plural, scientific rationality, since it limits itself to contradiction. Inhabiting the borderlands that separate and adjoin new and ancient forms of knowledge in their discontinuous complementarity, the dialectic is destined to lead the life of a vector, like railway points that only control a limited length of track. The Bachelardian 'non' cannot therefore be assimilated to the 'non' of Marxism and still less to that of traditional Hegelianism.

Nevertheless this question of the possible articulation between Marxian dialectical materialism and Bachelardian materialism has to be re-examined. Yet such a debate can only take place when we have examined in turn the impact of this philosophy of 'non' both on the field of ideology and on some symptomatic realities and signs, which together form as it were the skyline of Western metaphysics.

What we have to do now is characterize this break and the epistemological blossoming that resulted from it, and so as to put the methodological structures of the question of the subject into place, we shall restrict ourselves to the term of *envelopment* with which Bachelard designates the relationship between traditional forms of knowledge, X, and other forms, non-X:

A philosophy of 'non' whose only terrain is juxtaposed systems which at a precise point enter into complementary relationships with one another, must first of all take care never to deny two things at the same time. It lacks confidence in the coherence of two negations.

Negation has to remain in contact with a primary formation. It has to allow a *dialectical generalization* to take place, one which must include what it denies, and indeed the development of scientific thought over the past century has depended on such dialectical generalizations that *envelop*[4] what they deny. Thus non-Euclidean geometry envelops Euclidean geometry; non-Newtonian mechanics envelops Newtonian mechanics: wave mechanics, envelops relativist mechanics. In the domain of physics Planck's *h* constant appears as a factor disobeying the rules of science and common sense. As has often been said, one has only to remove this *h* from the formulae of wave mechanics to find the formulae of classical mechanics. Micro-physics, or to put it another way, non-physics, therefore includes physics. Classical physics is a particular non-physics corresponding to the zero value attributed to *h*.[5]

Bachelard proceeds to show this generalization at work in the establishment of a new and fertile coherence between scientific fields and various forms of rationality:

Several dialectical generalizations which at first were independent have cohered. It is thus that the non-Newtonian mechanics of Einstein was quite naturally expressed in Riemann's non-Euclidean geometry. But philosophy must experience this coherence in its proper order, for it is neither automatic nor easily come by. The philosopher who wishes to understand super-rationalism must not therefore immediately make himself at home in it. He must test the openings of rationalism one after the other. He must research for the axioms to be dialecticized, one by one.[6]

With this promise of generalization and coherence not only is dialectical reason of a Hegelian and perhaps Marxist variety relativized and planed down to strict limits – 'The traditional doctrine of an absolute and unchanging reason is only a philosophy, and an outdated one at that'[7] – but also and most importantly the possibility emerges of a general formalization that would utilize in its transfers, variations and translations, as well as its 'metaphors', the structural tool that formalism provides it with. If a structure is defined as a self-regulating and self-regulated system of formal transformations and operations, then the possibility arises of producing a formal epistemology in which the structural network would not just be the discourse of 'pure' science in process of formalization, but also the discourse *on* science, provided of course that one carefully maintains the structure's operating and operational role and avoids petrifying it into a naïve ontological realism, into 'thing-worship' – that is to say, if one avoids taking structuralism as a philosophy or a doctrine.

Alongside the structural understanding so productively at work in the fields of the exact, logical, mathematical and mechanical sciences, as well as in the human and social sciences following in the wake of linguistics, a new scientific discourse is establishing itself, one composed of translations, transfers, regulated exchanges and coherences, of formal communications, and a generalized discourse of structural epistemology may take shape in formal continuity with it. For the first time in the history of the sciences, the scientist and the epistemologist speak the same language, that of structure as the logic of all objects. Scientific language and metalanguage both find a place on that immense loom of Penelope, that mobile, differentiated and unstable structural network which now presents itself as the general matrix of discourse.

Hermes

Following in the visible wake of Bachelard, Michel Serres's work *Hermès ou la communication*[8] is more directly concerned with mathematical science, as it recognizes in modern mathematics the emergence of a pure *formal discourse*, which through the generality of its ensembles dismisses any treatment by way of the symbolic. All this however would only be a reflexive echo, a useless repetition of mathematical activity, if Michel Serres had not clearly announced the possibility of generalizing such a transition to the rest of culture, demystifying in the same stroke the cliché of mathematics' splendid isolation. In all fields where there is language – mathematics included – the era of the symbol ends, and the formal stage emerges.

Serres begins by making light of that scholastic partition

between the sciences and the humanities upon which our universities thrive and which is unknown for example in the United States. The installation of such a barrier has unpardonably screened us off from what, on the contrary, has to be boldly thought through, namely, the alliance in the 'Greek miracle' between mathematical thought and a monstrous, resplendent flourishing of mythologies. It is thus quite naturally in the *communication* of the Platonic dialogue that Serres finds his point of departure for the proposition that the dialectic is both a dialogue regulated by the norms of spoken discourse in which the idea as a universal is fixed and communicated to us, and a mathematical method that deals with the universal in itself through 'a progressive refinement of abstract idealities in the style of geometry'. In the same movement therefore we may conceive of form and understand one another.

As we have said, Bachelard was able to repeat this same movement, thereby hoping to drag us out of the nineteenth century. The coexistence in Bachelard of a pure epistemology and of a psychoanalysis of the elements enables what underlay the 'Greek miracle' to re-emerge, but his work suffers from a fundamental division and the two projects, one 'delineating a pure form' and the other giving meaning to the obscure potential of a cultural content, continue to be distinguished, and even opposed or seen as antidotes to one another. Bachelard the epistemologist, the philosopher of 'non', and Bachelard the psychoanalyst of the elements continue to exist in a state of non-communication, although there is no shortage of sites for a possible unification, such as in the psychoanalysis of the physicist's knowledge or the questioning of the archetypes of material reason in rational materialism.

What Serres announces, and this is why his book deserves to be mentioned here as one of the texts that make our era bring to fruition the seeds of the epistemological break and the Bachelardian philosophy of 'non-', is the abandonment of the polemical meaning of that 'at the same time' which marked the coexistence of the two projects by forcing them into the mould of a cold war, even of a peaceful coexistence, and, with it, the promise of a return to the unity of one and the same approach. From then on, the establishment of modern mathematics' pure formalist language is better than a guide or index, for it is what makes possible a clear and rigorous construction of models and structures in the field of cultural matters only recently considered irremediably opaque. It is the first sign of the general emergence of the purely formal, ensuring 'a limitless development on the base of Bachelardian shortcomings', the finest and most successful examples of which can be seen in the work of Lévi-Strauss or the patient research of Georges Dumezil in the field of Indo-European mythologies. Bachelard was necessary, his *Philosophie du non* and his *Matérialisme rationnel* just as much as his psychoanalyses of the elements, to ensure that all possible variations had been examined and exhausted: 'Bachelard choose his archetypes in the ultimate myth of the ultimate science. He is therefore the last romantic. He reunites in a daring fusion the clarity of the form to be extracted and the density of the content to be understood – he is therefore the first neo-classic.'

The formal versus the symbolic

Taking the rupture further in relation to the Bachelardian 'Ur-symbolic', Serres announces the classical epoch of the 'pure, formal model' which is completely indifferent to the concrete determinations of its elements or to the regional, empirical description of its relations:

A structure is an operational whole with an indefinite signification (whereas an archetype is a concrete whole whose signification is non-defined), grouping together both any number of elements whose content is not specified, and a finite number of relations whose nature is not specified but the function and certain results of which are defined in relation to its elements.

Here the notion of structure which had become more than suspect through the play of entropy and delirium is clarified and restored in its primacy, and it is significant that Serres shares Piaget's conclusions in his short book *Structuralism*,[9] which also represents a valuable attempt to clarify structuralism. Piaget writes:

As a first approximation we may say that a structure is a system of transformations. Inasmuch as it is a system and not a mere collection of elements and their properties, these transformations involve laws: the structure is preserved or enriched by the interplay of its transformational laws, which never yield results external to the system nor employ elements that are external to it. In short, the notion of structure is comprised of three key ideas: the idea of wholeness, the idea of transformation and the idea of self-regulation.[10]

Further on, in his conclusion, Piaget emphasizes that structuralism must remain a method or else it will founder in a reification of structures, in a caricature of positivism, and we recognize the necessity of heeding the following caution as a kind of principle regulating the employment of a logical, structural account for a given object:

Briefly, the permanent danger threatening structuralism when one tends to make a philosophy out of it is that an ontologically privileged status will be accorded to structures; it is a danger that emerges as soon as one forgets the latter's connections with the operations of which they are the product. However, if we remind ourselves that structures are essentially bundles of transformations, then it is impossible to dissociate them from the physical or biological operators inherent in the object or from the operations realized by the subject of which they represent only the law of composition or the form of equilibrium and not prior entities upon which they stand. In contrast to any other type of action, it is in effect the peculiar property of operations to coordinate and organize themselves into systems. It is then these systems which, through their very constructions, constitute structures and not the latter that pre-exist actions and constructions by determining them beforehand.[11]

The 'non-' of psychoanalysis

The question that now has to be asked is, if it is true that the end of the nineteenth century brings about, thanks to psychoanalysis, to Freudian theory as well as practice, a relativization in the rule of the Cartesian subject, then what form does this relativization take? Does it assume the shape of an englobement in the sense that Bachelard gave to this term in *La philosophie du non*, and may a non-subjective theory be obtained through psycho-analysis, as there has been a non-Euclidean geometry since Lobachevsky and Riemann? Or on the contrary, following in the trail of Michel Serres' discovery of a network of communica-tion, and instructed by Bachelard, though radically contesting the latter's stopping at the 'symbolic' stage so as to move on to the formal Leibnizian one, do we have to see, again by means of a Freudian epistemology, the subject as being inscribed some-where in a combinatory structural network and in this case, is its position, discerned once more through a Leibnizian *analysis situs*, homogenous to structural space, or on the contrary, is it radically different from it, situated in the impossible space of a heterotopy in relation to the structural model of language and the combinatory impulse?

If we are ready to recognize also that scientific knowledge had until then been produced within the horizon of the trans-cendental ego, it is legitimate to ask ourselves how this hegemony of transcendental subjectivity was contested by the appearance of a structural model of interdisciplinarity, and how also the irruption of the heterogeneous with Freud and psychoanalysis managed to shake these certainties to their foundations? The problematic of the unconscious does not in fact threaten from the outside that circle of certitude identical to itself that the transcendental horizon installed, but it displaces in an irrever-sible way the subject's own relationship to itself. Or rather, as we shall see, it discloses it as always having been split. Such a display of the split subject could not leave the horizon of clas-sical scientificness undisturbed, for it opens up the question of the subversion of categories. We can however at this stage say that one of the results of the irruption of the unconscious in the twilight of the positivist epistemology of the nineteenth century was not only to restore the powers of the imagination in scien-tific research and invention, but also to show that there has probably never been within its own domain a scientific discourse capable of being isolated and thought of independently as

Science, but that, in spite of the transcendental ego's absurd anxiety to rule over all and sundry, literature, science and philosophy have never been separate from one another. There are not two Riemanns, one the rigorous formulator of axiomatics and the other the delirious Baroque fabricator of sweeping metaphysical dreams. What we know since Freud, and the irruption of the dehiscence that he occasioned into the closed field of transcendental subjectivity, is that there is no pure discourse subjected to a syntactic, combinatory scientificness, but that the most scientific of proposals is grafted onto a *Begriffdichtung*, onto an imagistic generative mechanism whose production always exceeds and corrupts the supposedly transcendental and objective positions of its pronouncements. And in an undissociable way, all languages, even that of clear and objective knowledge, are riddled through and through by the cracks of the unconscious.

The consequences of this corrupting irruption of the unconscious on the formal Leibnizian-type network which Serres has rehabilitated as a challenge to Cartesianism will also have to be thought through and questioned by means of a deep semantic of the whole *syntactic superego* which has reigned over mathematically inspired knowledge. Is Leibniz's thought open to the heterogeneous, to heterotopy, to the Other, or does it remain servile to the principle of identity? Is there a place for Heraclitean discord in the subtle networks of Leibnizian harmony?

A minimal definition of structuralism

First let us recognize the importance of the convergence between Piaget's definition of structure as tied to a system of transformations and operations, and Serres' notion of the logic of any given object that works upon the mobile and differentiated network of structure. In fact an analysis is structural when, and only when, it brings to light a content in the form of a model, that is, when it is able to isolate a formal set of elements and relations upon which one can then argue without having to appeal to the significance of the given content. Serres goes on:

Structural analysis therefore gives rise to a new methodical intelligence which means nothing less than a revolution for the problem of meaning, because a structure once isolated as such (with its abstract relations and elements) enables one to discover all the imaginable models that it can generate. In other terms it is possible to construct a living cultural being by investing a form with meaning.

Serres calls this pure formal system a network of communication. Its structure can be likened to the subtlety of the network woven onto a chessboard through the reciprocal situation of the pieces and their spatialized relationships along potential lines of force. But the chessboard metaphor remains insufficient because it is planar, whereas a differentiated and unstable network of forces interacts with another formally similar network in all the spatial dimensions. On this new 'Penelope's loom' the traditional dialectical argument, as with Bachelard, is thus:

... that singularly restricted and impoverished instance of a continued struggle between the only two remaining pawns, which have the same power to move in only one direction and which enter into open conflict with one another at the precise moment when one of them gains an equal footing with its adversary through labour and culture (which shows, curiously enough, that it doesn't see through the other's game), and this conflict finishes by the capture of a privileged point (and that is an impasse because the linear series is broken) that was occupied by the now vanquished other side.

Here then there is essential unilinearity and a univocal determination of the high points of the game.

The conquest of pure formalism by mathematics also has the effect of shutting up a very voluble character, namely, the epistemologist who, from the outside, lorded it over the object, method, status and limits of science. This character is now reduced to being no more than the belated historian of an already 'outworn' practice, the anachronistic naturalist of an ever-moving science that will always frustrate his own classifications.

For this new mathematics contains a twofold paradox. First, in a self-regulating movement, it becomes its own epistemology, its own metalanguage and its own independent logic. It takes itself for its own object, the object of its own discourse. It is from within that it asks itself the Kantian question *quid juris?* and it is in its own language that it replies: 'Mathematics tries to discover the maximum number of points of view from which it may speak about itself.' Here, there is that 'constitution of an epistemology, at first positive, then rigorous and finally generalizing'.

The second paradox is attached to the first. This narrative, descriptive and methodological independence could be a refusal, a form of self-enclosure. But it is however at the very moment that this epistemological enclosure takes place that an opening also reveals itself for a possible generalization. It is the conquest of this natural and no longer artificial language, enabling a self-directed discourse to emerge, that ensures, through homogeneity, the progression to generality. 'There is no longer any over-arching epistemological system; thought now rests on its own mobility.' And this displacement by means of which mathematics reappropriates itself for itself, entails the proposition that 'mathematics is an internally open and externally closed theory'. The latter aspect delivers mathematics from all references to the Husserlian burden of a constituent ego or an antepredicative grounding for experience. Hence that 'liberating movement towards universality'. The former aspect, on the other side of the fence, is that path, that never-ending progression (method, *odos*, road) towards its essence, mathematicity. 'Mathematics,' writes Serres, 'is not open towards something other than itself, it has opened up *on* itself and for itself.' A sort of 'essential history' of mathematics thus becomes possible, and at the same time the quarrel between ancients and moderns is done with. Mathematical polyphony gives itself free scope within the horizon of its self-transparency.

The return of Leibniz

Serres is right to situate this 'coming of age' of mathematics, achieved through its autonomy and inner dynamics, under the aegis of Leibniz – and of a Leibniz admirably considered as the perfect point of congruence of a self-referential system.

Mathematics, dynamics and metaphysics all merge and converge with Leibniz into a finely adjusted harmony. The recognition of this perfection of the Leibnizian model is situated yet again in the space of a communication, between the works of Leibniz of course, but also inasmuch as these operate together, between the fields of thought. Let us take as an example 'substantial communication demonstrated *more mathematico*'. Serres reveals the numeral economy of the connections, the communications, between the famous 'windowless monads' and pre-established harmony. 'The bundle of relations with God is made up of fewer lines of communication than are in the network of reciprocal expression, and far less when the number of monads is increased.' And from here Serres constructs a theorem: 'As soon as there is a substantial pluralism it can be demonstrated by means of the combinatory that pre-established harmony is the most economical solution for establishing full relations within that multiplicity.' What is important here is the self-reference of the system in a harmonious congruence: 'The thesis of pre-established harmony is implied in pluralism by the mediation of the combinatory.' Michel Serres is right to see in the Leibnizian system the ancestor of the models of modern mathematics, of that logic of 'any' object, since it consists in a mathematization of univocality or a *system of continuous isomorphies*. With this, we are reminded that scientific knowledge is a discourse composed not only of subordinations and hierarchies but also of coordinates. The end of this remarkably clear and elegant book concerns the possibility of a reading of 'empirical' cultural fields by the formalization of 'regional networks' whose pure formal structure is that of analogy. All due praise has to be given to Michel Foucault for his attempt in *Madness and Civilization* to establish a 'geometry of the uncommunicable'. Serres recognizes in the trajectory of this book, in this 'system of all possible variations of the negative', this 'structural genesis of all possible alienation', the quality of an epistemological catharsis, and the promise of constituting a general organon of the sciences which presently remain at the stage of description.

But the epistemological problem that Michel Serres poses, the one that haunts all similar attempts at conceiving of the Same in the categories of the Other, is this: can we ever shed the universe of Sameness? Serres asks the question as a Leibnizian: 'We lack a criterion enabling us to maximize the number of necessary and sufficient strata for exploring the totality of a culture, or even for defining it as such. We do not have the criteria for establishing a firm and steady table.' It is a problem for Lévi-Straussian methodology as well. How can we escape from this situation, from the fixity of its own gaze in the Same?

The moral of Serres' book therefore tends to show that if formal thought in the human sciences approaches a mathematical status, it could not be reduced to the usual tools of the geometrician. There is a chance that this thought may invent new structures, and beyond the ambiguity of a project whose proposed goal is to reduce phenomena to the quantifiable, to calculations, one may hope to see an original mathematics produced.

This has been a necessary detour via Bachelard's thought and that of Serres, who brought it to fruition while nevertheless contesting it; necessary too was the recapitulation of Jean Piaget's generalizing and formal epistemology, not only to remind us that structuralism is not a philosophy, a doctrine or a dogma, but a method whose fertility and rigour are capable of formally generalizing the statements of a philosophy of 'non', but also to describe the stakes of the epistemological break which characterized the end of the nineteenth century, a moment of discontinuity when various points of view proliferated. This recapitulation has enabled us to trace the outlines of the framework in which the following question, hitherto deferred, will have to be formulated. If it is true that an epistemological mutation effects the scientific discourse of mathematics, physics and logic, that is those discourses whose whole existence lies in formalization, then can the same be said of the human sciences and philosophy? Can we say that in the field of these discourses,

which we can momentarily agree to name ideologies (by local-
izing the sphere of application of the Marxist division ideology,
science), a comparable revolution has been produced?

2   The subject in crisis

This is where our question leads to, for it seems to us that the
problem of the subject functions here in a critical way: it is
the point around which a certain ideological practice turn
and comes apart and where the possibility for a new scientific
practice emerges, namely, psychoanalysis. I say the possibility
and not the positive reality given the essentially *problematic*
character of the advent of psychoanalysis, due to the resistance
it has encountered and to the necessary *delay* with which the
effects of this epistemological revolution have made themselve
felt. It is thus retrospectively, that is, after this delayed action
has had its effect, that we can finally take note of the possibility
of a modified problematic in philosophy and the human sciences
If we do not falter we are presented with the opportunity of
measuring, in this temporal displacement, the far more radical
scope of a question about the very possibility of scientific dis
course in general, to the extent that through its unprecedented
articulation between the clinical and the theoretical, psycho
analysis places a question mark over the gains of both pre- and
post-axiomatic scientific discourse.

   In other terms, the question arises of that formal and harm
onic congruence which, following Serres, we have been able to
say is symbolized by the Leibnizian text. If it is true that the
epistemological break produced at the end of the nineteenth
century reintroduces us to the age of Leibniz, as a structural
epoch, then where exactly does the subject stand in all this –
question delayed by the difficulties encountered by psycho
analysis in its journeys through scientificness? But are we still
dealing with the same scientificness, and is the closure of the
epoch of subjectivity to be tidied away with others in the formal
and coherent network of the philosophies of 'non', or, on the

contrary, does this question of the subject carry a certain *excess* with it as regards the philosophy of 'non', one which through its outgrowths changes the basis elements of the problematic? Through thus functioning as a problematic *supplement*,[12] does the Freudian question of the subject perhaps upset the most structured of structural classifications and operations, as well as Piaget's notion of an *epistemic* subject, the formal but centred producer of structural operations and transformations that are realized within the multidimensional network of the new sciences and epistemology? The persistence of a Leibnizian harmonic coherence and the centrality of a subject, however free the latter may be of substantialist metaphysical contents and the phenomeno-existentialist burdens of 'consciousness' and 'concrete experience', are two crucial issues calling for an exploration of the genealogy of subjectivity.

With Descartes then the possibility emerges of a problematic of the subject which was suppressed, that is, relativized by Freud at the end of the nineteenth century, in the context of the explosive proliferation of axiomatic fields. How did this break happen and is it completely comparable to the epistemological break that relativized the Euclidean field, or are we confronted with an even more profound break with more far-reaching and disturbing consequences for the position of the subject in the field of the identity and the ontology of matter?

Logic, especially with the rediscovery of formal logic foreshadowed by Aristotle, was completely emptied of its ontological implications, and in particular it rejected the notion of a foundation as well as a self-identity of being. The somewhat circular problem by which the question of subjectivity could at this level be highlighted is the following. Is a transcendental subjectivity tied to the metaphysical principle of identity necessary for a formal logic to be postulated, or is it, on the contrary, one of the avatars of an ontological determination of the history of metaphysics of which structural and other contemporary formalisms will have to purge themselves? In other words can a formal logic be envisaged without any recourse to a constituent subjectivity of either an empirical or transcendental nature?

It would obviously be wrong to think that from Descartes to
Freud the field of subjectivity is quite uniform with no inflec-
tions. On the contrary, the differences between the Kantian 'I
think' and the Cartesian *cogito* or the Husserlian transcendental will have to be gauged, precisely as differences or *Nuancier-
ungen* whose scope directly touches the question of the Subject.

This restructuring of the problematic of subjectivity along the
diverse 'epistemes' that mark the history of Western rationality
and knowledge is conditioned by various fundamental elements,
including the notion of time and that of identity or property,
defined in relationship to its *Others*.

In order to put the question of subjectivity in Descartes in its
right place, it has to be seen against the background of an initial
impossibility for thinkers to conceive of the notion of the subject, an inconceivability that begins in Antiquity and continues
throughout the Middle Ages, in spite of hints of a possibility of
such a notion in such currents as Thomism.

The absence of the subject in antiquity and the Middle Ages

One of the best vantage points for considering this absence in its
a contrario activity is provided by the question of fault and
error, seen in all the diverse connections that they have with one
another. Plato, Aristotle, and even Aquinas put forward no
theory of the subject responsible for his errors, such as emerges
on the contrary in the dialectic of Cartesian will and understanding. In ancient thought no subject exists that is free to
deceive itself, and the problems of fault and error are resolved
by considering the nature of the object, *a parte objecti*. Furthermore, the analysis of fault comes completely under the heading
of error. The Socratic doctrine that 'no one wills to be evil'
assimilates moral fault to an error of judgement, but in Plato
judgement itself never brings into play the freedom of a subject.
On the contrary, it is within the domain of the object that a
wrong proposition may be substituted by a right one, as is
illustrated by the metaphor of the dovecote developed in the
Theaetetus. The black dove lets itself be taken in place of the

white one by the hand that gropes inside in search of a prey. The erroneous or unknowing judgement is formulated in the same way, i.e. in place of the truth, as the wrong action is accomplished instead of the right one. And medieval scholasticism inherited the Socratic maxim: *omnis peccans est ignorans*.

Within this perspective therefore, fault is reduced to error and has nothing to do with the responsibility of a subject predetermined as free, and the dynamism of the will, first introduced by Descartes, is also absent. In addition, moral fault, represented in its extreme form by the tyrant, the Platonic figure of alterity, corresponds to a total lack of will, a sort of degree zero of liberty. 'No one wills to be evil' in the Socratic problematic could easily be translated in the *Gorgias* by the tyrant who does not do what he wishes to, precisely because he does what he pleases. This rule of desire which binds the tyrant to his whims is the very figure of alienation in Plato. At the heart of the City it is the seed of disruption and subversion, since in the subjection of the powerful to their passions, the lower instincts, *epithumia*, gain the upper hand over the cerebral *nous* and over the thoracic *thumos* where the heart as well as military valour and virtue are to be found. The soul tyrannized by pleasure and desire, the tyrannic soul, the soul of the tyrant, in effect, corresponds to the City fallen into the depths of political decadence, where there is no more city, since in this progressive deconstruction the social groups made to be controlled by the dominant classes have gradually taken over. Tyranny is the final moment in this catastrophic evolution, this 'catagogy'. It follows the democratic phase, or the reign of the merchants and artisans of the marketplace, with their shopkeeper mentality, the counterparts of *epithumia* and the lower instincts, of libido in the soul. With these people in power, the philosophic noocrats and the virtuous warriors no longer have their say in affairs, and the phase thus corresponds to the soul when it is a prey to the passions. One desire that is stronger than the others will soon monopolize all energy in the furtherance of its aims; one demagogue more powerful or seductive than the rest will also soon enslave the masses in the furtherance of his, thanks to rhetoric, that dangerously debased supplement to philosophy and the logos.[13]

It is worth taking the trouble to examine what is involved in this metonymic apparition of tyranny in the soul and in the City, achieved through the victory of a passion or a man over that crowd of others, characteristic of the preceding phase, the democratic one of potential tendencies, the Gidian one too of the equipollence of desires and pleasures when one is not confronted with a choice, and where one position is worth as much as another, in a freedom that Descartes in his system called 'the lowest degree of freedom' – that of indifference. This multitude of desires, this polyphony of seductions that for Plato characterize the democratic city and the soul of the democratic position, are, in their gratuitousness and dispersion, the prelude to the emergence of tyrannical arbitrariness which will have an easy job in hogging the stage, reducing all things to the monotony of the tyrannical discourse, the univocality of dictatorial orations, to the unidimensionality of obsessional neuroses. The pessimism found in this Platonic genesis of tyranny, seen as a reduction to the univocal of what was an unbridled excess of the liberty of indifference, finds a sort of echo, a symmetrical image in dissymmetry, in Freud's analysis of obsessional neurosis, where it functions as an impoverishing and metonymic levy upon libidinal richness. But this time, law and order are no longer, as with Plato, the conceptual matrix of the logos, through which the transgression or subversion of desire that leads to tyranny may operate. Law and the castrating reality principle form another figure in the same structure, namely that rupture in desire that, through metonymy, ends in obsessional neurosis. The 'innocent' anomic moment in Freud therefore, when the infant Eros, before running up against the harsh reality principle, the iron law of guilt and repression, can still merit the versatile and glittering title of *polymorphous pervert*, would correspond to the gleaming multitude of desires in the Platonic democratic man. More than one connection can therefore be made between the seventh book of the *Republic* and Freud, for in the space of this encounter the absence of a Subject, of any conception of free will, as well as the presence of Eros the showman, fabricator of tricks and tropes, are both apparent. On one side metonymy, and on the other as in *The Interpretation of Dreams* and the Platonic myth, metaphor. But the angle of incidence as regards the axis of law differs fundamentally from Plato to Freud. With the former it is the subversion of the ontologically determined law which, as the final phase of decadence, brings about the tyranny of the passions, whereas with Freud it is the reading of the outlines, tropes and figures of desire that allows for a deconstruction of the law as that which succeeds the expression of desire. In Plato, a subversive and tyrannical Eros *bends* the law that pre-existed him, thus enabling one to condemn him on the basis of an *a priori* and ontologically determined law. On the other hand, with Freud it is through Eros's sleights of hand, his tropes and somersaults, that one may both understand neuroses and dreams as types of compromise between elements struggling against each other, and the law as a form of acquiescence in one of these types, namely, obsessional neurosis. The latter is a metonymic source of belief in the law, the exasperated figure of a Superego seen as an ulterior derivation in relation to the original libido and Eros. This difference has to be accounted for by the interplay between castration and the death wish whose role must be examined in each of the camps. Between the two there is an overlap, namely the myth of Gyges' ring, which we deal with elsewhere.

It is therefore not in terms of free will or the liberty of a responsible subject that fault and error are considered in the Platonic framework, but as tyranny generated by ignorance, by the proximity of non-Being. Only an ontological knowledge, the maximum of enlightenment obtained through the episteme, can cure this ignorance, this commerce with non-Being. Here it can be seen how much Spinozism would owe to Plato, in spite of its Cartesian terminology of the clear and distinct idea. The clarity of knowledge and of Platonic being, like Spinoza's adequate idea, have enough internal energy to assert themselves without there having to be some exterior dynamic will that would move them. Error then, in relation to this positivity *a parte objecti*, is nothing more than a deficit, a lacuna, a lack of being. The hand that gropes in the obscurity of the dovecote in search of a white dove is the victim of a simple *misapprehension*, as fault and error are the product of *inattention*. The subject, properly speaking, does not enter into it at all.

The lacuna of the subject: the first Oedipus

The subject is thus the locus of an absence, or lacuna, in which one statement is substituted for another, without the question of their impact ever being raised. A whole system of determinations in Ancient Greece reinforces this adherence of fault to the domain of error as a deficit in the world of objects or of being. The tragic fault establishes an order of guilt that becomes apparent in the upsetting of another order, and not in the responsibility of a subject. This upsetting of an objective order is seen as a transgression of the law, but this transgression is not expressed through the will of a subjective centre; on the contrary, it remains the consequence of an *ananke*, a destiny outside of man's control. The only knowledge that it falls to Oedipus to obtain is found precisely in the reconstitution of that chain of causality exterior to himself, which is not freely desired by him, and whose other side is the recognition of the subject as a lacuna, or the definition of man – the reply to the riddle – as irremediably out of step with himself. Far from being a quest that redresses this displacement in the ideology of repentance or in the act of 'becoming aware of one's responsibilities', the Oedipal quest can only aim at an objective purification, a correction in the disturbed order, an elimination of the physical scourges and evils that are the product of the blemishes entailed by his fault and which are cast over the city like a large shadow.

The question posed by the Sphinx and the one Oedipus asks himself about his own origins have the same answer. This answer is the fusion of man and fault, as something predetermined and not as the result of a choice, a plan, or of any kind of wager. Further, the privilege that is Oedipus's because he was able to reply to the Sphinx's riddle will make him a king and the lover of his mother as well as the usurper of his father's throne, and this privilege is bound to his very guilt, of which it is merely the other, supplementary side. The fact that the encounter with the Sphinx and Oedipus's *sophrosuné*, his sapience, both take place in the time gap between the murder of the father and wedlock with the mother bears witness to this strange interdependent relationship between the privilege bestowed by the reply and an objective and unwitting guilt, as if the possession of such knowledge, which momentarily rescues Thebes, resided in that infinite gap which both separates and binds the synonymous events of Laius's murder and incest with Jocasta. This far-seeing reply thus appears as the painfully inadequate suture of a fundamental absence, as the 'stop-gap' ideological solution that with its illusive positivity tries to plug up the underlying, irremissible, infinitely wide, abyss, or what amounts to the same, brings together in a total coincidence the two events whose synonymy makes up the Oedipal enigma – the enigma of a guilt without responsibility. In one and the same supplementary gesture, Oedipus delivers Thebes from the evil that the Sphinx had cast over it and brings the plague upon it through his guilt. The genesis of such a curse, lurking in the very 'nature of things', opens up a bottomless space with no location, namely the very absence of the substratum identical to itself that could be called a subject. It is through such a movement that Hellenism, which established with Plato and Aristotle a substance or substratum upon which Cartesian or philosophical self-identity could come to rest, at the same time undermines the very solidity of these foundations. In the caesura between the murder of the father and marriage with the mother, one that is chronologically determined as the product of a dilaceration between two synonymous and interdependent acts, into this caesura there slips the announcement of a humanism, the definition of the universal, of a human essence upon which all the humanist and anthropocentric discourses from Descartes to Sartre will sustain themselves. Now, at the very moment when the reply to the Sphinx – the definition of man – is uttered, any basis for identity slips away, and in a mocking gesture the very possibility for an ideology of the human subject is dashed to the ground. Because of the Oedipal ignorance of fault and culpability, ignorance of the unconscious, ignorance of the strange, illogical, but non-metaphysical relationship that shall always bind together in a non-mediatizable and non-dialectical conflict the death wish (Laius's murder) and incest, there can be an indefinite expansion of desire (union with Jocasta), 'before' the reality principle. The two poles of these antagonistic and interdependent moments will have had to be projected upon the sham axis of an illusive chronology, as two moments separate from each other and in whose untenable interstice the poverty of the humanist discourse would settle, so that the metaphysical impossibility of the definition may break apart in the same stroke that the humanist discourse reveals its fragility as the troubled and ridiculous stop-gap of a guilt engraved within the nature of things.

Oedipus is the first to make the humanist pronouncement; he is also the first to witness its ruins at the moment it is erected. The punishment that he inflicts upon himself for his crime, in the apperception of a deferred knowledge, must not be seen in terms of a personal responsibility, the attribute of a subject, but as the paying off of an economically determined debt or deficit whose void only being may fill.

The 'eye too many'[14] by which this knowledge is freed is the equivalent or supplement of that eye which Oedipus must remove if the plague is to stop ravaging Thebes. We have come full circle, but by following a kind of Moebius strip. The knowledge of the reply to the Sphinx's question will banish the monster: the removal of an eye, the metaphorical source and organ of the light of knowledge, will clear away the plague. It is the price that has to be paid for redressing a fault, the knowledge of which emerges simultaneously with the recognition of its victorious and fatal entailment by the first reply. With Oedipus's blindness, the humanist reply disappears in the haze of a ridiculous illusion. In this circuit of knowledge and apperception, in which the 'eye too many' cancels itself out, Freud was able to trace the anguish of the primitive stage on which all fantasmatic and theoretical machinery is put into motion. But this history of the eye is also a history of the subject, of the supplementary subject, whose shifting guilt will never settle in a definite site.

The discourse of personal responsibility is therefore one of vanity, the vanity of that speck in the midst of being that would constitute the Cartesian/Sartrian ego. The absence in Ancient Greece of the subject prefigures, through its treatment of fault, the furrows in which the Freudian problematic was to take root.

The Cartesian ego as stop-gap

Such is the abyss that the Greek Eros in its relationship to fault had let develop and which Cartesian thought tried to cover up, by erecting in place of the Oedipal tangle a subject who, armed with an infinitely free will, ensured the functioning of that circular argument that links up attentiveness with the decision-making process. But the operation that in turn allowed for this extraordinary fetishization, as well as the Cartesian fiction's undeniable beauty, consists in spurning the gains of the theory of Platonic reminiscence, in abandoning the original enigma of the status of Ideas and the Essence in relation to the cognitive mind, and in inscribing within the understanding a substance or substratum, an active *cogito* as the receptacle of those celebrated seeds of eternal truths which till then had not site or support from which to display themselves.

It will be remembered that in Platonism the status of the idea is fluid, oscillating between exteriority and interiority . . . One may travel towards it, although only metaphorically, when the shadows and *doxai* in the depths of the cave are left for the sunlit brilliance of the Idea. But inversely the maieutic operation achieved by Socrates, the son of a midwife, consists in delivering souls of the truths and ideas that lie within them. Where? Certainly not in any subject, seeing that there really aren't any and that substantiality, far from having encountered man, is still found within the domain of essences. Plato gave a magnificent portrayal of this oscillation in the myth of Reminiscence. To know is to remember, to travel towards ideas which are not absolute discoveries, since it appears they had already visited us in a time whose origins remain hidden. It should be emphasized in passing how modern this theme of reminiscence is as regards the status of mathematical truths, explaining as it does the ambiguous fate of scientific discoveries from Thales to Einstein which, given their emergence at the historical level, must be thought of as events, but at the same time ones that will escape from history so as to belong, *de jure,* to the whole republic of knowledge. Plato conceives of that lightning movement by which scientific truth passes through its 'discoverer' (leaving precious little to his transcendental subjectivity and nothing to his empirical subjectivity, if not the illusory mask of a proper name) in the enigma of reminiscence, that is, he temporalizes what had been a (metaphoric) spatiality. To be in a state of reminiscence in relationship to the idea means that a problematic bridge of remembrance has been cast towards it and that one is in the process of inventing or rather of being delivered by it (in the sense of giving birth to something). This mythical time functions as the analogue of that strange displacement between simultaneous possession and dispossession that a cognitive subject maintains with scientific truth. In any case the enigma of reminiscence spares one from having to posit any subjectivity. Descartes's operations put an end to this torsion between exteriority and interiority, and, by converting the subject into a substance he implanted the seeds of truth, the 'clear and distinct ideas' of that sanctuary, the *cogito*, which only Freudian psychoanalysis would fracture and uproot.

The subject therefore presents itself as a force, a hub of intellectual activity where ideas group together. The *cogito* comes forth as a fetish temporarily masking the gaps in the processes of desire and decision making. The problematic of fault and error is inverted within the new context of the subject. Instead of fault being thought of in terms of ignorance and error, as is the case from Antiquity to medieval scholasticism (*omnis peccans est ignorans*), things are now turned upside down and it is now the field of error that is relativized in terms of fault. To make a mistake in virtue of the duality between the under-standing and the will is to assert by means of one's free and infinite will contents of meaning within the understanding that remained confused. I am no longer deceived. I am responsible for my errors. The subject endowed with a will is now the master and it is up to him to reform himself, to take the decision to accept only clear and distinct ideas into his understanding, and which have the further quality of directing that understanding. But in their absence, as in the liberty of indifference, I would remain free to commit errors that are due to two principal causes (*Regulae*), namely, prejudice and precipitancy, i.e. to that propensity of my will to affirm things when clarity is lacking in the understanding. There is just one remedy against this fault – attentiveness, which is also a question of will. Everywhere on this circuit the will is to be found, and through it the *cogito* fore-shadows the famous Sartrian aphorism: 'Consciousness is consciousness from beginning to end.' The *cogito* and free will are to survive right up to *Being and Nothingness* where, losing their strictly cognitive value, they reappear in the form of an existential philosophy of consciousness and freedom. And it is no surprise that this philosophy has a bone to pick with the unconscious and psychoanalysis.

Certain well-intentioned people whose impenitent humanism cannot be consoled for that death of man announced by Fou-cault, Lévi-Strauss and structuralism – although, as lovers of structure, they confirm that that is the only tenable solution at the present time – have sought a support for structurality in the figure of God, and having bestowed the role of the Great Other upon Him, have seized upon his presence in Descarte's Third Meditation to make him serve as the refuge for the attributes of a dispossessed mankind. We shall say later on what has to be made of this ingenious ideological sleight of hand by which the son of man is substituted for Man. *Ecce homo; ecce Nemo.* But we can state here that the God of the Third Meditation does not function as some would have us believe as a prefiguration of the Freudian unconscious (in spite of the able developments of this theme by P. Nemo in *L'Homme structural*, Coll. Figures,

Grasset, 1975). If it is true that an interesting and analogous argument can be drawn from the fact that Sartre (who disposes of God by making his attributes descend into human consciousness) has a terrible struggle with structures and the unconscious, then that is no reason for making God the receptacle of structures, and by closely following the texts we shall see how far structuralism is from a Pascalian episteme in the sense that the flag-bearers of a structural Christology would have it. At the very most all that can be said is that there is no notorious incompatibility between a Foucauldian vision of history and the non-intervention of God in Pascalian history. But that is no justification for hurriedly reintegrating God into the fabric of structure and for confusing him with the Lacanian Other. A double insult is being committed. The first is not only to ignore the transcendental character of the Pascalian God but also his hidden, *absconditus*, nature, causing him to speak figuratively, the God who is both absent and present and who would sooner choose to occupy the place of the signifier than the substitute role of the Great Absent Signified. The other insult, with more serious consequences, consists in ignoring the importance of the multi-layered symbolic analyses performed by structurality and which constitute a key moment in the irreversible epistemological process by which structures have taken over the role of any subjectivity, even a divine one.

It is precisely this process that we are describing here, but first we have to take note of what is produced by the Cartesian fiction of a free and substantial subjectivity; first, free will; secondly, the centrality of the *cogito*, and thirdly the assimilation of error to fault, thereby entailing the metaphysical notion of responsibility. This fertility of the *cogito* however, with its clear and distinct ideas and its power as a heuristic tool and epistemological model, could not function in solitude. It needs a God as a guarantor of the truth so as to definitely exorcise the perils of doubt and chase away the Evil Genius who casts a spell of uncertainty over the existence and knowledge of all things, making the *cogito* inoperative as a criterion of truth. The God of the Third Meditation, far from functioning as a corruptor of the subjectivity of the *cogito* in all its plenitude or as a sort of deferred Lacanian Great Other, ready to shake the unconscious apart, is only – and this is hardly negligible – the epistemological guarantor of truth, the undoubtedly indispensable auxiliary for knowledge of the physical world (he guarantees the existence of the exterior world in the Fifth Meditation) and perhaps of the mathematical one as well (to the extent that knowledge of mathematical ideas can be deduced in a more analytic way from the *cogito*, but needs a divine guarantee all the same). In any case, between the *cogito* and God there exists a pact of epistemological cooperation which in no way can be considered as the prefiguration of the relationship between the Ego and the Unconscious Other.

The virtual image of the unconscious can be seen at work in that peremptorily dismissed extreme point of madness which, as the argument between Foucault and Derrida shows, functions in the hubris of the hyperbole of doubt, in that insane convolution by which the *cogito* suddenly manages to spring forth: 'I doubt, I think.' This madness is accompanied by another piece of irrationality, a far more fertile one from our point of view, and which may be gauged by the extent to which the *cogito* operates as a fetishizing denial of the problematic of the unconscious, or, in other words, by finding out how Descartes even if faced with the burning problem of the unconscious would not have had the epistemological equipment to enable him to deal with it, except by falling back upon mythological images and flights of fancy. And it is precisely within the domain of the imaginary, in the difficulties posed by the problem of the knowledge of extension, or in the 'novel of anatomy' represented by the story of the pineal gland, that, in the shape of a figurative anamorphosis, of an over-precocious image, the problematic of a literally *unthinkable* unconscious is to be found. We shall show how narrative and fictional processes generate these mythical pronouncements in another work where we shall also see what extraordinary *Begriffdichtung*, what conceptual scenography, is at work in Descartes's text, whose scope scientific modernity must rediscover.[15]

The omnipotent Cartesian subject therefore had to appear so that man could be made master and owner not only of nature but also of meaning and signs, thus forming the ensemble of knowledge. Foucault has admirably shown in *The Order of Things* as well as in *Madness and Civilization* the over-arching character of this advent of the Cartesian episteme:

> Between Montaigne and Descartes an event took place concerning the emergence of a *ratio*. But the history of a *ratio* like that of the Western world falls far short of exhausting itself in the progress of 'rationalism'. To an equally large but more secret extent it is composed of that movement by which Unreason has embedded itself in our native soil, undoubtedly to disappear in it, but also to take root there.[16]

3   The return of Oedipus, the repressed

We shall now have to deal with this return. Cartesian subjectivity, well entrenched, with its fetishization of the *cogito*, thought that it had chased away unreason and with it the problematic of the unconscious which inhabited that fissure perceived by Greek philosophy and mythology in the place of the subject. From the end of the nineteenth century up to the present day we have been witnessing the return of Oedipus, in spite of Sartrian denials – the last, but not the least important bastion of Cartesianism. We have to examine the implications of this return of Oedipus whose relationship to that crevice constituting subjectivity as an absence was inscribed in the Greek episteme.

To fully take into account the importance of Oedipus in the structural problematic and to see how much the Freudian and Lacanian perspectives have contributed to the question of a semantic and symbolic approach capable of critically examining the positions of a hegemonic syntactical analysis, we have to measure the impact of the violent ordeals and incisions that Lacan, interpreting Freud, has had to undergo at the hands of Deleuze and Guattari's pyrotechnical work *L'Anti-Oedipe*. We will thus be able to gauge if the stakes of the psychoanalytical Oedipus still stand, or if they disappear.

The subject split

It has to be understood how Oedipus and the subject as a divided phenomenon, long denied through the erection of a centralized and pivotal subjectivity, are now returning in the abrupt unevenness of our most recent modernity, this return having been prepared by the axiomatization of subjectivist and substantialist psychology, a contemporary of the other axiomatic revolution of the end of the nineteenth century. The Lacanian conception of the mirror-phase, through its presupposition of the break in the unconscious, is, as we have seen, the most critical place where the demarcation line passes between a *cogito*-type subjectivity and the fragmentation – which does not mean the eradication or the end – of the subject. That the 'human offspring, at an age where he is for a time, however short, outdone by the chimpanzee in instrumental intelligence can nevertheless already recognize as such his own image in the mirror' and that this 'recognition manifests itself in the illuminatory mimicry of the *Aha-Erlebnis*' means that a nodal point has been uncovered where both the deconstruction of the *cogito* and the advent of the symbolic as the essential structure of the unconscious are at issue. And in this delay or anticipation, the question of the difference between nature and culture plays the same role as the incest taboo in the structuralism of Lévi-Strauss; Oedipus is the name of that semantico-syntactic operator setting rhetorical and symbolic figures into motion, ones that are extremely rich in polysemy and plurivocality.

The thesis that we shall here defend against some extraordinarily telling objections is that to accuse Oedipus of being the residual terminus of an exclusive family triangle, is to fail to recognize the originally diffracted and plural, even schizophrenic, character of that operator of the profound tropological motion of the unconscious for which family structure is a mere opportunity for its inscription and manifestation, one that is always derivative and symbolic and which in no way exhausts the former's potential. If one chooses to ignore all these aspects, then one is up against the fantasy of a causalism for which Freudian and Lacanian psychoanalysis are in no way guilty.

So as to understand the efficacity and symbolic productivity of Oedipus, the scope and implications of the Lacanian analysis of the mirror-phase have to be carefully examined. First of all its specalur structure is the mark of a fatal non-coincidence with oneself, of a gap between ego and imago, delineating the trace of an original divergence where traditionally subjectivity in all its plenitude had been located. And the fact that this non-coincidence is accepted in a mood of jubilation points to the introduction of an ambivalent enigma which is by no means an affective one in the existentialist sense, but rather a structural and symbolic one to the extent that it reflects the riddle of the strange and unpredictable relationship between Eros and Thanatos. It is a relationship of mutual inherence, but also and at the same time one of radical antagonism that founds a non-logic, or at any rate one that is neither Aristotelian nor Hegelian, that is to say where contradiction and identity play no central role and only figure as axiomatizable sites that can be integrated into a network whose inter-relationships surpass them in many respects.

Mirror splits

The mirror-phase functions as the point where this relationship emerges, dissolving and circumscribing logic and the dialectic and presenting us with a schizo-logic which we shall have no trouble, as shall be seen, in naming Oedipus. This Eros/Thanatos relationship even finds a guarantee for its ever pre-given symbolicness in that delay, or if one prefers, in that prematurity by which an atopical and achronic temporality establishes itself. This unplaceable temporality means that the structure of the mirror-phase cannot be interpreted in terms of a barren existential experience as some would like to do. Yet it is nonetheless an event with a specific date, one that can be assigned to a period in the development of the subject: 'the human offspring, at an age which he is in for a time, however short . . .' In the enigma of this structure that is also an event (between six and eighteen months), there is already a displacement, a metaphoric precocity, a fissure or lack, an inadequacy by which a profound semantic process is set into motion. And exactly the same applies to the celebrated Oedipus complex which is neither an event nor a structure or which is rather both at one and the same time, and which exists in a relationship of non-coinciding mutual generation that activates, at the centre of the syntactic combinatories of desire, the trajectories of a rhetoric and of a profound semantics. In dreams, in neurotic symptoms or in schizophrenic transhumance, *it* ('ça')* speaks.

We can already perceive a threefold displacement in the analysis of the mirror-phase and we wish to maintain that this displacement, this differential divergence, forms the basis upon which the trajectory of desire is stirred into action as a process of signification and mobility on the part of the tropes or rhetorical figures scanned by the unconscious. The first displacement, constitutive of the ego, is the *non-coincidence of oneself with oneself* in the dehiscence between ego and imago that falls back upon itself in a movement of rotation, since the symmetry of Ego/Imago is produced along an axis perpendicular to so-called 'sagittal' symmetry. In his remarks on the paradoxes of symmetrical objects Kant revealed how dissymmetry is superimposed upon symmetry. My left side and my right side, although symmetrical, are neither similar nor interchangeable, but it is this reconstructed and reversed imago that I must accept in the mirror; a lozenge-shaped optical image opening up an abyss in such a way that to speak of the *cogito* as a complete centrality becomes absurd. Borges also brings into play in 'Death and the Compass' all the *tropological* resources (ones that revolve, like the statues of Daedalus) of this enantiomorphy; and the same process can be seen at work in the *Mythologiques* of Levi-Strauss.[17]

The second relevant displacement is no longer found in the

* 'Ca' is also French for the 'id'.

difference between ego and imago but in what one may call, after Derrida, 'differ*a*nce', that is, the temporal distancing effect which produces the *Aha-Erlebnis* at that fragile moment when the human offspring is 'behind' the chimpanzee from the technical point of view. Behindhand, but the process also points to the infant's prematurity, his over-advanced development. And as this compulsion, this joyful yet mortal recognition (see Mallarmé's *Hérodiade*), is repetitive, we are faced with an unparalleled temporal structure, where difference and the act of deferring ('différer'), that of according a reprieve in the process of repetition, combine. It is a reprieve whose tortuous itinerary is a challenge to the presence and the maintenance of the present. Backward and premature, the child passing through the mirror-phase peremptorily fragments – and forever – what Kantianism tried to reunite under the name of pure and transcendental temporality. But such an enterprise will appear derivative in relation to the original fragmentation of difference.

In the same way Cartesian and phenomenological subjectivity always tries to reconstruct a unified human subject by bringing together in a compact way the two moments that the ego/imago relationship had separated from the beginning. This reunification is only a secondary recuperation. *Diffraction* comes first.

The subject, pure time, and indeed all 'personal' attributes are forever deferred and non-coincident with oneself. It is in this third displacement, that of language, a derivative of the preceding one, that one finds the origin of the symbolic as something tied to the generating function of tropes, that is, of displacements of meaning and names which constitute the self as being always derived and secondary, as an obstinate reconquest and desperate attempt at reunification and fixation on the basis of an initial dissemination. This displacement determines one's relationship to names. Lacan is right to emphasize that the relationship of the imago to the ego is produced at this highly noteworthy stage when the infant is still, etymologically speaking 'in-fans', that is, when he does not speak, yet finds himself in the uncomfortable and partially mortal position of hearing his own name caught within a signifying chain that englobes him and in which he plays no role as a speaking subject. It is the same anamorphotic and optical displacement that relates Eros to Thanatos and introduces both a dissymmetrical image within the domain of symmetry and the impertinence of metaphors within that of analogy and property. We are here faced with a scheme comparable to the one Plato developed in the myth of 'Gyges' ring', which we deal with elsewhere.[18]

In the same way that the child perceives in a jubilatory mood the mortal displacement that separates him from himself in the optical imago, so too the 'infans' who hears people 'speak about him as if he were not there' rejoices at listening to his 'own' name in the Other's discourse, as an object of this desire that is forever lost and irrecuperable. It is the erotic assumption of a mortal non-coincidence which, though it is not definitively a Thanatic somnolence, must nevertheless allow the trace of castration to pass over it. Lacan tries to show that the mirror-phase summarizes the fertile articulations of Oedipus and castration, that is, the other side of Oedipus; hence, the privileged position of this structure through which the irremediable symbolicness of Oedipus is realized, its irrepressible function as a semantico-syntactic operator enabling culture, or in other words the symbolic, to detach itself from naturalist or organicist theses. The process brings about the same Copernican-type revolution which Lévi-Strauss has brought to light in the prohibition of incest, the enigmatic law of exchange which has the after-effect of modifying the structure of the substance in question so that it assumes a different nature.

This same distancing function draws a definite line of demarcation between, on the one hand, symbolic and Freudian psychoanalysis, and on the other all the theories that are subject to the metaphysics of the subject whether the latter be Cartesian-cum-Sartrian ideologies or Chomskyan dreams of an immanent self-transparency on the part of the subject harbouring innate ideas. This 'line of fiction, asymptotic to the subject', this schism or internal split that riddles the subject from the beginning, invalidates any general theory of the symbolic that does not go beyond a syntactical matrix destined to the greater glory of the principle of identity. It thus shifts the position of that gap between the ego and the Other in which the Sartrian displacement of a dialectic without synthesis was situated. It is no longer between two subjects that this gap is produced, but the fissure, the crack, the *Spaltung*, lies open from the very beginning between the subject and himself or herself.

Let us recall Lacan's position on this point:

> An existential negativity has been reached the reality of which is ardently promoted by the contemporary philosophy of being and nothingness.
>
> But the latter unfortunately only grasps this reality within the limits of a self-sufficiency of consciousness, and, being one of its premises, adds the illusion of autonomy in which it places so much confidence to its constitutive ignorance of the ego. It is a purely mental game, one which through having taken so much from analytic experience, culminates in the claim of having founded an existential psychoanalysis.

This radical critique of Sartre and existentialism joins up with the one Lévi-Strauss delivers on the subject of existentialism and history. What is at stake here is the pathetic operation of denial by which existential philosophy, because it is entirely a derivative of a philosophy of the free subject and consciousness, tries to come to grips with the reality of the unconscious without however having to posit its epistemological existence – for if it did, then it would lose face by having to reject its own positions. Phenomenology tried to outwit and resist the unconscious in a triple movement of encirclement and denial. The difference between the thetic and the non-thetic consciousness was the first of those manoeuvres. The introduction of 'bad faith' was the second, and the final strategy was the proclamation of an existential psychoanalysis which, bent on the project of preserving creativity and the subject's freedom, was substituted for traumas (read and interpreted by Sartre in causalist terms). The caricatural nature of the Freudianism presented by Sartrian philosophy as the enemy should not escape attention. Not only does the id function as a substantialist hydra with the annoying and unbearable consequence of cleaving the personality in two (whereas *cogito*-type conciousness is consciousness through and through), but what is welcomed in the trauma, that productive infantile event, is the initial fillip (seen in causalist terms) that troubles the life of the subject and engulfs the significance of his or her actions. The demiurge of the project or fundamental choice would substitute the humanism of liberty for the causalism of a supposedly traumatic destiny.

One should also be wary of any reifying reconstruction of Oedipus which, using strategies similar to Sartre's and making too facile a critique, attacks an adversary that has been previously distorted, thus paving the way for the demolition of the original and remarkable implications of the Oedipal situation as well as its tropological fertility, which goes far beyond the family circle.

In any case the Lacanian theses have to be recorded in all their detail to show how much they herald the advent of that schizo-analysis which Deleuze and Guattari thought they were the first to prophesy in *L'Anti-Oedipe*. As a profound syntactical operator, this 'dehiscence of the organism at its centre', this 'primordial Discord' first of all confirms the conception of man as being specifically premature at birth. The mirror-phase was thus to be interpreted by Lacan as a:

> drama whose internal dynamics rush precipitately from a state of insufficiency to one of anticipation – and which for the subject caught in the trap of spatial identification plots the series of fantasies going from a fragmented image of the body to that of a form, which we shall call orthopaedic, of its totality, and then to that of the finally accepted armour-plating of an alienating identity, which will stamp its rigid structure on the whole intellectual development of the subject. The breaking of the circle that runs from the *Innerwelt* to the *Umwelt* thus generates the inexhaustible and futile attempts to patch up the scattered fragments of the ego.

The riddles of the mirror

The mirror-phase, because it definitively shows that the subject is marked by a spatial and temporal schism, thus functions as the universal syntactic operator of all other occurrences of the subject's fragmentation, of its pulverization and disintegration. And as we shall see, one of its avatars is, through the mediation of Oedipus, the symbolic. We wish to emphasize that there is no question here of the eradication or the end of the subject, but that the operation ensured by the specular structure is that of an original disjunction which can vary from the production of the double to that disintegration of which the canvases of Bosch, with their *membra disjecta* and organs painted in exoscopy, 'combining and arming themselves for intestinal persecutions', are the culminating representation. It can be seen here that a schizo-logic (which Lacan rightly reminds us is one of the loci where psychosis and neurosis, far from remaining separate from each other in their different compartments, form a mutual articulation in the symptoms of spasms and schisms in the hysterical person) is one of the particular instances of the open structural functions whose very fabric resides in the symbolic and whose deep generator, tied to Oedipus, is the mirror-phase.

We can thus understand the inertia characteristic of the formations of the 'I' and find there the most extensive definition of neurosis – as the ensnarement of the subject by the situation which gives us the most general formula for madness, not only the madness which lies behind the walls of asylums but also the madness which deafens the world with its sound and fury.[19]

Through the mirror-phase Lacan manages to break apart that other, unsilvered, mirror which in the imaginary impotence of Freudianism separated neurosis from psychosis and assigned to psychoanalysis, as Foucault has so brilliantly shown in *Madness and Civilization*, the continuing institutional role of the asylum and of all repressive confinements. In limiting itself to the neurotic patient waffling on a couch, psychoanalysis once more repressed madness, by locking it into the shackles of nosographical classifications, by casting it into the dark Outside. The mirror-phase is the enjambment that challenges the closed space between neurosis, the locus of significance, and psychosis, where insignificance reigns in all its 'sound and fury'. Lacan is truly the founder of schizo-analysis. Deleuze and Guatarri have not failed to note the importance of the mirror-phrase, but only in passing. But when they take off their hats to Lacan in *L'Anti-Oedipe* it is like that Korean in James Bond who takes off his lead-lined headgear only to aim it at his adversary's neck, with fatal intentions. But what they seem to have failed to recognize in a work whose arguments are in many ways most welcome is the scope of the schizo-analysis founded by Lacan. We in our turn have to examine the implications of their arguments, given the disjunction they perform on the one hand between a mirror-phase which they see Lacan as having been unable to profit from ('You know how to conquer, Lacan, but you don't know how to profit from your victory'; or: 'The illustrious Lacan, like Hume in the prefaces to Kant's *Prolegomena*, has beached his boat, but only to let it rot there'), and on the other hand what they name Oedipus. Not only can it be said that this reproach is unjust as regards the supposed sterility of the mirror-phase, which is a fully functional operator just as much in the analysis of schizophrenia as constitutive of tenderness and aggressiveness caught in a double-bind as in the practice of irony – not only that, but what we must also question, while agreeing with criticisms that are often justified as to the use of Oedipus, is precisely this disjunction. The mirror-phase, castration and Oedipus are to our mind closely bound up with one another, and on the basis of these three schemata, not only do we see the necessity for recognizing the gap or split that works upon the process of desire at the deepest level of its supposed dynamic, but also why the Unconscious is expressed in terms of a liberating combinatory symbolicness that takes the shape of tropes, preserving the structurality of its field of application from any substantialist return towards the immediateness of mystical thing-worship.

The cracks that appear at the mirror-phase and the metaphorical originality of Oedipus are to us in a relationship of synonymy whose implications we shall soon have to study. But first let us examine in close detail the objections of *L'Anti-Oedipe*.

Is Oedipus a despot?

It is especially in the chapter 'Psychoanalyse et familialisme' that the strongest arguments are made against Oedipus, who is taken to task for having expropriated the rich profusions of the psychoanalytic discovery, for having confiscated the freedom of a *productive* Unconscious for the benefit of an *expressive* one. The imperialism of Oedipus is seen as the structure-event starting from which psychoanalysis and the problem of the Unconscious begin to 'go sour'. 'Psychoanalysis is like the Russian Revolution: one doesn't know when it started to go sour.' This perversion or rather betrayal of the Freudian discovery of the unconscious has a name: Oedipus. Who is Oedipus for Deleuze-Guattari?

The effects of Oedipus' intervention are first of all characterized by the act through which the wealth of the unconscious as a productive unit is overlooked and abandoned, the 'free syntheses where everything is possible, endless connections, non-exclusive disjunctions, conjunctions lacking any specificity, partial objects and pulsations'. What Oedipus makes us fatally forget is the direct confrontation between desire-based and social production, between symptomatological and collective formations, as well as that point where psychological repression meets up with the social repression of machines based on desire.

In sum, the Oedipal situation, through the family triangle that it implies, disconnects desire from the social and collective machinery of the drives which traverse the space of the social, reductively confining it to a stifling role in the theatre of petty bourgeois individualities. The consequence of this oversight or reductive effect of the sovereign position occupied by Oedipus is to impoverish the field of symbolic expression itself:

> Free association, instead of opening out on to polyvocal connections, shuts itself up in a univocal impasse. All the chains of the unconscious are bi-univocalized, linearized, and made to depend upon a despotic signifier. Any *production* based on desire is crushed and submitted to the demands of representation, to the dreary games of the represented in the representation. The productive unconscious

gives way to an unconscious that only knows how to *express* itself, in myths, tragedies and dreams.[20]

To make the wrong epistemological break, one that assumes the form of a fetishizing stop-gap enabling Oedipus to install himself, is finally to reduce and stunt the field of investigation and practice of production based on desire, by setting up limits and barriers everywhere – a break that shuts off psychosis and neurosis, family and society, and the regions of the unconscious *topos* from one another. It is as if Freud, confronted with the extraordinarily frenzied flourishing of unconscious productions based on desire, including schizophrenia, *quite simply didn't have the nerve.* Freud recoiled in horror when faced with the seething raw reality of the unconscious. He wanted to file away in cramped series what, through its very nature, could not be caught up in the coils of representation and the theatrical. With Oedipus there emerges a theatre, a stage, where the props of a classical scenario are erected. 'It is only gradually,' say our authors, 'that he made the family novel a simple dependency of Oedipus, seeing to it that everything in the unconscious turned neurotic under his rule, at the same time that the family triangle was enclosed within the unconscious. The schizoid is the real enemy.'[21] Oedipal denial, a sweeping movement through which the despotic signifier is installed, would thus mean that the richness of the workshop and factory has been replaced by the poverty of a theatre of expression: 'Production based on desire is personalized or rather personologized, imagized and structuralized (we have seen that the real difference or frontier does not pass between these terms, which are perhaps complementary). Production is only production of fantasies, of expression.'[22]

Deleuze-Guatarri, and the cure

We shall have to follow the general direction of this critique which, before attacking certain theoretical developments of Freudianism and especially Lacan, strikes a blow at the use made by the psychoanalytical institution and the couch of Freud's discovery. The strategic position of Deleuze-Guatarri is complex. It assumes the trajectory of an anabasis and consists in an anxiety over the function of the psychoanalytic establishment in its reductive practice; this first gesture is reminiscent of the healthy impatience, the holy wrath, that leads another team, Cooper and Laing, to assault the asylum-fortresses of Great Britain. 'On the door to the consulting room, these words are written: leave your desiring machines outside, abandon your orphaned and celibate machines, your taperecorder and your little bike, enter and let yourself be Oedipalized. Everything flows from there, starting with the unspeakable character of the cure, its highly contractual and interminable nature, a flow of words against a flow of money.'[23] How, at this level, can we resist being seduced by Deleuze-Guattari's critique of a practice that is too frequently shamanistic and whose hermeneutic approach too manifestly becomes a bi-univocal translation reducing the patient's history to what can be derived from his traumas, envisaged in the most causalist and trivially anecdotal way?

In this respect and in many others *L'Anti-Oedipe* is a liberating work because it cures the intelligentsia of a number of prejudices and taboos. The hammering of schizophrenia as a kind of psychoanalysis in its shattering and clastic irruption definitely bring some fresh air onto the theoretical and ideological stage, throw the windows wide open, and to the fetishists, sectarians and maniacs of workerism and stultifying 'militant' practices says, as to psychoanalysts: 'There is a bad smell surrounding you, one of death and of petty personal concerns.' This deliverance can be rightly compared to Lacan's impatience vis-à-vis the use made of his theses and the theoretical apparatus he has invented by certain of his disciples for whom the 'letter' is no more than the punch-mark or stamp that metaphorically inscribes a character, a type, on the flesh of the subject, within a suffocating family history: the same holy wrath, the same scorn.

The divided Lacan

Lacan's irritation over certain aspects of psychoanalytic practice and the importance of the mirror-phase are without doubt two of the 'initial fillips' of the book. In any case these themes inevitably pervade the reading of that fiction or poem, *L'Anti-Oedipe*. We are here at the second stage of that anabasis which structures the itinerary of the work, marked by the authors' ambiguous relation to Lacan. There is for them a good Lacan and a bad one. The good Lacan, although this due merit is not entirely recognized in a thematic, but only in an operational way, is the unwitting inventor of schizo-analysis, the man of the mirror-phase whose importance we have just described. This Lacan also inspires our authors over the irritation he experiences with psychoanalysts. But the bad Lacan, distinct from the first and impossible to interiorize, is the one who lets himself be completely dominated by Oedipus, who has fallen into the Freudian basket and reconciled himself with the Odeipal reductions. With the latter: 'Oedipus has appropriated production based on desire as if all the productive forces of desire emanated from him. The psychoanalyst has become Oedipus's coatstand, the agent of anti-production in the domain of desire. The same history as that of Capital and its enchanted, miraculous world (in the beginning too, Marx used to say, the first capitalists could not have been unaware).'[24]

The same history too as in the Russian Revolution, to take up the metaphor proposed by Deleuze-Guattari, where the schizophrenic, creative and prolific swarm of desires finds a surprising analogue. First the soviets were everywhere, decentralized assemblies, molecular and shifting. Then came Lenin, who put everything into order. The smothering action of the Bolsheviks led to the Stalinist Great Fear and to the despotism of Gulag, just as between Oedipus and the foreclosure of the couch and the cure there reigns the same padded-cell atmosphere which as Foucault has shown in *Madness and Civilization* accomplishes the selfsame motions of confinement as are to be found in nosographical classifications. In addition, only one step separates the texts of Foucault dealing with the repressive, cloistering function of psychoanalysis at the end of the nineteenth century and the sarcastic remarks of Deleuze-Guattari on analytic practice. And the stigma of this second stage of the anabasis is the epistemological break between psychosis and neurosis, the ever-vigilant frontier guard in the service of repression.

Emptying out the negative

Hence the necessity of returning to that strange gesture, reminiscent of a potlatch, by which Freud allowed Oedipus to rule the roost, installing the massive* terror of the symbolic. And this is not so much Lacan's fault as Freud's. Enamoured of positivity, Deleuze-Guattari cannot bear negativity, which already in Freud started to work upon desire. That desire should be equated with a lack is inadmissible here. The inscription of castration, the complementary other side to Oedipus, drives out what gain the unconscious and sexuality might have made from bisexuality: 'One must speak of castration in the same sense as Oedipalization, for it is its crowning glory. It designates the operation by which psychoanalysis castrates the unconscious, injecting castration into it.'[25]

Deleuze-Guatarri by opposing the pre-eminence of castration and lack wish to bring about a Ptolemaic revolution, one that would be antagonistic and liberating as regards the Copernican revolution that Freud produced by subjecting bisexuality to castration:

Certain analysts, following Melanie Klein, tried to define the unconscious forces of the female sexual organ in terms of positive characters that are a function of partial objects and flux. This slight edging away, which did not suppress the mythical castration, but which made the latter depend only in a derived way upon the organ instead of the other way round, met with much opposition in Freud. Freud maintained that the organ from the point of view of the unconscious could only be understood upon the basis of a primary

* Deleuze-Guatarri use the word 'molar' which they oppose to molecular'. (Trans.)

lack or deprivation, and not the reverse. Here we find a properly analytic paralogism (that is found to a large extent in the theory of the signifier) which consists in passing from the partial detachable object to the position of an entire object as detached entity (the phallus). This passage implies a determined subject as fixed ego in either sex, who necessarily experiences as a lack the subordination to the complete tyrannical object.

It is thus in one and the same gesture that Deleuze-Guattari denounce Freud's act of denying the primary fact of bisexuality, his constitution of the relationship between desire and the signifier as one of lack and negativity, and his phallocentrism. The war machine that *L'Anti-Oedipe* sends charging against these ideological traps amounts to a liberating Ptolemaic revolution through which the rights of bisexuality are reaffirmed by positing castration as something derived and partial. The workings of the machine motivated by desire are supposedly obtained through a synthesis in the Kantian sense between the organless body upon which the partial object is placed or between the ego thereby obtained and the drives. Here too there is the expletion of a certain subject, through the deliverance of the ego away from the phallus's and the signifier's grip. From then on, we are only faced with positivities which, as with Matta, enter into relationships of connection, disjunction and conjunction with other partial objects: 'Each element of the corresponding multiplicity can only be defined *positively*.'

The little structuralist and symbolic theatre is thus broken up into tiny fragments. The fine multipolar and scalene network has been replaced by the noisy jumble of desiring machines, similar in their stochastic dispersion to what Foucault calls in the *Archéologie du savoir* discontinuous pronouncements, or to what Nietzsche had already realized through the dispersion of his aphorisms. A molecular space which thwarts the tropes of the network in which the demon of massiveness was hidden. To plug into another machine is a paranoiac act. Deleuze-Guattari's balista disconnects and dissolves, yielding the fluidity of the molecular in the milieu. The Oedipal and structuralist theatre was at best a Vasarely and at worst a Millet. Deleuze-Guattari claim to have restored us to the sound and fury of the molecular discontinuities of the unconscious. We are back in the age of Bosch and *The Garden of Delights.*

It is tempting, even seductive, to follow this iconoclastic thought to the end, attacking the movement of territorializing denials brought about by Oedipus in contempt of the decoded, fleeting impulses of desire. But where exactly do they take us? 'Such is the nature of neurosis, displacing boundaries so as to secure just for itself a little colonial plot.'[26]

The Song of the Sirens

It is also tempting to go on board what is presented to us as a sort of 'bateau ivre' and jeer with *L'Anti-Oedipe* at the kulaks on the bank who are quite content with the little parcels of coded signifiers that they have been left to cultivate. The final moment of the anabasis goes right to the heart of the theoretical and denounces the symbolic as the enclosed circularity of exchange. Deleuse-Guatteri set out to discover the unconscious investments of desire in the social domain and they also wish to modify the relationship between exchange and gifts on the one hand and debt on the other. Here too there is to be a Ptolemaic revolution in anthropology, for Oedipus is to be hunted down as the despotic guardian of the symbol and of exchange. The habitual relationship between Oedipus and the incest taboo, as Roheim conceives of it for example, will be torn asunder. 'The incest taboo is said to imply an Oedipal representation of the repression and return from which it emerges. But the opposite is clearly the case. Not only does the Oedipal representation presuppose the prohibition of incest, but also one cannot say that it emerges or results from it.'[27] To demonstrate the inanity of the proposition that 'incest is desired because it is forbidden', Deleuze-Guattari force a disjunction between Oedipal representation and the incest taboo. This elision is methodologically necessary for our authors so that they may re-establish within a positivistic framework the relationship of direct libidinal investment with social production 'with no suppression of the sexual character of symbolism and its corresponding effects, and especially with no reference to an Oedipal representation assumed to be originally repressed or structurally enclosed.'[28]

Setting aside for the moment the surprising reasons that have led Deleuze-Guattari to reduce Oedipus to a representation, let us salute the stand they take in the debate with culturalism:

The conflict of the culturalists and the orthodox psychoanalysts has often been reduced to these evaluations of the respective role of the mother and father, of the pre-Oedipal and the Oedipal, without ever leaving the family circle or even Oedipus, always oscillating between the two celebrated poles of the maternal pre-Oedipal stage of the imaginary on the one hand, and the Oedipal and paternal pole of the structural order on the other; both are on the same axis, and both speak the language of a familialized 'socius' of which one designates the maternal dialects, the other the iron law of the father's word.[29]

This text, although it places a troop of quite unreal shadow boxers on the stage, since it sees Oedipus as an empirical entity, has nevertheless the merit of putting us on guard against the involuntarily ethnocentric gesture by which we transpose familial schemata on to ethnographical realities which are not to be subsumed under it. But in the same gesture we are invited *a contrario* to detach the Oedipal situation from any identification with the family so that it may be generalized at another level which, consequently, is not an ethnocentric one.

Exchange and debt

Even more basic is the critique of exchange and the symbolic order against whose circularity Deleuze-Guattari stress the importance of debt, that fissure in the domain of exchange which restores the body's dimension as a depository of inscriptions.

Society is not based upon exchange, the 'socius' is a recorder; not to exchange but to mark our bodies, which are of the earth, is what matters. We have seen that the order of debt flows directly from the exigencies of this savage inscription. For debt means unity of alliance and alliance is representation itself. It is through alliances that the impulses of desire are codified and that, through debt, man is given the faculty to remember words. . . . That is why it is so important to see in debt a direct consequence of a primitive inscription instead of making it (and the inscriptions themselves) an indirect means of universal exchange.[30]

The body, the impulses, dynamics and desire are re-imported where structure and exchange once stood as the squanderers and founders of the latter which, through a reverse movement, subordinate themselves to debt as a cruel inscription in the flesh. 'Desire knows no exchange, it knows only theft and giving, sometimes one in the shape of the other, in the form of a primitive homosexuality. Hence the loving anti-exchange machine that Joyce portrayed in *Exiles* and Klossowski in *Roberte*.'

It could be added that all of Shakespeare's plays function along the lines of this structural model and we shall study elsewhere the relationship he sustains with the circulation of a negative quantum: refusal of the loss of virginity, potlatch, mask, expenditure and the pound of flesh are all bound together by this economy of the debt – which is more than an economy, as it brings into play the relationship of desire to emptiness and uncertainty. And it is here, precisely, in the importance accorded by them to debt, that Deleuze-Guattari admit the fundamental necessity of allowing the gap of a negativity, the incision of a lack, insinuate itself into the space of an asserted plenitude. They are under the illusion of opposing debt and exchange, of rehabilitating Mauss against the closed structurality of a Lévi-Strauss, but what they do not see is that no parallel can be made between these two levels and that debt when inscribed onto the network of exchange certainly brings about a transgression, as we know since *The Genealogy of Morals* and Bataille's *La Part maudite*, and that it is the site where exchange in a sense thwarts its own rules (Serres' analysis of Molière's *Dom Juan* brings this out very well).[31]

It may be said though that debt forms a sub-set of exchange, or rather that it is only a particular case of exchange, to the extent that exchange presupposes syntactical and semantic operators whose effect is to be found in a transgression between the continuous and the discontinuous. But inversely, debt, because it presupposes negativity and uncertainty, i.e. the introduction of a negative magnitude or of a non-mediatizable and non-dialectic negativity, is at the very root of the symbolic and the active processes of exchange. It is debt that enables the passage from restricted to generalized exchange to take place, from the local to the global, where the continuous and the discontinuous, instead of being firmly established points of view, are recorded in their difference and kinship. Its negativity enables a disinvestment to emerge that in turn activates the domain of the symbolic.

When Deleuze-Guattari take up the question that Mauss had at least left open – 'does debt come before exchange or is it only a type of exchange, a means serving the latter?' – they accuse Lévi-Strauss of having 'apparently closed the matter in a categorical way: debt is only a superstructure, a conscious form in which the unconscious social reality of exchange is circulated.' They do not seem to be aware that this question cannot be framed in terms of an alternative or an opposition. Far from there being an incompatibility, even an antagonism, between debt and structural exchange, there is on the contrary a complementarity, an essential, two-layered relationship of mutual implication. Debt and the gift (in the form of a potlatch) are in effect two borderline cases of exchange, sites where exchange unfolds itself and where its contours undergo an anamorphosis; it is therefore a particular example of the law of exchange. But inversely, structural exchange is subordinated to a mode of debt, to the extent that the differential gap produced by debt is a necessary precondition for the structurality of the symbolic. From the outset dissymmetry works upon organized, structural exchange, paving the way for symbolization because it is that which puts a check on and mutilates the fullness of positivity. It is thanks to the operation of debt that metaphor can corrupt the combinatory functioning of the syntactical matrix. Debt therefore accounts for the possibility of the emergence of restricted exchange from generalized exchange as well as for the 'reality' of structure.

A factor in diffraction, the inaugural lack producing poly-semy, the negativity whose metonymic emblem is debt, brings to the combinatory indefiniteness of structurality the definiteness of a reality principle which is not a return to the univocal, but a selection from the range of possible combinatories. If it is true that the structural approach can well escape from that reduc-tionism for which structure is a mere hollow form or mathe-matical grid, then it is clear what an essential role the domains of the symbolic and the semantic play in giving the structural schema its dynamic force. And it is with debt that one may discern the site from which a semantic process corrupts and shifts the syntactic and combinatory arrangements. *Far from having cast debt aside therefore, structuralism has always welcomed it as an indispensable part of its functioning*, since the negativity it implies is at the heart or source of the production of the symbolic as that which detaches itself from the plane of the real and the mists of the imagination.

It is through the presence of debt within structure that structuralism remains open-ended, as Lévi-Strauss has admirably shown in relation to myths in *L'Homme nu*.

It can thus be seen upon what basis we interpret *L'Anti-Oedipe*. It is correct to say that we agree with Deleuze-Guattari in seeing in debt an opposition corrupting the law of exchange, but we also maintain that it is within and not outside the structure of exchange that this corruption takes place. Better still, authentic structuralism has always been able to harbour in its diverse ramifications a problematic both of the continuous and the discontinuous, of circularity and openness.

That is why we shall in all friendship contest a certain number of points concerning Oedipus. Far from seeing any sort of solution of continuity between the propositions of the mirror-phase and the advent of Oedipus as basic operator of the symbolic, we shall affirm their necessity. Before Oedipus there was not a desire that Oedipus then mutilated, repressed or triangulated. By Oedipus we mean a semantico-syntactic relationship and operator universal enough not to be reducible to a real family, to the history of the subject. The paradox of Oedipus is the same as that of the incest taboo in Lévi-Strauss: *it overlaps onto a structure whose divisions it also founded*. To say then that the Oedipus theme goes no further than the family triangle comes down to saying that the incest taboo can be reduced to exogamy or to its contrary, endogamy, or to whatever figuration these two give rise to. Deleuze and Guattari have taken the easiest way out by affecting to reduce the function of Oedipus to a family triangle. In the same way, by reducing exchange to a simple modality they impoverish its structurality, and having pared it down to an empirical expression can put an equals sign between it and debt, which they also reduce to the dimension of a hypostatized inscription oblivious of the negativity that it nonetheless contains. Oedipus in its function as a semantico-syntactic operator of desire pre-exists that structure-event traversed by the subject in the development of its libido which psychology has called the Oedipus complex.

The poetics of Oedipus

For us, the Oedipal situation, in its structurality, is what presides over the entry of the subject into the order of the symbolic, the site where the possibility of a detachment from the order of the real may emerge. The passage through Oedipus, far from being the site of a deeply rooted fixation in the hebetude of a family relationship, functions in fact as the *structural opportunity* where not only the ambiguity of the parental relation as something pre-derived and polysemic, but also the absence of attributes peculiar to any one relationship, may be experienced. Because a specular structure has always diffracted the constitution of subjectivity, the Oedipal relationship is always corrupted by it; it is affected semantically, giving rise to the impossibility of constituting a point of anchorage in the initial effect other than in a symbolic way, i.e. derivatively, in a way that is 'not its own'. None the less, the traversal of the Oedipean field is necessary so that the structuration through the schism or initial split in the subject may find its inscription in the 'real'. It is, in effect, because Oedipus is put into contact with parental prohibitions that the reality of the limits placed upon desire is experienced. Castration therefore has to be connected to Oedipus as the metonymic function by which the essential negativity of desire is realized or resurfaces into the 'historical' domain.

It is this negativity, as we have seen, which is the driving force of the poetics of the unconscious, and which establishes the reality principle as well as the possibility for the symbolic to emerge. If desire is not to remain in the hebetude of a positivity in all its fullness that nothing can diffract, then it must accomplish its symbolic vocation as trope or figure, a process that presupposes both a lack and a displacement. *The Interpretation of Dreams* and all of Freud's and Lacan's analyses have brought into the open the 'poetic' nature of the unconscious where generative structures are no more than displacements governed by tropes. And their full meaning resides in the recognition that there is no primary Oedipus, that any mark of Oedipus is already metaphoric and derived. It was through disregarding the originally displaced and diffracted character of Oedipus – that is, its *semiotic deficiency* – that Deleuze and Guattari thought they could attack Oedipus. They have abusively reduced him to a representation and a historicity.

But what they fail to notice is that the Oedipal situation goes beyond itself in each of its determinations. To the extent that it is the absent figurative operator, it escapes from any given modality of a present structure to which it cannot be reduced and in which its potential cannot be exhausted. Far from being the operator of a family triangle, Oedipus enables this triangulation to *symbolize* with any other social determination which must not however be relativized in relation to it. There is no right formulation of the Oedipal situation that has priority over others seen as its pale reflections, distant copies or subordinate images. They all symbolize among themselves upon a structural network that marks them all. Semantic activity commences in this network through the ambiguity or plurivocality generated both by the work of debt or, as here, the specular structure as original diffraction, as well as through the ambiguity, surfacing into 'history', of the relationships that are 'internal' to the triangles but which exceed them in all respects. As Green has shown in *Un oeil en trop*, Oedipus is also Orestes or Othello and many others besides. The axial structure called Oedipus is open to many other variants, depriving it of any privileged central theme. *No one element is dominant in the Oedipal situation* and the Greek hero is merely the eponym of a simple structurality open to all the arrangements of the symbolic and poetic orders; an operator of deep structures that are nothing other than tropes.

What Pouillon says of structuralism we can thus say about Oedipus:

Structuralism implies plurality of organizations. There is thus no sense in speaking of a structure peculiar to every whole, or of an archetypal structure that would in some sense be their composite image. Each variant is a variant of the others and not of just one of them occupying a privileged position, nor is it a variant of an 'ideal' type. The variables, which explain the differences, refer to no other invariant save the rule of invariability. Structure is essentially the syntax of transformations allowing for the passage from one variant to the other, and it is this syntax that explains their limited number, i.e. the restricted exploitation of theoretical possibilities.[32]

It could be added that in the case of psychoanalysis, as in anthropology, it is the impact of a 'history' that enables one to explain the non-exploitation of all theoretical possibilities and what one may call the particular semantic selection. But this option must not be referred back to a causalist conception of events. It is because it is a 'history' that has been always symbolized by the original diffraction of the optical 'I' that is out of step with itself, that it enables one combination rather than another to emerge. The structural 'reality principle' is not to be found in the real but in the efficacity of the symbolic itself, if one bears in mind that this symbolic order is affected from the outset by a 'disinvesting' negativity that contests all forms of the 'personal' and the real, even the illusion of a familial archetype, wrongly promoted to the rank of event or inaugural trauma.

Through the inscription of castration and repression which, we state openly, function as forces liberating all the power of the symbolic, it may be said that the Freudian Oedipus fully accounts for the schizoid structuration of the mirror-phase as posited by Lacan, enabling one to *go beyond* what the concept of sign and of linguistic structurality still owed to a trans-cendental determination of subjectivity. It is because a certain structuralist ideology thought that a blank had to be installed in place of the subject (a place that had been hastily evacuated), that generative grammars of a Chomskyan type saw fit to reimport the dimension of the subject as the site where deep structures and invariables would take root and find support.

This Cartesian avowal translates a clumsily constructed 'abreaction'; and the return, in all its force, of a central empirico-transcendental subjectivity becomes a stop-gap, a fetishization, stepping over the question of the unconscious in the name of a substantialist positivity. Repression and castration, on the contrary, in the sense given them in the work of Freud and Lacan, enable one to perceive that in a space more profound than Chomskyan deep structures there is a generating apparatus composed of tropes and figures that are to be found moreover, in the analysis of the symbolic space in anthropology (Crocker on the Bororo) and which is at work in the unconscious through an original, constitutive lack. *L'Anti-Oedipe* which reads like a work of fiction with all the latter's charms, confronts us with an imaginary version of the Oedipal situation, reducing it to being no more than the enclosing operator of a family triangulation. But we have to recognize, on the contrary, that the familial Oedipal process undergone by every subject is only one actual-ization, among many others, of all the symbolic possibilities of which the Oedipal operator is capable, and which it activates on the basis of the fundamental lack that constitutes the sym-bolic and the trope as inaugural displacements.

Only if one yields to a one-dimensional positivism and

asymbolia therefore can desire be called a positivity that invests the social domain. In that case it is hard to see how Deleuze-Guattari can still speak of the *polyvocality* of desire and production based upon desire, starting from the ideological site of positivity that they intended to conquer. By accusing Oedipus of flattening out the 'polyvocalities' of desire, not only do they subject him to an unfair trial (for he has done nothing of the sort, since from the beginning he goes beyond any familialist determination), but they also deprive themselves of the means, when speaking of positivities, of spelling out how and from where the formations of desire are recognizable as polyvocal. Unconscious Luddites, they wreck the trope-making machine only to put in its place a simple semantic chain where desire is spoken of as an infrastructure of the unconscious, as a workshop or factory, and the formations of machines based upon desire as so many positivities.

The boomerang effects of transcendental materialism

Despite all our cordial feelings for Deleuze-Guattari and – why not? – the recognition too of the various sites of liberation that *L'Anti-Oedipe* has brought to our attention, we must, so that the pleasure that this text produces may increase, bring to light the status of its conceptuality and metaphors. How can it be said, in fact, that desire belongs to an infrastructure? If it is not to try and paint white roses red, like the gardeners of *Alice in Wonderland* before the arrival of the Queen of Hearts, a decapitating innovation (off with their heads), and to please certain supporters of an outdated Marxism, why do Deleuze-Guattari still use this vaguely spatializing conceptuality (infra, super), whereas we know, since Gramsci, that it has become impossible to speak in such a binary way and that even those who borrow their concepts from the domain of a Marxist conceptuality have abandoned the linear and bipolar differences of a space naïvely sandwiched between infra- and super-structure? Just as they have gone, along with Althusser, as close as possible to boldly renouncing the epistemological fetishism of 'causality in the last instance', so they have recognized too, thanks especially to anthropology, that the function of the last instance is not necessarily performed by the economic. Thus Godelier, studying African societies, has been able to pluralize the concept of the last instance to the extent that this role may be held by the political or religious spheres, according to the structure of the society under study. The final operator of the complex structure of the contradictions of a Mossi society, for example, must not be sought, as Michel Izard has shown, in the economic domain. The latter is merely a moment, a site in a network whose apex 'in the last instance' is to be found in the over-arching political and state systems of the Yatenga, which structure the identity of groups and individuals as well as the other modes – religious, ideological, economic, etc. – of their existence.

A methodological step forward was thus made, thanks to anthropology, on the road to the constitution of an open 'Marxism'. Such a step would have been even longer if anyone had dared to interrogate the causalist and metaphysical totem-concept of the last instance. No one did dare, for Marxism still functions in the hope of scientificness. But at least it has been noticed that the economic does not exercise its hegemony every-where, and thanks to the post-Althusserians we have to be grateful for this liberating step forward, for it has rescued a good number of researchers from a linear, mechanical and causalist materialism that hindered their studies by making them repeat in never-ending chorus the theory of the 'reflection'. The chief stages on this road are first the work of Althusser (*Contradiction and Overdetermination*) and also Mao Tse-tung's article on contradiction, which has been taken up in the field of Marxian studies. The latter in fact, as we have seen, by proposing the distinction between secondary aspect of a principal contradic-tion, principal aspect of a principal contradiction, and secondary aspect of a secondary contradiction, has pluralized the structure of contradiction and multipolarized the dialectic enough to bring us close to the structural axiomatization of the notion of contradiction. Here though we are still certainly in an archaic domain where contradiction retains its hegemonic and abusively privileged position of power, sterilizing real processes through an impoverishment of mental ones from which schizo-analysis and the work of Lyotard have shatteringly cut us free in their turn, by relativizing in the discontinuity of aphorisms à la Nietzsche the type of impoverished relationships that dialectic negativity represented. And in such a way the two outermost limits of the dialectical field are drawn, beyond which everything is still possible. On one side the Leibnizian combinatory that *polytopizes* the field, but leaves enough space for the multi-faceted linearity of a network of multiple relations. On the other, the archipelago of distinct and separate pronouncements, the *schizo-topy* made up of a collection of points of singularity, the logic of non-relations, the invention of chance happenings – the stochastic other side of structurality.

It is good that the processes of a stretched and distended dialectic should have broken asunder between these two poles. But in both instances the question of the corruption of the syntactic order or of the symbolicness of the discontinuous had not been raised. It is, on the contrary, with the concept of *over-determination*, a semantically charged concept of Freudian origins, that the dialectic has been able to avoid being re-absorbed back into the idealism of a pure combinatory, and has been fragmented into discontinuous and stochastically silent positivities. The dialectic, like any relational fabric or generative dynamic, begins when a *clinamen* comes and blocks the discontinuous and autistic flow of the elements, forcing them to enter into joint combinations and to weave the thread of a relationship. Now, this relationship would have been quite content to incorporate the negation formerly proscribed by the logos of identity and would have pursued its pluralization of the modes of contradiction, going as far as a multi-layered and highly mediatized analysis as regards its terms but remaining repetitive as to the modalities of its relations, if Althusser – taking his cue from Lacan, Freud and Mao Tse-tung – had not perpetrated the violent but productive act of introducing over-determination into contradiction, and allowing a semantic 'corruption', a semiotic chora* to pervert the logos of (non-) contradiction. And it should not be forgotten that the danger which the dialectic incurs through Althusser, and which Mao had the courage to face up to, originates from psychoanalysis and the Freudian heritage.

The fecundity of Oedipus as a semantico-syntactic operator, in its figurative poetic function of the generator of tropes, produces overdetermination and continues the effects of *The Interpretation of Dreams.* 'Dreams are unaware of the logical *non* wrote Freud. Overdetermination as a relativization of a logic of (non-)contradiction and of a dialectical logos which is just one of its subsets operates as an inscription of the unthinkable dissymmetry of the relationship in which Eros and Thanatos are inherent and antagonistic, and functions within the domain of rhetoric and Oedipal poetics, to the extent, as we have seen, that the incisive mark of castration is written into them, an inscription of which the mirror-phase is the perpetual witness; the unforeseeable reinscriptions of lack.

Consequently, to define desire as an infrastructure is to bring into play a defunct conceptuality whose status has been rethought by the recent developments of Marxism. We shall not go as far as to say that we hear the echo of that Stalinist decree by which, fortunately for him and Soviet researchers, language through the munificence of the tyrant had been baptized an infrastructure in a famous article. Deleuze and Guattari's proposal functions here rather as part of a metaphorical chain which constitutes the conceptual texture of *L'Anti-Oedipe* and in which, Oedipus having once and for all been assimilated to the stage of representation, we are invited to go and look in the wings of the symbolic theatre and to find what? A factory, a workshop where machines are ticking over.

---

* *Chora:* a concept employed by Plato to describe what is unstable and amorphous but nonetheless necessary to the subsequent emergence of distinct ontological forms and the possibility of naming them. Now often used in a psychoanalytical context to describe the state of primitive energies and drives before the structuralization of the unconscious at the Oedipal stage.

This detour has been productive since it enables our authors to install themselves on the skyline of a dynamic, Cartesian mechanism and a 'rejuvenated' Marxism. To substitute the metaphor of desire as production for the theory of an expressive unconscious is to put off for ever the question of the pluralization of the dialectic and its fragmentation into a multidimensional symbolic order. The problematic of the axiomatization of negativity and contradiction is thereby eluded. The war-machine of *L'Anti-Oedipe* resembles those 'entropic' machines of Tinguely, and we welcome the polemical verve that it exerts against the apparent temptations of the Leibnizian combinatory that founded one of the aspects of structuralism – syntax and the network. A little schizophrenic dissemination does no harm when the combinatory and multidimensional network risks being identified with a continuum of paranoiac branchings. In any case this victory of the discontinuous is a Pyrrhic one, as it is doomed to reinstall the real, and especially the self-referential identity. Desire as production produces asymbolic and positivistic flows which, certainly, connect and disconnect and combine and cross over one another but whose positivity appears to us to bring about the involuntary movement of a substantialist regression which, in relation to the potentialities of structuralist and Leibnizian formalism and the death wish, takes us back to the silent opacity of a collective subject of enunciations.

In addition, if we advance further in our examination of the sites of production of the conceptual scenography of *L'Anti-Oedipe*, if we examine the apparatus of its *Begriffdichtung*, we shall notice that its most innovatory concepts are of *substantialist* descent. 'Desire as production', as we have said, accords a privilege to the real at the expense of the symbolic. It can no longer be said that it (ça) speaks but that it (ça) produces. By placing a question mark over the signifier, Deleuze and Guattari fall back to the level of a causalism of real production which, in an unmediated way, invests the social body and excludes any form of void, of negativity or lack, creating an impasse for the death wish.

But as we have seen, the gap, the lack, the difference, that is the inscription of the void, are necessary for the polytropic functioning of the unconscious as a structure that generates displacements, condensations and the whole poetic rhetoric of the unconscious. That is the lesson of structuralism, bestowing upon it the trajectory of an itinerary similar to the one which had led Leibniz from a combinatory analysis (*Ars combinatoria*) to a topological one (*analysis situs*). This itinerary is a correlative, at another level of inscription, of the one which operates through the extraction and corruption of a semantic process out of the syntactical matrices where in principle everything was possible. Structuralist semantics with its *analysis situs* therefore functions as a structural 'reality principle' that inscribes the divergence of a particular profile of structure in the indefiniteness of the combinatory which had remained at the ludic level of a pleasure principle: a generative selection which presupposes, at its roots, lack and delimitation through difference, i.e. the dissymmetrical inscription of Thanatos.

To substitute the machinery of desire for structurality is to conflate the semantic and symbolic dimensions and to peremptorily switch off the machinery of tropes. And if one applies to the text of *L'Anti-Oedipe* the concepts and images it proposes, one will be able to see, through the lack that pervades and fractures it from end to end, that the symbolic is far more nomadic than the producer unconscious. Hermes travels further than Prometheus bound.

For Oedipus

Deterritorialization, what Deleuze-Guattari call with a seductive conceptual nonchalance 'decoding', resides in the trope, the machinery of the symbolic and the deep rhetoric of the Unconscious through which it is accomplished. By way of proof we may mention the prohibition that Aristotle, making sure that things kept their own proper meaning, placed upon the *metabasis eis allo genos*, the conveying or act of translation that lightheartedly skipped from one type of being to another.

Oedipus, the eponym of a displaced and inadequate translation, the one into which lack and repression insinuate themselves, is the nomad 'par excellence', the wandering vagabond
of the open metaphor. Gaily contesting the family as original
society, he is the operator of ambiguity and polytopy; and so
we can see that the passage through the Oedipus complex is only
a secondary episode as regards the structure of the cloven subject who is always out of step with himself. We shall therefore
prefer to see the unconscious as a nomadic transduction, rather
than adopt the workerist metaphor of the unconscious as factory.
The semiotic body, supposedly blocked by the symbolic, is none
other than that tropological operator that speaks through combinations of fantasies, words and spaces that joyously code,
decode and semanticize themselves. Sade saw this, and with him
the postures and articulations of bodies acting together, the
subtle and polysemic pyramids of their various positions, form
the unstable graph and combinatory of a rhetoric whose
alphabet consists of sexual organs, faces, hands etc. We have
here an immense emblem of the fragmented body that with its
many permutations forms a text whose semiotic and structural
articulations, through the rhetoric that they set in motion, are
the expression and inscriptions of desire. Bodies in the process of
writing, the text of the parts of the body that never revert back
to an amorphous mass, but which welcome divergencies and
distances in and between them – the intertext. There is no place
here for a production of flows, but there is for the dynamics of a
graph and trope that mutually combine. The typology of Sadian
positions is a treatise equivalent to Du Marsais's theory of tropes.

In choosing to ignore the nature of this combinatory of desire,
one lacerated by lack and negativity, worked upon by Thanatos
and uncertainty, and in placing an impasse in front of the death
wish, the authors of *L'Anti-Oedipe* have confined themselves to
a substantialist description of desire whose origins are Cartesian.
But of a curious Cartesianism, since in its imaginary field the
mechanism of the *res extensa* and the activity of the *res cogitans*
are telescoped together. Deleuze, let us not forget, has given an
admirable interpretation of Spinoza's texts. He has retained

from his author the dynamism of the substance as *conatus*, itself a descendant of what for Descartes was thinking matter. But Descartes, through his theory of animals as automata, as well as his treatises on anatomy and medicine, or again in the *Principles of Philosophy*, makes the body and the *res extensa* a piece of machinery. As a Spinozist bent on reducing the Cartesian dualism between the two substances by overcoming the difference that separates them, Deleuze forces together the two substances: 'machines' is the heritage of the Cartesian *res extensa*; and 'based on desire' is the transformation of Cartesian will into a Spinozist *conatus*.

Now, if there is in Descartes a masterful anticipation of the problematic of the unconscious as order of the symbolic then it is to be found, as we have said, in the mythological flights of fancy by which Descartes transgresses the opposition which he had first of all postulated, in the interests of an epistemological necessity between the two substances and consequently between the soul and the body. These transgressions are three in number. First of all the problematic of the dream and its denials, as given in the first meditation. Then there is the provisional hypostasis of that third substance made up of the 'union of body and soul', destined to explain the impact of effects and the fact that 'my soul is not lodged in my body like a pilot in his ship'. There is finally the extraordinary 'novel of anatomy and physiology' represented by the problematic of the pineal gland, supposed to paper over the chasm between the soul and the body by ensuring the mimetic inscription of the traces or engrams of one substance (the body) on another (the soul). It was through tearing away this mythological stop-gap that Freud managed to introduce the problematic of the unconscious, ensuring, in the same stroke, that the subject was out of step with itself. He thus revealed the importance of the symbolic order as generator of those semantic and syntactical processes that speak forth on the basis of a deficiency and of the extraction of the physiological function (*res extensa*) from matter in all its fullness. It is in this Cartesian site/non-site, in this papered-over crack, that the unconscious might have been situated; but it was only to arise later, when the epistemological conditions bound up with Leibnizianism emerged in turn.

By borrowing their conceptual apparatus from the transcendental materialism of the machine-cum-*res extensa*, animated by all the prolix subjectivism of the ebb and flow of desire, Deleuze-Guattari omit, in their Cartesianism, the enigmatic site where the latter had profoundly felt the effects of the symbolic fissure of the unconscious, that bizarre place where all desire is rooted in a lack and its denial. Their dynamism, contrary to Leibnizian dynamism, whose job it was to conciliate and articulate the mathematical graph with energy, is a mute one because it is caught up in the solid substantiality of flows. It (ça) flows, it does not speak. Their most recent book has fortunately cut loose from this humoral conception of desire and all the power of transversality is gaily reinvested in this *Kafka*,[33] a Balkanized text devoted to the translations and transductions of language where machinery is at last restored to the vocation of its multiple inscriptions, of language and desire, that is to a structured functioning through tropes. We are no longer in a space of post-Cartesian transcendental materialism that the machinal configurations of a Fernand Léger might illustrate. We find once more, especially through the problematic of the Balkanized and lacunary overdetermination of languages, a Baroque space where the social domain is only an eclipsed symbolic site with no fetishization of positivities. And it is Hans Bellmer who stands out as the emblem of this other stage on which the curtains are drawing apart.

The subject – ever-present thread in the web of the symbolic

A hope nourished by those who had thought that structuralism had consummated the final expulsion of subjectivity and the body was to see these two philosophical themes reappear in the wake of *L'Anti-Oedipe*. But neither of them had disappeared as a fault of structuralism, as we have shown. The body, which threatened to return to the muteness of a substance, has been restored to its function of symbol in a site where semiotic and symbolic transformations are rooted in the basic drives. And the subject, far from being caught in the alternative of all or nothing, a Cartesian relic, is inscribed, through structuralism's Leibnizian combinatory method, as a function in a lacerated space of which it is no longer the master or owner. The Baroque plurivocality of desire completely pervades it in its position of self-displacement, in the split that generates the activity of the profound rhetoric and tropes of the unconscious. This Oedipal function is in no way an accomplice of a representative conception of language but on the contrary challenges it, through the process of signification that permeates subjectivity and constitutes the pulverized (i.e. schizophrenic or ironic) subject of enunciations. The metaphysical poets, Donne especially, as well as the Nouveau Roman (closer to ourselves), realize this subversion of the subject through an Oedipal operation: 'Oedipus is, at root, just one cultural form amongst many others, that are equally viable provided they accomplish the same function, namely the act of castration in the psychic order.'[34] We have pointed out one of these forms in the incest taboo as Lévi-Strauss has framed it in its enigmaticness, spanning the rupture between nature and culture while simultaneously wrenching the latter from the order of nature.

We are now in a position to examine what is involved in the crisis of meaning and the subject which structuralism has brought about, by asking ourselves if the structurality whose conceptuality we have seen enriched by a profound, figurative semantic process, that corrupts syntax, is still capable of thinking through that crisis, or on the contrary if the latter goes far beyond its problematic.

Our starting point shall be an amalgamation, performed in *L'Anti-Oedipe*, which misguidedly lumps together Oedipus, the family triangle and structuralism, denouncing them 'en bloc' as exerting a repressive weight upon the non-Oedipal schizophrenic drives of the unconscious:

How many openly or covertly pious interpretations of Lacan have thus spoken of a structural Oedipus so as to produce and close the double impasse, to lead us back to the problem of the father, ever to Oedipalize the schizoid, as well as trying to show that a gap in the symbolic referred us back to the imaginary, and inversely, how imaginary confusions were part of structurality . . . That is why we can personally see no difference in kind, no frontier or limit, between the imaginary and the symbolic, any more than between Oedipus as crisis and Oedipus as structure, or between problem and solution. We are faced here with a double impasse which is analogous to the movement of a pendulum responsible for sweeping away the entire unconscious and which, unremittingly, swings from one pole to another. The unconscious is crushed in the vice of an exclusive disjunction.[35]

This process is based on a fantasy that distorts Oedipus and the symbolic in the sense that it causes both to lose their value as operators of figurations tied to lack and to the generation of images, monograms of impulse in the shape of tropes as Freud and Lacan have described them. Producing an amalgam between the symbolic and the imaginary and flattening out the semantic distance that articulates them together as genotext and phenotext, Deleuze-Guattari are thus reduced, in a dualism that borrows not only its structure but also its content from Cartesianism, to draw a demarcation line between a composite imaginary-cum-symbolic on the one hand and an all-powerful Real on the other, hypostatized in the same way that Descartes, as a consequence of his dichotomy, constitutes the *res extensa* as a substance with all the aporias that arise from this. We are thus well and truly in the reign of transcendental materialism – which our authors readily admit to.[36]

The schizoid in Lacan

The opposite position that we shall defend consists in taking up the challenge of Oedipus and the symbolic as both the operators of the real/imaginary distinction and producers of a topo- and tropological machinery which has no need to fetishize the Real and the body in their mute 'In-itself' opacity, in order to activate the function of the real and the lacunary grasp of the subject upon it. The chapter 'D'une question préliminaire à tout traitement possible de la psychose'[37] pioneers this new frontier of the labour of the symbolic and shows that the supposedly impassable wall of the rupture between neurosis and psychosis, at which Freud is claimed to have stopped short like Moses at the threshold of the promised land, can be surmounted by way of the Oedipal foothold that the closure of the Name of the father already ensures upon it, that is, through the problematic of the signifier which in the Other, in its role as the site of the signifier, is the signifier of the Other as the site of Law. Familialization has almost no role to play in this process, for this moment has already been cleaved and riddled with holes by the symbolic which, snatching it from the field of 'personal property' has already set the dance of the tropes into motion with other dispersed elements. For Deleuze and Guattari there is no triangulation but the promise of a schizo-analysis in the pulverization of the paternal in its diverse facets; 'father inveighing, father as good-natured, father all-powerful, clumsy father, ridiculous father, household father, father on a spree'. The Oedipus here, who has nothing to do with any causalism, has always been permeated by a symbolic order that decentres and displaces him, making him the errant, nomadic operator of a semantic corruption where the cleaving of the subject's identity does not fail to show its combinatory machinations and syntax as displaced by the work of the Other along the unforeseeable lines of metonymy. This is the labour that is undissociably Oedipus's, through the castration that subverts the subject and through the cardinal difference between the symbolic and the imaginary. The alliance between Oedipus and castration and the convergence, posed by Lacan and reaffirmed by M. Safouan, between these two instances whose labour cannot be surpassed at the level of the specular function, will enable us not only to recall the body into the field of the symbolic, but also to show that there has never been any other question on the entire agenda.

Symbolic/semiotic

That is why, far from seeing Oedipal structuralism as expelling the subject and the body, we can now state that there has never been a question of anything but them in Oedipal poetics. The subject is certainly diffracted and never quite 'itself', subverted or pulverized by the specular lacuna, the syntax of the chasm which from the outset works upon it. A body whose semiotic drives, as we shall show, dislocate language, is one of the aspects of what we still claim should be called the Symbolic.

First we shall adopt the methodological distinction proposed by Julia Kristeva in an article whose theoretical programme assigns a novel place respectively for the semiotic and the symbolic.[38] For Julia Kristeva:

> the semiotic processes that introduce the fluid, shifting effects into language and, *a fortiori*, into poetic language are from a synchronic point of view the marks of basic drives (appropriation/rejection, orality/anality, love/hate, life/death), and from a diachronic point of view go back to the archaisms of the semiotic body, which before recognizing itself as identical in a mirror (and consequently as a signifying entity) is in a state of dependency vis-à-vis the mother. As drives orientated towards the mother, these semiotic processes pave the way for the entry of the future speaking subject on the path of signification in the symbolic, but the latter, that is, language as nomination, sign, syntax, can only constitute itself through breaking with this anteriority, which may be reverted to in as much as it signifies primary processes, displacements and condensations, metaphor and metonymy, but which is however always subordinate and subjacent to the principal function of nomination-predication.

The basis for this distinction between the symbolic and the semiotic arises, according to Kristeva, from the repression of the basic drives and the unremitting, incestuous relationship with the mother which constitutes language as a symbolic function. The poetic, semiotic process that causes the heterogeneous to resurface in the symbolic, through effraction, would therefore mark the return of the basic drives and of repressed incestuousness, the return of 'le mal' (to situate this problematic in the texts of Bataille).

Now for Julia Kristeva it is the subject of poetic language who thus challenges the transcendental subject by which the symbolic is regulated. The binary opposition proposed by Kristeva is in fact that of scientific language (including linguistics) regulated in turn, willy-nilly, by the operations of the transcendental subject, constitutive of the symbolic. For Kristeva, this symbolic order constitutes a logic of the sign which poses the problem between signifier and signified, but which preserves as a necessity the placing between parentheses of the speaking subject, the corollary of 'personal identity, that sorry treasure' which Lévi-Strauss speaks about at the end of *L'Homme nu* (p. 614):

The fact remains that in the displacement opened up between signifier and signified, giving rise to the interplay of structure, *a subject of enunciation* emerges which structural linguistics ignores. As we know, generative grammar fills in this gap by reviving general grammar and the Cartesian subject so as to justify the generative and recursive functions of syntactic graphs. But in fact, generative grammar is a prop, an avowal of linguistic structuralism's shortcomings, rather than a new departure.

We are in full agreement with this remark too, for as we have already stated in a previous chapter, Chomsky's introduction of Cartesian subjectivity as a support for innate ideas and deep structures corresponds to the fetishistic filling in of a gap perceived as a blank. According to Kristeva it was Husserl, with the theory of the transcendental ego, who laid the foundations of linguistic (structural or generative) thought by suggesting that 'any signifying act, to the extent that it remains an act that has to be elucidated by knowledge, is no longer supported by the "sorry treasure" of personal identity but by the transcendental ego'.

'Let us stop,' writes Kristeva, 'and consider the Husserlian signifying act and transcendental ego but without forgetting that linguistic thought is to Husserl what philosophical thought was to Hegel. A reduction, perhaps, but also concrete realization, i.e. the realization of an impasse.' She then proceeds to show that any predicative (syntactic) operation which constitutes consciousness in the process of forming judgements at the same time posits the signified being (and thus the object of meaning and signification) as well as the operating consciousness itself. 'Let us first recognize with Husserl the thetic character of the signifying act, introducing the transcendental object and the transcendental ego of communication and hence of sociability, before going beyond the Husserlian problematic to search for what produces this operating consciousness, what works upon it and exceeds it (as we shall argue when confronted with poetic language).' This stopping point at the transcendental ego as constitutive of communication and scientificness is necessary, for otherwise one would regress through believing one could dissolve the metaphysics of the signified or of the transcendental ego to a negative theology denying their necessity.

Julia Kristeva first establishes therefore the correlation between meaning, science, communication and a transcendental ego which, in the last instance, she sees as the constitutive operator of the symbolic. This correlation functions as a circumscription aimed at conserving a certain type of metaphysical relation, establishing its territory upon the denial of what is heterogeneous to meaning, here, the basic drives and the body, which must resurface and break the circle of the symbolic by the eruption of pulsations, of the poetic and the semiotic. This semiotic 'chora' thus constitutes a modality of signification ('significance') that is heterogeneous to meaning ('sens'), 'but always in a relationship of negation or surplus with it'. This chora contains what the process of acquiring language in children signifies in its prelanguage phase, one that is 'prephonological, antepredicative, coming before the mirror phase, as well as what the psychotic dicourse produces from the drives of the body.' Julia Kristeva opposes this *chora* or *hyle* to the symbolic function of signification, not without delineating zones of mutual contact where this semiotic heterogeneity resurfaces, in poetic language for example, at the level of socially communicable discourse. 'Language, as a social practice, always presupposes these two modalities, which nevertheless combine in different ways to constitute types of discourse, of signifying practices. The scientific discourse, for example, aspiring to the status of a meta-language, tends as far as possible to reduce that component part I have called the semiotic.' On the other hand the signifying economy of poetic language has the following characteristic: in it, the semiotic (that logically precedes the sign and predication) is not only a restriction in the same way as the symbolic but also tends to gain the upper hand as *the* major restriction, to the detriment of the thetic and predicative constraints of the 'ego' in the process of forming judgements.

We shall thus recognize the fertility of this operational division between the symbolic and the basic drives of the semiotic, a fertility that brings it into relation with a political problematic to the extent that psychosis and fascism are borderline territories where poetic drives, as in an anamorphosis, risk seeing their maximal effect produced. And here, in the analysis of Céline (whom the French left has just taken off the Index, so as to gorge on the delicacies of a finally authorized banquet after a long period of self-denial), Julia Kristeva integrates and announces the full scope of the violent eruptions that the fascist upsurge brought about in the domain of the rationality of the human sciences. Strategically speaking her gesture can be compared to the impatience with which Deleuze-Guattari described both that closure supposedly brought about by Oedipus and the power of the heterogeneous which they wished to put into action. Julia Kristeva, by making this operational division, also has the merit of activating the function of the heterogeneous whose sluice-gates she opens up, pitting it against what for her is the reductiveness of the symbolic: 'Poetic language, having profoundly modified the position of the signified and of the transcendental ego, nevertheless puts forward the thesis, not of a being and a meaning, but of a signifying apparatus. It offers its own procedures as an indefinite process between sense and non-sense, between the symbolic and the semiotic.' This text therefore arrives at the right moment to harvest what *L'Anti-Oedipe*, the seductive but clumsy advocate of the heterogeneous, had sown in the supposedly barren field of structurality. It has the immense merit of not falling into the substantialist trap of the transcendental materialism of schizo-analysis, and of perceiving in psychosis one outermost limit of the semiotic drives (from the point of view of the subject) and in fascism the other (from the point of view of institutions). Here the contributions of Wilhelm Reich are brought to fruition, and Céline's text is, semiotically speaking, exculpated (which does not mean that its appeals to murder are empirically absolved) without any regression to the materialist Cartesianism whose blind alleys we have criticized in *L'Anti-Oedipe.*

Consequently it is perfectly natural to see Kristeva crediting the Freudian break with having dealt the first blows to the fortress of the transcendental ego. The nuanced and non-dogmatic position that she develops, in contrast to Deleuze and Guattari, in fact enables her to integrate and axiomatize the contributions of his theoretical position, without being bound to a clastic denial:

It is, as you know, the Freudian theory of the unconscious that enables one to conceive of the subject in such a way, for through the surgical inroad that it has made into the operative consciousness of the transcendental ego, the psychoanalysis of Freud and of Jacques Lacan has brought about the possibility, not (as some reductionist interpretations would have it) of some typologies or structures in which the same phenomenological reason is to be situated, but of heterogeneity, which, under the name of the unconscious, works upon the signifying function.

Ubiquity of the symbolic and of the $-\phi$ *function*

We may leave this operational division to play its role while we shall attempt a structuration of its field. The question that we might nevertheless ask, given this binary analysis whose antagonistic logic proposes a fascinating and radical inter-rogation of the subject, is that of the whereabouts of the site from which the division is constituted. To the very extent that Julia Kristeva recognizes the major part played by the 'surgical inroad' of psychoanalysis into the operative consciousness of the transcendental ego, it is legitimate to ask on what basis this heterogeneity which 'under the name of the unconscious works upon the signifying function' brings about the overthrow of subjectivity. We believe we have recognized this site in the operation of the symbolic, in the sense in which Lacan defines that semantico-syntactic operator which provides the grounds for the distinction between Real and Imaginary and subsumes through the specular structure both the Oedipal function that cannot be reduced to a family level and that of castration as the split in the subject. There is for us, bridging and dialecticizing the surface difference between the symbolic and the semiotic, and explaining their production, an S, or Symbolic Function deeper than the symbolic function recognized by Julia Kristeva, in as much as it does not elude the relationship between language and body, but on the contrary is found at its very roots.

Here one of the avatars of the Lacanian function ($-\phi$, minus phi) may be recognized: 'It is because we can only speak of that which may alter something's place, i.e. the symbolic, that we can say, literally (à la lettre), that it is not in it. Because for the real, however much it may be shaken, the symbolic is always there in any case, in its place; it carries it about stuck to the sole of its shoe, knowing no way to get rid of it.'[39] This symbolic function as Oedipal operator worked upon by *lack* appears to us to have been brought to the front of the stage by Deleuze-Guattari in their *Kafka*, as we have said. In any case it seems to maintain its supremacy over the real and the imaginary which it constitutes in depth, and to be not without some connection with the basic drives in such a way that the difference between what Kristeva calls the symbolic and what she calls the semiotic or poetic drives is for us *a surface effect of that Oedipal symbolic-ness* to the extent that it begins by being a figure of discord and separation; that is that, arising out of the lack whence it speaks, the poetic force of the heterogeneous has always been a part of the imagery and profound rhetoric of the unconsciousness: 'an original organic disarray' writes Lacan, 'that must be thought of as a vital dehiscence, constitutive of man, and making un-thinkable the idea of a milieu formed before him – a "negative" libido which makes the Heraclitean notion of Discord as being prior to Harmony shine out once again.'[40] Structure and the interplay it contains, burrowing deep into it from the outset,

form the profound symbolic matrix from which may be understood and generated, through metonymic displacement, all the
gaps, deficiencies and discontinuities which not only leave their
mark on the profound figures of the unconscious, the tropological trajectories, but in the very act of prising them from the
mutism of 'real' physiological functions, also inscribe in a
series of extrasystoles, hiatuses and uncertainties, the infantile
and psychotic stammerings of a body always fragmented already
and cloven by its symbolization. Between the symbolic and the
semiotic we shall thus readily distinguish with Julia Kristeva two
functions or *modus operandi* of the 'minus phi' function, but on
condition that we see them as local and topologically situated.
Familialist Oedipalization is always secondary and derivative in
relation to that deep Oedipus which is the primary symbolic
structuration emerging during the mirror-phase; it is 'im-proper'
and metaphorically out of step. Lacan is thus right to see in it a
mere 'normality of sublimation which designates an identifying
modification of the subject, and, as Freud wrote as soon as he
had felt the necessity for a topological coordination of psychic
dynamism, a *secondary identification* through introjection of the
imago of the parent of the same sex.'[41]

It is because this fracture, this primary gap in the subject
(emerging at the mirror-phase whose syntactical matrix it is), is
absolutely fundamental, that not only does a kind of emptiness
and *cenology* affect the profound figuration of the tropes of the
unconscious, producing a structural network, a Hermes upon
which overdeterminations concentrate as semantic effects, and
sublimations as versatile displacements of the unconscious-cum-
language, but also a secondary identification becomes possible
in the form of an extraction or disinvestment always temporally
out of step with the 'self', even at the time of its first historical
emergence in the development of the subject. To have taken it,
as the authors of *L'Anti-Oedipe* have done, as a fundamental
triangulation is, alas, to miss and ignore the spatial and temporal
displacement that works upon it, it is to mistake the effect for
the cause, and, by giving priority to a hypostasis of the real, it is
finally to hold the schizoid fairly cheap. 'Structuralism is the

real enemy', the anti-Oedipean motto, turns against schizo-analysis, since the constituent schism of structural interplay is missed. The operational distinction suggested by Julia Kristeva between the structurally symbolic understood as a transcendency and the semiotic drives, the poetics of the body, enables one to conceive of the history of ideologies as breaks and meta-morphoses in the problematic of the subject. Nevertheless this division must be seen as a sub-set of the Oedipal Symbolic and Topology in which the body and the subject have always been caught up. That is why, far from seeing, as Kristeva does, figures and tropes, metaphors and metonymies, condensation and dis-placement as the corollaries or simple subsidiary appendices of the nominative and predicative functions, and consequently of the ever-dominant Name of the Father, we consider them as profoundly *constitutive* (yet in an *indefinite* site) of the difference between the semiotic drives and the symbolicness of language.

This deep poetics, hidden in the empty spaces of the un-conscious for which it is just the other name, is also the operator of the transgressions of this difference. At the very moment that we accept that scientific discourse takes place within the frame-work of a transcendental subject, it should also be recognized that the delirium of tropes, evidence of a whole series of somatic inscriptions (orality/anality, exclusion/inclusion), is already in the process of corrupting it, as the delirious metaphysics of Riemann or the paranoic frenzy of a Ferdinand Ledoux will show. The transcendental subject is always subverted and out-flanked by those profound figurations, the corrosive tropologies of the unconscious which consume it. That is why far from seeing in the maternal Oedipus an archaic moment, a site of prehistoric happiness which the semiotic drives hark back upon to subse-quently besiege the circumscription of the symbolic arising from the 'backward' mirror-phase, we shall dare to maintain that this incest is only a borderline case of prohibition, and of the figurative Oedipus. Childlike burblings, prephonologies and antepredicative formations can indeed be arranged along the temporal axis of an infantile genesis of which the mirror-phase would only be a subsequent stage. This is what J. Kristeva proposes as a methodological strategy, and we accept it within that limit. But we shall still abide by our notion of a profound *equalization* of the psychotic body with its drives and tropes, worked upon by the schism of the mirror.

We shall thus uphold the rights of an *anaphora* so as to affirm that the process of signification and the generation of the formula by a genotext, all concepts proposed recently by Julia Kristeva, function as a non-teleological pre-emption, as a structural matrix making selections out of the stock of information and phonemes, including the 'chora' which has already been striated by that vital dehiscence constitutive of desire – the specular. There is no need to fictitiously create that node of identity, that *real* immediacy. The symbolic is ever pregiven. Might we venture to perceive it in the inscription of sites announced by Daniel Sibony's book *Le Nom et le corps*?

Inseparable from those word-shapes that swarm upon the silent body, desire hooks itself onto them so as to accomplish its trenchant incision and to fix meanings from which senseless and unpredictable words spring forth. Of course, the wanderings of these word-seeds upon the body tallies with their wanderings in my gaze, with a sense of being adrift in my thoughts, but their halfway presence on my body is what enables desire to search and find them, and even to create them.[42]

This mutual entailment postulates an ambiguous entity which we shall name Oedipus and which, from the site of its lack, relativizes all the divisions between the symbolic and the semiotic, the real and the imaginary, between neurosis and psychosis. It is through this enigmatic site, called the symbolic by Lacan, that Freudian structurality and its interplay, torn through with gaping holes, surpasses any metaphysics of the logos and sees in rhetorical figures the primary movements of the inscription of desire.

The subject, as well as the fracture, has always been seized in this decentred and lacunary network, *the difference of libidinal potential*, whose effects we have already pointed out, to the extent that they are related to the *Verneinung*.[43] That the *undecidable* inscription of desire as language upon the body sets a fundamental dissymmetry into motion upon the basis of which it (ça) speaks in tropes, points to the locus of a re-inscription of the dissymmetry which founds the Eros/Thanatos relationship as a logic beyond (non-)contradiction. By refusing to recognize this dissymmetry and the *hubris* by which Freud goes beyond any metaphysics of subjectivity, we shall be back with a hypostasis of the subject à la Sartre, whose fidelity to a Parmenidean metaphysics of being need not be stressed. On the other hand, and this is the hope upon which our proposal rests in its 'return' to Lacan and to the recognition of that schism forming the order of the symbolic from which the subject has never been absent, we shall have the opportunity once more of joining up, beyond the metaphysics and theologies of man, of the Real and of positivism, with the shattering intuitions of a de-ontologized Heracliteanism free of any fixed position on being, and whose principles and primary motor will be discord or separation, against the background of a topology of unstable and ever-shifting forms that are always, like desire, that joyful Hermes or trope-maker, in the process of construction and de-construction. 'War is the father of all things, of all things the king; some he designates as Gods, the others as men; some he makes slaves, the others free.'

Retrospectively, the knowing subject reveals itself as being always affected by tropes and a figurativity whose *emblematic* shirks any allegiance with the principle of identity. There is not on the one hand the circle of the cognitive transcendental ego, and on the other a heterogeneity and heterotopy assaulting it from without. On the contrary, it is upon the mobile graph of a Leibnizian network that the tropes and traces are inscribed, but also the sites, the *topoi*, in which the subject has always given its share to the heterogeneous by which, in its appointed place, the specular gap, it is kneaded and split.

6. The Art of the Fugue

Following on his *Le Cru et le Cuit*, *Du miel aux cendres*, and *L'origine des manières de table*, the fourth volume (*L'Homme nu*) of Lévi-Strauss's *Mythologiques* winds up a series of analyses of myths and completes a quadrilateral, or rather inscribes a tetragram within the intended figure of Lévi-Strauss's recent work. This book, whose complex musical structure makes it an immense pleasure to read, is therefore one element of a series, a staging post on a journey of exploration, but it is also a concave mirror designed to capture the reflections of its predecessors, and to show them up in a new, synchronic light that brings out previously unexplained relations. It must be read as a continuation and a summa. It is the aleph or microcosm of a sequence and also its final term.

It is moreover this specular relationship, this looking-glass structure of dissymmetry within symmetry, which *L'Homme nu* displays as one of Lévi-Strauss's leitmotives: we shall see it at work in those crucial modulations that would be reminiscent of a symphony were it not for the breaks in continuity. *L'Homme nu* may, in fact, be called a play of echoes. Thus while *Le Cru et le Cuit* offered a vertical analysis of the passage from nature to culture, opposing man to nature or animality, the present book situates the relationship between nature and culture in a complex horizontal field stretching from the naked to the dressed, and back again, whose profuse corpus of myths is, thanks to this change in approach, capable of absorbing the myths studied in

Le Cru et le Cuit. The stage, too, has been changed by the same law of reflection: while *Le Cru et le Cuit* dealt with South American myths, *L'Homme nu* concentrates on California, on a part of North America whose gradual unfolding, from the 'overture' onwards, by the parallel development of its geographical infrastructure and mythical superstructure evokes the structure of a fugue.

Le Cru et le Cuit looked at South America and at the differences between man and beast: man eats cooked food, animals eat raw. The present work, by contrast, deals with the naked and the dressed or adorned, with California, with the problems of exchange and circulation. This is how Lévi-Strauss himself puts it:

> To those people who hold large intertribal, principal and secondary fairs at which neighbouring friendly or occasionally even hostile people can intermingle, the mark of civilization is no longer, as in South America, the opposition between man and animal, but the opposition between people whose commercial skills provide them with a varied menu and those who are forced to live on their own produce.[1]

But, behind the discontinuity of the two territories, the perpendicularity of the two axes and the irreducible differences they entail, Lévi-Strauss discovered a congruent relationship between the basic structure of the myths of two cultures thousands of miles apart; and it is precisely by starting from their separation in space that we can learn what they have in common. As the magnificent 'finale' of *L'Homme nu* puts it, it is the 'preference for a certain mode of cooking that strikes me as providing the deep reason for the identity, at first sight so incomprehensible, of the myths from north-western North America with those from central South America'.[2]

This common preference is reflected in the use of the earth-oven; but far from being one of those empirically determined universal invariants that gladden the hearts of modern anthropologists and biologists, and far from succumbing to the essentialism of *human nature* in which certain generative linguists have been trapped, Lévi-Strauss's invariant is a relational constant, a *formale quod sub lumine quo* at the level of the deep structure, whose modulation – presence, absence, actualization, rejection and restoration – presides over a whole structural range of mythical configurations, in their abundant diversity. As we shall see, Lévi-Strauss does not resurrect *human nature* as a Platonic essence (in the manner of biologists anxious to substantialize the genotype); rather does he proffer a decentration which, in the name of the unconscious and of structure, vitiates all attempts to posit a human essence in the form of a purely conscious subjectivity: in revealing the basic structures responsible for the congruence of apparently unrelated myths or surface structures, Lévi-Strauss proceeds towards simple and general elements, final and naked invariants that lend the title of his work yet another connotation. But these invariants 'stay put'; they can only be apprehended by a structural topology that eschews the ethnocentric crossing of boundaries, and bars access to the manifestations of a *noumenon*: nature or human essence. It is Lévi-Strauss's great merit that he has guarded against this substantialist regression, defending the claims of relational if not of relativistic thought.

The title *L'Homme nu* thus receives an ironic justification in two senses: the opposition of naked *versus* clothed is part of the deciphering of an omnipresent reference to adornment, as exemplified by the string of human hearts described in the story of the *Loon Woman* (M546). And Lévi-Strauss goes on to show that this story has the same deep structure as the South American myth of the *Bird's nester*, a discovery that led him to the earth-oven and thus helped him to repatriate the *Raw* into the *Naked*. The second irony is that Lévi-Strauss never arrives at the 'nakedness' of human nature as such, a fact that few humanists will forgive him. *L'Homme nu* is also a masterful tone poem, and above all a clear and serene manifesto proclaiming the fruitfulness of structural analysis and its capacity for transformational innovation.

In reading *L'Homme nu*, we must therefore try to bear in mind all the various strands, woven together like the elements of a fugue, no less than the egregious elements, those dissymmetrical factors thanks to which structural analysis can remain an 'open' method even when applied to the most circular and involuted structures:

> Structural thought is a form of thought that keeps trying – and I believe this explains its attraction at least during the recent past – to reconcile the sensible with the intelligible, and refuses to compartmentalize man, in the manner of the philosophers, by introducing a distinction between the domain of science and another alien to it, and hence falling outside their province.[3]

The articulation of the sensible with the intelligible is introduced during the prologue. Here, drawing the geographical boundaries of the Klamath and the Modoc, and setting out the geographical conditions of their mode of life, Lévi-Strauss already shows that this infrastructure is symbolically reflected in the non-mythical stories told by his informants, playing the part of retrospective witnesses, and also in myths incorporating geographical and physical notions that cannot possibly be reduced to the infrastructure, since each of the two levels is deployed autonomously, though not in such manner as to exclude the symbolic impact of the other.

Lévi-Strauss's structural and musical approach thus constitutes a method based on demonstration, though one that is fully open to heuristic illumination. He is at great pains to stress that there is a fundamental difference between the human and the physical sciences – that the former cannot have the same truth value as the latter because each follows an experimental method of its own:

> The only demonstrations we can adduce are those helping us to explain more things than we could previously. This does not mean that they are true, but merely that they pave the way for further demonstrations that will explain even more, and so on indefinitely, but without these demonstrations ever becoming established truths.[4]

Nevertheless, this structural system open to constant enrichment and renewal contains privileged sites, zones of pregnancy and denser polysemy: those elements of the Brazilian myths which *Le Cru et le Cuit* had shown to be problematical persuaded Lévi-Strauss to look towards North America for a solution, or rather to look to the privileged site of California for 'empirical' confirmation of what deduction had enabled him to foresee or suspect, but in such manner that his empiricism remained relativistic or relational and never pretended to the status of a truth. This suggests a close affinity between the approach of Lévi-Strauss and that of Kant: empirical realism is always the correlate of transcendental deduction. Just as Mendeleev's periodic tables enable us to 'foresee' a chemical substance from the possible combination of its elements even before that substance has been discovered empirically, so the structural system of continuous isomorphisms introduced in *Le Cru et le Cuit* enabled Lévi-Strauss to foresee that Indian groups in the North would provide myths corroborating a number of earlier hypotheses.

However, like Chomsky's transformational grammar, Lévi-Strauss's Kantianism in its heuristic effect introduces a series of operations and transformations in the course of which the formal texture of the myths and their similarities serve as a vehicle and itinerary for the invention of a new sense. Lévi-Strauss asks us to consider a methodical set of *translations* of myths into one another, a set of dynamic and musical translations in which the structural *method* discovers its sense of *transport*. Its mediators are the deep structures of the corpus of myths, seats of resemblance opaque to empirical description, matrices of dynamic transformations:

We are not looking for the why of these resemblances, but for the how. In fact, the characteristic feature of the myths we are comparing is not that they resemble one another; indeed they often do not resemble one another at all. Our analysis tends rather to bring out common properties in the face of differences that are sometimes so great that the myths we have combined into a single group used to be considered totally distinct entities.[5]

But far from ending up with universals, as Chomsky unfortunately does, and far from adhering ethnocentrically to Kant's list of categories, Lévi-Strauss reserves a relational value for those deep-level homologies between cultures whose surface structures remain irreducible to one another: 'The resemblance does not exist as such: it is only a particular case of the difference, the case where the difference tends towards zero.'[6] Similarly Leibniz, in his *Remarks to the Cartesians*, had argued that rest was only a limiting case of motion, with zero velocity.

And it is indeed an instrument of Leibniz's structural order that Lévi-Strauss places in the service of his Kantian resolve to 'reconcile' the sensible with the intelligible.

Instead of treating similarities as experimental data we must apprehend them as entities of reason. They cease to be merely observable and become demonstrable to the extent that there are distinguished, in degree not in nature, differences whose reduction invariably calls for a demonstration. The need for demonstration thus extends to the entire field.[7]

This forceful stand against empiricism goes hand in hand with a persistent attack on those anthropologists who confine themselves to the isolated empirical description of a single ethnic group:

The fact that an anthropologist withdraws for a year or two to a small social group, strip or village, and tries to grasp it as a totality, does not justify the contention that, at levels other than those in which necessity or chance have cast him, this unity will not make way to a lesser or greater degree for what are often quite unsuspected aggregates.[8]

Hence the important operational and Leibnizian distinction between strong and weak group interactions. In this generalized structural transport-economy, Lévi-Strauss pays particular attention to the production of differences and variations between sets of myths, which he treats as the equilibrium shift of a system and as the continual readjustment of the grid by the mythical operator, an effect whose causes must be sought in the relations or interactions obtaining between peripheral groups or mythical aggregates: though the basic logic of myths became formalized, it is first of all a logic of otherness, the formal thought of the *Other*. This explains the double error of the functionalists and other empiricists who, having steeped themselves to the point of hallucination in a single ethnic group or in a single code, surrender first to the constraints of identity, to the tautological thought of the *Same*, and who, going even further in pretending that the products of their empirical observations can be raised into universals, fall victim to a substantialist illusion and commit, this time in the name of Western rationality, the error of ethnocentrism which invariably means reducing the Other and the Different to the Same. *The naked man is not man per se*, and Lévi-Strauss is right to observe: 'It is high time that anthropology rids itself of the illusion manufactured by functionalists mistaking the practical limits set by the kind of studies they advocate for the absolute properties of the objects to which they apply them.' Lévi-Strauss avoids these functionalist and subjectivist traps (which, as I have pointed out elsewhere,[9] also threaten linguists and biologists) by concentrating on a structural and orderly movement from the Same to the Other. We shall have occasion to examine several stages of this process.

Before we leave these methodical questions, however, we must first stress once again the marked similarity between the strategy and range of Lévi-Strauss's thought and that of Kant: just as Kant's adversaries were empiricists and dogmatic metaphysicians whose collusion reflected a shallow ontology, so Lévi-Strauss too is being challenged on two fronts, by empirical functionalism amd substantialism, of which the first is readily shown to be a consequence of the second, empiricism 'avowing' its hidden dogmatism the moment it rises, with the help of a mystifying and substantialist rationality, to the heights of universality and 'Cartesian' innatism.

Does this mean that Lévi-Strauss ignores the whole problem of innatism or the rootedness of deep structures in a human nature? We shall see that this is not so, but that, perhaps, there is good reason to question the metaphysical residue in Lévi-Strauss's concepts, and quite particularly in his idea of *nature*. But we should also bear in mind that if a measure of innatism is involved in these concepts, it is a kind of innatism stripped of all the subjectivist connotations besetting, for instance, some of Chomsky's thought: Lévi-Strauss's is a *relational* innatism close to that of Piaget,[10] and not a substantialist, subjectivist innatism, let alone a philosophy of consciousness. When Lévi-Strauss draws attention to the importance of structure and the unconscious in the very sphere where mystified 'humanists' expect to find the subjective and conscious *cogito* intact, under the label of human nature, he is not trying to destroy the philosophy of consciousness, but simply to axiomatize it, and at the same time to set it free, to break its enslavement to the object. The great contribution of structuralism is that it presents thought as *thought about a relation* and not as *consciousness of an object*.

In short, systematic decentration and structural shift have led Lévi-Strauss a long way from Husserl's *zu den Sachen selbst* and from the 'all consciousness is the consciousness of something' of the phenomenologists.

Lévi-Strauss likes to stress that the *a priori* of the deep structure can no longer be fitted into a substantialist *cogito* of the Cartesian type, because the subject constitutes a major epistemological obstacle:

> Hence we see how much the effacement of the subject is what may be called a methodological necessity: it reflects the determination to explain no part of the myth except by the myth itself and to eschew the viewpoint of an arbiter inspecting the myth from the outside and hence inclined to find extrinsic causes for it.[11]

The formal and self-regulatory character of the myth, this structural shift of 'translations without an original text', thus invites us to replace a formal *cogito*, even of a Kantian type, with a formal and self-transparent *cogitat* or *cogitatur* whose fundamental operators, relativizing the distinction between conscious and unconscious, operate at the level of the mutual articulation of the sensible and the intelligible, that is in a relationship akin to what Kant in the *Critique of Pure Reason* has called the *schematism of the pure understanding*. This schematism, lying as it does halfway between intuition and conception, being neither one nor the other, but partaking of both in depth, would seem to be the equivalent of those fundamental operators Lévi-Strauss presents at the end of *L'Homme nu*. Here, going beyond the entire system of binary and specular oppositions, he proposes to end his quest for the 'unique myth', i.e. the myth that would subsume all prior mythical oppositions, symmetries and dissymmetries, by treating the earth-oven as the formal and primary root of the entire system of myths, as the archetypal schema presiding over the intertextual network of the myths of North and South America and explaining their deep homology. This schema is the focal point of the whole *Mythologiques*, of the formal overdetermination which, because it articulates the sensible and the intelligible no less than the infrastructural and the conceptual, is analogous to the Kantian schema and defends, by way of a *passage à la limite* of the structural quest, the rights of a 'transcendental' imagination:

> On the plane of myths, this conceptualization of the infrastructure is expressed by an ideology in which the conquest of fire alone could reflect the primacy of the earth oven, and the combined conquest of fire and water that of boiling. The Ge myths tell of the first, the Bororo myths of the second, and the Salish, who have the most complete culinary system, combine both tales in their myths. . . . But right across the board of the immense mythical field we have been exploring, it is indeed the earth-oven which, by its presence or absence, plays the pivotal role.[12]

As the pivot, or cardinal point, the earth-oven, that ultimate structural operator which weaves the threads of the deep structures into the homologous tissue of the myths of North and South America and consolidates the story of the *Bird's-nester* in its central function – this basic schema marking the end of a musical adventure – is unlikely to fall into the trap of simple and substantial originality, comparable to the Bachelardian archetype derived from the psychoanalysis of fire, or to the Jungian archetype, in which heraldic and emblematic substantialism continue to reign triumphant: by virtue of a double corrective Lévi-Strauss's schema remains purely formal and proffers the concept of decentred innateness:

An apparatus of oppositions somehow built into the understanding functions whenever recurrent experiences, be they of biological, technological, economic, sociological or other origin, take control, much like those innate forms of conduct that we attribute to animals and whose phases succeed one another automatically whenever an appropriate combination of circumstances triggers them off. Similarly elicited by such empirical combinations, the conceptual machinery is set in motion, ceaselessly extracting meaning from every concrete situation, however complex, and turning it into an object of thought by adaptation to the imperative demands of a formal organization. In the same way also, it is by the systematic application of the rules of opposition that myths are born, rise up, become transformed into other myths which are transformed in their turn, and so on until insuperable cultural or linguistic barriers, or the inertia characteristic of the mythical machinery itself, lead to the appearance of eroded forms changed beyond recognition. Then the characteristics of the myths make way for other modes of reality elaboration which can, from case to case, be compared to a novel, legend or fable fashioned for moral or political ends.[13]

Not only does this passage explain the erosion of the corpus of myths by entropy more lucidly even than did *La Pensée sauvage*,[14] but it also presents a genesis of a schema transcending the opposition between the innate and the acquired.

This internal shift, or decentration, thanks to which the radical schema of the corpus of myths eludes tautology and identity to leave itself open to a form of otherness more radical even than the dialectic, is also reflected in Lévi-Strauss's assertion that there is an initial *dissemination* of a schema, an original factor of pluralization: 'Far from denying the uniqueness and exclusivity of a mythical schema, I realize that every schema, however fundamental it might seem to be, normally engenders its contrary, either by direct reflection or else by a terminal elaboration.'[15]

We may therefore say that a dynamic enantiology, or rather an enantio-logic, presides over the work of mythical elaboration and that its modalities are akin to the work of dream elaboration. As Freud has shown in his *Interpretation of Dreams*, the work of dreams disregards logical negations and introduces a logic of contraries involving a dissymmetrical factor. 'The problem of the genesis of the myth' Lévi-Strauss points out 'thus emerges into that of thought itself, whose constituent experience is not that of an opposition between the Self and the Other, but of the Other apprehended as opposition.'[16] This, moreover, is not the only congruence between the Freudian approach and the work of Lévi-Strauss; there is also the role both attach to the unconscious: it is 'structured like a language' and bound up with the decentration of the subject. The manner in which the unconscious combines significant elements to build up dreams is in fact reminiscent of the mythical operator's combinatorial faculty to compose myths from simple figurative elements which Lévi-Strauss has called 'zoèmes':

> Eagle and his sister Loon, their brother or cousin Lynx are already known to us, as is Coyote who continues to play the part of deceiver but is changed from the simple commensal he is in the Yana version into the father of two heroines and also into the kinsman and colleague of the old chief Cocoon, owner of the communal house.[17]

All 'zoèmes' constitute permutable elements, so many *letters* by which the mythical operator expresses himself, but instead of unfolding, like the text of the dream, the history of the wishes of an individual subject, these mythical 'texts' have a schematic origin in which an economy of exchange is articulated with an ideology of adornment. This occurs in a mysterious site: the structural junction of infrastructure and concept. Whether or not this schematism devoid of subjective support involves a principle of displacement is something we must now investigate.

This too means following the path leading from *Le Cru et le Cuit* to *L'Homme nu*, from the centre of Brazil to the northwestern coast of California, from the myth of the Bird's-nester to that of the Loon Woman. On it, we shall discover, in fire and the earth-oven, the deep structural economy of their hidden homology. Throughout the 682 pages of *L'Homme nu* this path is staked out by structural transformations that represent both its map and its territory: the successive headings of 'Secrets de la famille', 'Jeux d'échos', 'Scènes de la vie privée', 'Scènes de la vie de province', 'Amers savoirs', 'Remontée aux sources', 'L'aube des mythes' link together parts that constitute so many musical movements, whose structure and key are reflected in a 'finale' that may be called a conspectus of the work of Lévi-Strauss and which, moreover, serves as a Discourse on Structural Method and a reply to his critics. This finale is, at heart, a projection of the structure of Ravel's *Bolero*, a transposed fugue that holds the key to the book's entire code and to Lévi-Strauss's mythopoietic and mythohermeneutic method; it celebrates the basic kinship of music and mythology: 'As a myth coded in sounds instead of words, the musical work supplies a decoding frame, a matrix of relations for filtering, organizing and replacing lived experience; as such it produces the happy illusion that contradictions can be surmounted and difficulties resolved.'[18] This elegant passage in which Lévi-Strauss, despite his opposition to the philosophers, shows how literally he takes the dream's injunction to Socrates: *poieson ten musiken* – (to) make music, (to) engage in a structural labour of a piece with the systems of transformation to which mythical stories serve as so many signposts or graphs, so many *stretti* of a fugue – this passage holds the key to the perusal of the whole book and to the entire mytho-logical corpus: the harmonic interference and the structural and musical articulation of myths, the transparency of the tissue or formal network on which this interference takes place and which explains why myths can be translated into other myths, also explains why Lévi-Strauss's writings display a self-regulated intertextuality, culminating in the finale of *L'Homme nu*. It shows that the same harmony and congruency presiding over the act of mythological genesis initiated by the schematic operator also presides over the task of all those who use analytical methods to rediscover the harmonic status and interlegibility of these myths, masked as they are by discontinuities and surface irregularities:

Myths about the origin of cooking fire (M 712) which become inverted into myths about the origin of rain, the celestial water which extinguishes domestic hearths (M 1), are transformed first of all into myths about the origins of adornments and trinkets, and then into myths about the origin of honey. The proof that this last transformation is real, is that honey, the original means of adornment, becomes an end in itself in myths that can be shown independently to have a transformational relation with the preceding ones. Their existence thus constitutes an *a priori* condition of the existence of the others, and when we study them, we find that they are possessed of all the empirical attributes the original hypothesis allowed us to postulate.[19]

From the laws governing the distribution of information in this system, and from the angle of distribution of the areas of light and shade, the student of myths can consider any given myth as conditioning or being conditioned by another. The hologram of these variations and chain of transformations is the demonstration of the proposition that there is 'a structure common to the myths of the two Americas in which the hero is a Bird's-nester.'[20] This central role of the Bird's-nester, first postulated in *Le Cru et le Cuit*, is verified in *L'Homme nu*, whose recapitulative and articulated course embraces in its formal figuration honey, ashes, water, fire, table manners, exchange and commerce. All these are finally placed on the synchronic graph of the harmonic transformation of myths into one another, with the heuristic order of their appearance, the *ordo cognoscendi*, functioning as an important operator, and revealing that, though symmetry and harmony are the laws presiding over the network, they have engraved in them an element of otherness and difference that introduces dissymmetry into their involute order.

The itinerary of *L'Homme nu*, like the writings of Raymond Roussel, thus covers the path, but in the order of a pertinent and reversible diachrony, that leads from the Bird's-nester to the Loon Woman and back, finally to reveal the operational character of the fundamental schema of the earth-oven: the starting point of this itinerary, which forces dissymmetry inexorably into the very heart of harmony and circularity, is the *decentration* of the primary ethnocentrism of the Klamath: 'The Klamath so-called by a name of unknown origin, refer to themselves as *ma'klaks* – men.'[21] This decentration is unavoidable because their 'weak interaction' with other groups heightens the operational importance of exchange and commerce as agents of otherness: 'The Klamath and the Modoc both contract marriages by mutual visits and exchanges of presents between families; there may be no relation of kinship between the couple who may, however, belong to the same territory or village.'[22] This minor escape from ethnocentrism is the first term of the decentration. Where the itinerary ends, in the finale, the laws of displacement and decentration are given free rein to make way for a non-symmetrical enantiology whose effects we have seen at work in the fractured construction of the fundamental schematism: 'Every schema, however fundamental it might seem to be, normally engenders its contrary, either by direct reflection or else by a terminal elaboration.'[23]

Between these two, a whole relay of transformational operations insinuates dissymmetry through specular reflection, and plumbs the various aspects of that reflection, be it direct or sagittal: the binarism whose inadequacies have so often been laid at the door of Lévi-Strauss, and incidentally of Jakobson as well, is here handled with a subtlety that lights up all the facets of dissymmetry-within-symmetry and recalls certain passages of Borges, for instance in *Death and the Compass* or *The South*. Borges, too, couples sagittal to direct reflection, thus introducing a principle of dissymmetry that Lévi-Strauss would be the last to disavow. The myth receives its initial impetus from that asymmetry which seems to run through the whole of the original schematism:

The world . . . is in the form of an original asymmetry that manifests itself differently depending on the perspective one adopts to apprehend it: between high and low, heaven and earth, near and far, left and right, male and female, etc. Being inherent in reality, this disparity sets mythical speculation into motion, and this because it moulds, not only thought itself, but also the existence of every object of thought.[24]

Along this road of continuous variations and regular transformations, Lévi-Strauss involves the American continent in a kind of geo-symbolism or geofantasy, establishing a specular relationship between Brazil and California, and thus reversing the direction in which the original migration probably took place. This 'topsy-turvy' absorption of America into the *ratio cognoscendi* illustrates once again, if further illustration be needed, by the heuristic importance of the territory of the Klamath and Modoc, the presence of a dissymmetrical factor in the very heart of specular symmetry. What matters at this level is the logic of supplementarity articulating this dissymmetry: the lozenge-shaped structures or graphs of the transformation networks result from a lack of surplus whose temporary elimination acts as a 'green light' to a heuristically engendered activity which, by the use of structural mimicry, makes possible the *phenomenological* reproduction of the formal generation of myths, such as it could or must have occurred.

However this reality remains a noumenon: we are left with a proliferation of geo-social cells calling to one another and which, as the biologists would say, are engendered by structural meiosis. Now, this chain of proliferations is subject to the law of dissymmetry: it is the missing element in a corpus of myths which, by a supplementary necessity, demands that its virtuality be actualized in the corpus of a neighbouring group. This law of decentration or of excentricity thus sets up a chain, or a whole congeries of supplements, leading from the ethnocentrism of the Klamath, breached or corrected by the return to the neighbouring Modoc, their original binarity already modified by dissymmetry. Healing the wound of this structural break calls for further exploration for a never-ending search that ranges over the entire geo-symbolic field. Because this supplementary search is a journey by fits and starts, a movement that is both diachronic and logical, it cannot possibly coincide with the proper meaning of a myth or its involutive completion: it leads to excentration with respect to the subject and to consciousness, robbing the anthropologist of any desire to achieve coincidence with an insular Self. This uneven and dissymmetrical chain is rooted in what Lévi-Strauss calls the 'splitting of the representation'.[25] This split is repeated perpendicularly in the relationship between culture and nature and hence hinges on the shift in meaning of the concept of exchange: 'True to its technique of systematic splitting, M 553 juxtaposes the natural and cultural aspects and leaves their incarnation to different personages.'[26]

But this binary specularization never leads to the holographic and flat reconstruction of a corpus of myths: there is no divine observer to whom everything is bathed in the synchronous light of absolute knowledge; as anthropologists or members of a group we remain moored to our particular anchorage or point of view:

> The symmetry of the Yana myth reflects this ambiguous attitude: it is as if the Yana betrayed, on the plane of the formal organization of the story, their pretence to see the territory of the Klamath in two simultaneous perspectives: one real, and orientated from the south to the north, the other imaginary, for it implies that they themselves are Klamath, and hence orientated from the north towards the south. In the final analysis, the reason why the internal symmetry of the Yana version concerns the axis of successions more than it does that of the simultaneities is because the Yana dwell outside the chosen land of the myth, and, in order to incorporate the myth into their legendary heritage, they must behave as if they lived within it.[27]

This fine passage, which once again explains the musical structure of mythopoietics and their interpretation in terms of an alliance between diachrony and synchrony, governed by dissymmetry within symmetry, challenges the idea of specificity and of self-identification: Lévi-Strauss makes us witness instead to the interplay of displacements, decentrations and continuous obstacles against a specular background. This poses the problem of the diachronic traversal of this network by a chain: there is movement in the structure, in the double form of involutive and dynamic transformations, and also of a trace or tracing crossing the perimeters and *templa* of ethnocentrism, of all that is specific and insular. It is no longer in all innocence that the Klamath can call themselves *ma'klaks* – 'men' – since by their side and bound to them by the structural interdependence of their corpus of myths there live the Modoc, the Achomawi, the

Atsugewi and the Yana. 'Compared with the Klamath and Modoc versions, the Achomawi and Atsugewi myths seem diploid forms, duplicating all functions.'[28] But this diamond-shaped structure is somehow deported, or rather deflected, and its displacement makes it clear that far from coinciding fully with its own centre of gravity, a particular version of a myth gravitates about a pole to which *another* holds the secret key. Hence the gradual enlargement of the field of action disturbed from the start by the Modoc-Klamath divergence and the dissymmetrical binarity whose very rules challenge the naïve ethnocentrism of the Klamath, those inhabitants of the 'Land of the Same'.

It is this principle of otherness within enantiomorphy that Lévi-Strauss develops to its limits when he draws attention to the *supplementary* character of a myth:

The myth cannot be reduced by any particular code, nor does it result from the accretion of several. Rather must we say that a group of myths constitutes a code of greater power than any it uses for ciphering complex messages. As a veritable 'intercode' it allows of the reciprocal convertibility of these messages by rules immanent in the various systems which, by their operation, reveal a global meaning distinct from their own.[29]

There is a whiff of Spinoza in this presence/absence of the myth, whose substance cannot be apprehended except in its attributes. Later, when dealing with his final recourse to the notion of a 'presence', we shall question the particular use Lévi-Strauss makes of the category of *globality*. Meanwhile we must stress that before it becomes a totalizer, this unique or central myth is an absentee or rather a fathomless operator, whose truancy offends against the principles of a (non-)contradictory logic by the type of otherness it introduces.

The emphasis is placed once again on the decentration of the myth, on the *disappropriation* accompanying its displacement: 'The myth is never of its own language; it provides a perspective of another language, and the mythologist who apprehends it through a translation does not feel that he is in an essentially different situation from that of the local narrator or auditor ('narrateur ou auditeur du cru').'[30] If we wished to indulge in the doubtful pleasures of a bad pun we might point out that the *Cru* is never the *Nu*, since the proper version of the myth does not exist and also because its indefinite translatability over this formal network of multiple exchanges occurs in the absence of an ontological foundation or unique referent. In the parallel he draws between music and myth – a parallel all of whose elements are not of equal merit – Lévi-Strauss has shown that while music involves transformational operations at the level of sound, the myth involves such operations at the level of meanings (or signifieds): no matter whether structurality affects the signifiers or the signifieds, it invariably does so in the *absence of a referent*. We might say that here, too, Lévi-Strauss brings into play that otherness which, as we saw, is responsible for the split in specular and symmetrical structuring: here it takes the form of a non-mediatizable negativity tending to displace the scene of sagittal or direct symmetries. But why is it that on the basis of this split, of this principle of decentration or deracination of the specific, Lévi-Strauss nevertheless continues dreaming of a globalizing structuration, of a unique and all-consuming myth?

This is one of the puzzles we have still to solve. The dream of re-anchoring cultural diversities in the identity or repetition of a non-human nature, one that is more physical or crystallo-graphic than it is anthropocentric, would in fact seem to be a relic of an open Marxist method projected into the symbolic and causal interplay between the geo-economic infrastructure and the ideological superstructure. When we recall Lévi-Strauss's declarations on this subject in *La Pensée sauvage*, we may ask ourselves whether the dream of arriving at a global signification distinct from myths does not reflect the pressure of a super-structure that has broken free and, in so doing, has become resubstantiated in the Same, or alternatively whether, if we remain attentive to the discovery of the earth oven as the original operator initially fractured by mythological variations, we shall not retrieve from this transcendental *schematism*, reminiscent of Kant, a radical otherness, a structural ambiguity whose non-coincidence with itself would be the rule, and which would suggest the idea of a dissemination or, in any case, of an alien element that, from the start, excludes any idea of specificity and hence of all forms of essentialism. This might well be Lévi-Strauss's challenge, or rather his sublime irony: that, when introducing an ambiguity comparable to the ontological ambiguity of Kantian thought,[31] he returns to the Same, to a globalizing structural identity in the very place where he has already sapped its epistemological possibility by the proposed admission of a non-dialecticizable otherness.

And Lévi-Strauss does not spurn recourse to logocentrism of a Platonic type: although he has long since had the courage to denounce the evolutionist illusion and the ethnocentrism of those armchair anthropologists who speak of 'primitives' (as if these people represented a phase in our own ancestral past), and who propel them quickly along the axis of our own history, only to rediscover them in the field of the Same despite their diversity, we are entitled to ask whether the price he had to pay for this demystification[32] was not too high. In 'History and Dialectic', the key chapter of *La Pensée sauvage*, and in another chapter entitled 'Time Regained', Lévi-Strauss has described history as the erosion and dispersion of the structural equilibrium by entropy:

The classification tends to be dismantled like a palace swept away upon the flood, whose parts, through the effects of currents and stagnant waters, obstacles and straits, come to be combined in a manner other than that intended by the architect. In totemism, therefore, function inevitably triumphs over structure. The problem it has never ceased to pose to theorists is that of the relation between structure and event. And the great lesson of totemism is that the form of the structure can sometimes survive when the structure itself succumbs to events.[33]

And turning his attention to the repercussions of history on systems of classification, he went on to say:

. . . human societies react to this common condition [i.e. that all societies are in history and change] in very different fashions. Some

accept it with good or ill grace, and its consequences (to themselves
and other societies) assume immense proportions through their
attention to it. Others (which we call primitive for this reason) want
to deny it and try, with a dexterity we underestimate, to make the
states of development which they consider 'prior' as permanent as
possible.[34]

But whether it be by this totemization of history, by attempts
to divine the future or, on the contrary, by the exclusion of time
through recourse to rites and the formal repetition of mythical
time, in either case it is clear that *history has been subordinated
to the system:*

Classificatory systems thus allow the incorporation of history
even and particularly that which might be thought to defy the
system. . . . And nothing in our civilization more clearly resembles
the periodic pilgrimages made by the initiated Australians, escorted
by their sages, than our conducted tours through Goethe's or Victor
Hugo's house, the furniture of which inspires emotions as strong as
they are arbitrary. As in the case of the Churinga, the main thing is
not that the bed is the self-same one on which it is proved Van Gogh
slept: all the visitor asks is to be shown it.[35]

This explains his courageous confrontation with Sartre and
the dialectic conception of history Lévi-Strauss advances in the
chapter entitled 'History and Dialectic'.[36] Denouncing the
privileged position the dialectic philosophy of history accords to
diachrony, and launching out at the metaphysical restoration of
anthropocentrism and at excessive concentration on the con
scious subject, albeit collective and the agent of history, Lévi
Strauss had this to say: 'A Cogito – which strives to be in
genuous and raw – retreats into individualism and empiricism
and is lost in the blind alleys of social psychology.'[37] What he
would have the anthropologist do instead is to welcome decen
tration, to abandon identification and to appreciate that if our
society can afford the luxury of treating history as a systematic
and meaningful progression along the diachronic axis, there are
others which cannot. Hence we must abandon the diffus

ethnocentrism inherent in all philosophies of history and adopt a new view of the relationship between history and anthropology:

The anthropologist respects history, but he does not accord it a special value. He conceives it as a study complementary to his own: one of them unfurls the range of human societies in time, the other in space. And the difference is even less great than it might seem, since the historian strives to reconstruct the picture of vanished societies as they were at the points which for them corresponded to the present, while the ethnographer does his best to reconstruct the historical stages which temporally preceded their existing forms.[38]

What Lévi-Strauss therefore proposes is putting diachrony 'in its place': 'in their [the philosophers'] eyes some special prestige seems to attach to the temporal dimension, as if diachrony established a kind of intelligibility not only superior to that provided by synchrony, but above all more specifically human.'[39]

The fact that he considers diachrony an erosion of the structure, a form of dispersal, and an agent of increased entropy, does not, however, mean that he himself thinks the structure is stable: in *La Pensée sauvage* no less than in the *Mythologiques* he has dwelled at sufficient length on the dynamic and transformational power of the structural whole constituted by a totemic classification or corpus of myths to silence the never-ending complaints by humanists of every hue that their beloved human subject has been impaired and that the system or structure is no more than an empty and static shell, a fossil, a reduction of the living to the skeletal aridity of an algorithm. God knows how often we have heard this anthem composed in the muddied waters of personalism, phenomenology, Teilhardo-Marxism and the notions of humanist splinter groups . . . What Lévi-Strauss rightly condemns in the modern aggrandizement of the philosophy of history is not so much the totemization of diachrony as such, of that pseudo-Heraclitean mirage and divinization of time, as the naïve ethnocentrism it reflects. What, he asks, do people without history do, or rather people without a history capable of being expressed in the same rational way as our own? ... Diachrony versus structure has become the battle cry and haven of the entire half-pay crew of the personalist ship, of all footloose humanist revolutionaries, of all outmoded phenomenologists determined to preserve the subject as agent of history, all wavering metaphysicists still awaiting their *cogito*. Let them be consoled: Lévi-Strauss has no wish to dispossess them of history or of Holy Diachrony. In this he resembles Althusser who, in quite another sphere – the perusal of the writings of Karl Marx – asks us to pay heed, in 'contradiction and overdetermination', to the complex relations between the infra- and superstructures. What both writers prescribe is greater detachment from the Same, a temporary withdrawal from the banks of the Specific, the better to apprehend the Other in his difference, instead of going out to meet him with reductive machines designed to acclimatize him, to enculture him and to enlist him for the great Pageant of History.

Lévi-Strauss does not destroy history and diachrony, as he has so often been accused of doing; he simply axiomatizes its status and tries to show that, however useful its strategic and mythical impact, it is not the only meaningful category: what must be overthrown, just as the despotic reign of Euclid's postulate was overthrown at the end of the nineteenth century to become one axiom amongst others, is the one-dimensional sovereignty of sense and diachrony. And it is precisely this relativization which is advocated in the decentration effected in 'History and Dialectic'. The consequences are considerable; it is now possible to conceive of an alternative to *cultural evolutionism*, that epistemological obstacle which poisoned anthropological endeavour in the nineteenth century and continues to prowl in culturalist studies, slyly maintaining the rash identification of the rites of 'primitive' societies with our own. Even the most resolutely empirical and Malinovskian approach is not free from this taint, and this despite precautions against contamination by otherness, or rather because of them – for this approach is immune to the corrective of translations or to changes in perspectives ...

The false antimony between logical and prelogical mentality was surmounted at the same time. The savage mind is logical in the same sense and the same fashion as ours, though as our own is only when it is applied to knowledge of a universe in which it recognizes physical and semantic properties simultaneously.[40]

Now it is precisely when we confront the discontinuity and difference he attributes to the strategic attacks of culture, in his cultural relativism consolidated by the study of myths, that we begin to wonder whether Lévi-Strauss's polemics against ethnocentric residuals, against the metaphysical illusions of philosophers of history and of the critics of dialectical reasoning, may not have carried him too far in his refutation of history to the point of restoring a philosophy of Presentness or Hereness, of exaggerating the idea of the eternally present.

What good, in fact, is this spiritual and ingenious refutation of time, worthy of Borges, the author of a *'nueva refutacion del tiempo'* (how can it be called new if time does not survive?), if it serves merely to fuse all periods of time, all histories and all transformations into the common matrix of a nature identical with itself? The decentration with which Lévi-Strauss opposes the fetishist reign of the subject, the reign of History; his belief that these ideological formations must be treated as myths and *read* as such – this view, alas, has as its reverse the replacement of cultural diversities on the common pedestal of a *nature* which, though it is non-human or ahuman, nevertheless reflects a kind of return to Cratylism, in the very places where Difference reigned supreme.

There appears therefore to be a strong Spinozist current in the work of Lévi-Strauss, and one that blends with the tendency of certain contemporary biologists to look for universal genotypes. Before we can assent to Sartre's objection that Lévi-Strauss is a 'transcendental materialist', however, we must remember how this return to the lost fatherland (motherland) of *nature* is effected: according to Lévi-Strauss it is only at the end of a methodological probe, more searching than any other philosophical excursion, into all the differences and complexities that we finally arrive at the scene of a general humanity, one that Rousseau glimpsed in his *Essai sur l'origine des langues* (London, 1783, Chapter VIII) when he wrote: 'One needs to look near at hand if one wants to study men; but to study man one must learn to look from afar; one must first observe differences in order to discover attributes.' 'However,' Lévi-Strauss adds:

it would not be enough to re-absorb particular humanities into a general one. This first enterprise opens the way for others which Rousseau would not have been so ready to accept and which are incumbent on the exact natural sciences; the reintegration of culture in nature and finally of life within the whole of its physico-chemical conditions.[41]

This reintegration of culture into nature, this repatriation (Hölderlin speaking of Aristotle and tragedy called it *vater-ländische Umkehr*), goes hand in hand with a radical hetero-geneity:

The idea of some general humanity, to which ethnographic reduc-tion leads, will bear no relation to any one may have formed in advance. And when we do finally succeed in understanding life as a function of inert matter, it will be to discover that the latter has properties very different from those previously attributed to it. Levels of reduction cannot therefore be classed as superior and inferior, for the level taken as superior must, through the reduction, be expected to communicate retroactively some of its richness to the inferior level to which it will have been assimilated. Scientific explanation consists not in moving from the complex to the simple but in the replacement of a less intelligible complexity by one which is more so.[42]

This attempt to recentre culture in physico-chemical nature, reinterpreted after a spiral shift, is vindicated by the actual state of biological research, and particularly by molecular biology which has discovered the combinatorial art by which biological events can be 'explained' or 'produced' without their diversity or complexity having to suffer. But these were living and self-regulating phenomena in the biological realm.

What Lévi-Strauss proposes is a reduction of culture to nature, a transition from practical gestures and human stories to an economic or biological infrastructure (which is characteristically structural, and not dialectical, as Engels would have believed).

It is certain that, once the humanist bolt has been drawn, once the ideological barriers of anthropocentrism and of subjective consciousness have been removed, Lévi-Strauss's attempt is highly tempting, the more so as it has unexpected reinforcement from the biologists, who have just patched up their ancient scholastic squabbles (vitalism *versus* mechanism and emergence *versus* reduction) to enter a new epistemological continent, structural in its problematics. Clearly, Lévi-Strauss has no intention of abolishing the complexities and differences characteristic of myths or the classifications he has attempted; rather does he denounce the transcendentalism inherent in the reductionist simplicism of historical and dialectical projects: 'A good deal of egocentricity and naïvety is necessary to believe that man has taken refuge in a single one of the historical or geographical modes of his existence, when the truth about man resides in the system of their differences and common properties.'[43]

We are, however, still entitled to ask whether Lévi-Strauss's dream of reinserting cultural diversities and structural differences into the common matrix of nature, albeit combinatorially and purged of its metaphysical residues, does not reflect, at an unexpected level, a kind of nostalgia for, and faith in, a matrix of Hereness, of the living present.

This is precisely what a certain passage in *L'Homme nu*, re-echoing the above passage from *La Pensée sauvage*, though no longer at the level of the re-insertion of matter into nature but rather in '*time regained*', seems to suggest: it is as if the impulse by which Lévi-Strauss rightly blames philosophies and mythologies of history for being tainted with ethnocentrism, and indeed for being tautological, drives him on, by sheer inertia, into a sphere in which cultural differences are abolished or made subservient to a material nature, but *formaliter spectata*, and to a Hereness reminiscent of Husserl's living present, thus never quitting the Platonic *ousia* against which we must undoubtedly advance the claims of a new Borgesian 'history of eternity' . . .

It is on reading 'L'Aube des mythes', which precedes the finale of *L'Homme nu*, that this suspicion becomes unavoidable. Commenting on the reparative and restorative function of myths in the face of the erosion of history and the entropic ravages of time, Lévi-Strauss emphasizes again that history is subordinate to structure: 'Carried to its conclusion, the analysis of myths reaches a level on which history abolishes itself.'[44] This replacement of history by a structure transcending all historical events, all demographic upheavals, is the other side of a general principle tending towards equilibrium, always destroyed and always restored, like Penelope's loom. This principle, a veritable Carnot's theorem in anthropology, is reflected in the analysis of the method by which the Dakota Indians of Canada 'recast the traditional version of a tribal myth so as to neutralize the contradiction between the ideologies of the Sioux and the Algonkins'. During a recent and historically attested migration, they came to appreciate an event which Lévi Strauss has generalized as follows: 'All the people of the two Americas seem to have conceived their myths for the sole purpose of being reconciled with history and restoring, on the plane of the system, a state of equilibrium, in which the blows delivered by events can be cushioned.'[45]

This 'bricolage' or readjustment engenders structural networks whose solidity, perpetually retrieved from the disorders and ravages of time, reflects the adamantine hardness of natural bodies as revealed by crystallography, and may explain why Lévi-Strauss feels impelled to invent the ground – or is it the heaven? – of an ahistorical and structural nature meant to accommodate the movable and transformational but homogeneous and self-transparent rules and schemata underlying the corpus of myths he has analysed:

Else, how could we ever appreciate that those elements of the system we call binary operators conserve their semantic function from one end of the two Americas to the other without our ever having the slightest need, when explaining this persistence, to take into account the innumerable demographic and cultural upheavals that took place over the centuries?[46]

But here the search for a natural structural ground is patently conducted under the sign of 'man released from the order of time'. It is from Proust that Lévi-Strauss has borrowed that expression, as witness this inscription at the head of 'Le mythe unique', the second chapter of 'L'Aube des mythes': 'Une minute affranchie de l'ordre du temps a recréé en nous pour la sentir l'homme affranchi de l'ordre du temps' (Marcel Proust, *Le Temps retrouvé*, II, p. 15).

This quotation which seals the connaturality of myth and music on which *L'Homme nu* is built, and perhaps also the entire work of Lévi-Strauss, thus constitutes a kind of break from diachrony, the hope of fusing diversities into the unity of Hereness, of achieving *re-presentation* on a closed structural stage, where the palace swept away upon the flood of history is restored in its full splendour: in a district of north-western North America. Here the play is finally revealed as a Parmenidean drama enacted in the living present, in a world structurally closed upon itself, where nothing can disturb the peace of the gods:

Thus we may say that the most thankless of tasks has been rewarded: without seeking or attaining it, we have located the land promised of old and in assuaging the triple impatience of a tomorrow yet to come, of a fleeting present and of a devouring yesterday that draws and fragments the future in the ruins of a present confounded with the past. Hence our quest will not have been one for lost time alone. For, in the final analysis, the order of time revealed by the study of myths is none other than that to which myths have aspired since time immemorial: the abolition rather than the recovery of time.[47]

And the wish to reconquer a presence in the present, whose essential calm is unruffled by the least wave of difference, by the swell of diachrony – this wish culminates in the statics of an involutive and reversible structurality rebutting the flight of time and the pretensions of history: 'In the very course of contemporary history, there persists a desperate and hopelessly vain attempt to arrest time and to reverse its direction.'[48]

The method by which Lévi-Strauss, that great demystifier of ideologies, has succeeded so courageously and lucidly in axiomatizing diachrony and history thus leads him inexorably towards the unification of a temporal axiomatics in an eternity whose pretensions may well be open to criticism: against that man beyond time, may we not have to rewrite a 'history of eternity' which continues that of Borges?

The dream of reversible time is, in fact, dreamed on 'a level where history destroys itself',[49] to usher in a world of plenty. It must be stressed that it is in the form of a *dreamed* abundance that this recovery of the presence is conceived, this 'desperate' and 'hopelessly vain' attempt to stop time. There is more than one echo of the despair and sad irony of Proust's *Temps retrouvé*, more than one forceful reminder of the negative determination of Beauty in Kantian aesthetics: the Beautiful that needs no concept to express its radiances, the Beautiful as finality without end, as disinterested pleasure. All these negative determinations, this negative theology, reflected in Valéry's dictum: 'Le beau est ce qui désespère', provide us with a kind of archetype for the desperate escape inherent in Lévi-Strauss's arrested time, in the eternally present. Yet this flight, though 'hopelessly vain', and hence like Borges' 'Approche d'Almotasim'[50] a promise that cannot be kept, this dream of vanquished time is nevertheless woven into the fabric of the present. In other words, Lévi-Strauss keeps to the stage of the Same despite all changes in scenery and the apparent shift towards otherness, as witness also his preference for figurative, i.e. *representational*, painting, and his refusal to admit dissonance as the splintered future of tonal music.

Further evidence that Lévi-Strauss's thought and practice are rooted in the metaphysical matrix of a presence and an essence can also be found in his recourse to the circular concept of *exchange*: the model of communication between codes and cultures whose omnipresence is revealed by the analysis of myths is in fact a circular and involutive form of symbolic exchange, representing the mobile structure of all modes of being, and an overall harmony. The economy is closed on itself: exchange of goods, exchange of words, exchange of women – *circulation* in the form of a circuit or circle. As against this Parmenidean aspect of anthropological thought, some have upheld the idea of the unpaid obligation, of the intrusion of a non-remissible difference which breaks the circle and circuit of exchange: Don Juan, admirably analysed by Michel Serres in his *Hermès ou la communication*,[51] is the prototype of the fanatic who sins against the circular law, never returning woman for woman, money for money, word for word, but spinning his scalene web, preventing the scar in the structure from healing and the circle from closing.

The case of a non-mediatizable negativity is argued most eloquently in Bataille's *La Part maudite*, and *a fortiori* in Nietzsche's asymmetrical reversal of metaphysics and of Platonism, which, as Bernard Pautrat has shown in a recent book,[52] eludes the rules of speculation and specularity, offering a non-circular but transverse abrogation of metaphysics, thus triggering off that decentration which has disturbed Lévi-Strauss's borrowings, deliberate or otherwise, from a metaphysics of Hereness and plenitude. And it is, above all, in the work of Jacques Derrida that the road leading back to the Specific is finally closed, the road to what may be conceived as proximity or adequacy, albeit with the property of accommodating, or being accommodated in, the constant but convolutive movement of exchange.

And man beyond time, that is, the circularity of communication, must then prove a metaphysical or ideological illusion.

Now Lévi-Strauss is much too precipitately accused of being caught in a spherical Parmenidean matrix, in a continuous chain of equivalences whose movement is reflected in a state of rest.

Because his accusers confine their attention to the dream of man beyond time, to the harmonic circularity of the closed exchange, they far too readily forget that the myth, which, for Lévi-Strauss is the anthropological 'object' par excellence, the privileged field of inquiry, has as its root, basic element or original letter an open or broken archetypal image non-coincident with itself. *The schema of the earth-oven*, that inter-space of nature and culture, does not preside over a complete ontology of Hereness and identity, and the graph of its distribution does not have a clear origin, a primary or archetypal element, but is rather a fissure, the back-shuttle in the web of myths, an original distortion or diffraction, split off from itself even before it starts out, engendering dissymmetries and discontinuities at the very moment when the idea of the Same and of simple repetition entrenches itself and believes it can take control. All the displacements, excentricities and decentrations we have discussed at such length do not suddenly appear *after the event* as the history of elements predetermined in their positive aspects; rather it is in their absence that displacement and dissymmetry do their advance prospecting for symmetry or simple specularity. Disappropriation, expropriation and excentration precede the Specific, the discovery of a centre, and the close-knit web of myths merely repeats, by illustration, the adventure of the genesis begun with the earth-oven, that simple element which can only be elevated into a universal on condition that the concept of universality adopted by our culture is first questioned and decentred with respect to itself.

The force of Lévi-Strauss's Leibnizian conviction, of that non-preestablished harmony, of that art of translation in the absence of an original text, resides precisely in the fact that it proceeds from no centre, no fixed point, only to reveal itself quite unexpectedly as the key element, as an original function, albeit diffracted, sundered and haunted by a non-mediatizable negativity that takes pleasure in crossing, thwarting and even cheating the much too highly structured circuit of exchange: the earth-oven is both the origin and the simple, omnipresent element, and also the principle of disruption, a defier of the very order it introduces. This initial disruption then informs a logic whose negative aspects affect unpredictable structural relations in so many different ways that we can readily appreciate why Lévi-Strauss, and Serres, too, for that matter, should not feel easy with a dialectic whose exchange and type of negativity, in their simple binarisms, provide a poor example of that mobile and dissymmetrical, open and receptive, form of cultural exchange which presents itself as the fabric of modern epistemology, in the manner of Bachelard's philosophy of the 'non', and in its rejection of mediatization on the grounds that it is too metaphysical an operation.

It is as a programme for future anthropologists and epistemologists that we must read Lévi-Strauss's ambiguous or ironic summons to guard against any regression to the Specific, a summons whose history we know, and which we can also see reflected in that enigmatic and decentring mirror where the schema of the earth-oven reigns over several realms and where Kant, majestically and ironically eluding the logic of the Same and the rational and transcendental universality of the categories and principles, suddenly presents us with the fragile and evanescent adumbrations of schemata that can free us from the traps of Specificity and Hereness:

This schematism of our understanding in regard to phenomena and their mere form is an art, hidden in the depths of the human soul, whose true modes of action we shall only with difficulty discover and unveil. Thus much only can we say: The *image* is a product of the empirical faculty of the productive imagination – the *schema* of sensuous conceptions (of figures in space, for example) is a product, and, as it were a monogram of the pure imagination *a priori*, whereby and according to which images first become possible, which, however, can be connected with the conception only mediately by means of the schema which they indicate, and are in themselves never fully adequate to it. On the other hand, the schema of a pure conception of the understanding is something that cannot be reduced into any image . . .[53]

To which *L'Homme nu* adds the following telling rejoinder: 'The myth is never of its own language; it provides a perspective of another language and the mythologist who apprehends it through a translation does not feel that he is in an essentially different situation from that of the local narrator or auditor.' Or again: 'To tell the truth, there never exists an original text:

every myth is a translation; it originates in another myth from a neighbouring but alien population, or in an earlier myth of the same population, or else it may be contemporary but appertain to another social subdivision. . . .'[54]

We could extend this tangled web even further: as Blanchot has put it so admirably, the discourse is infinite.

7. Conclusion.
The Site of Structure:
Heraclitus, Kant, and Hölderlin

'The work of Kant remains like a still unconquered fortress behind the new front line.'

Hölderlin

What then is the site of structure? It oscillates as we have seen between, on the one hand, the pole of a Leibnizian combinatory, a syntactic matrix, the logic of 'any' object whose range Michel Serres has shown us in his four *Hermes* books (discovering it even in the arcana of the living and in the constantly shifting rules of contemporary interdisciplinarity), and on the other hand the diffracted, disseminated pole of a dispersion into elements whose aleatory distributions Deleuze and Guattari have so poetically described, in spite of their propensity for a mystical materialism. Structuralism constitutes the most fertile epistemological break that the philosophy and human sciences of our time have known, carving out for itself a territory of knowledge in which the figurations of the imaginary, *set up by the network of the symbolic* and generated by the resourcefulness of tropes, ally themselves with the mathematical intuitions of the discontinuous and the relational so as to postulate, in accordance with diverse variants and in sites of which we have given some examples, a new relation between a formal syntax and a deep semantic process which simultaneously corrupts and constitutes in the 'real' the individual arrangements of this syntax, i.e. structures.

Bringing about a subversion of the classical ideological notions of subjectivity based upon the *cogito* and announcing, on the contrary, that the subject is caught in and cloven by the symbolic order, structuralism continually inquires what is the site of structure.

But before giving a full answer to this question, we shall first recapitulate some of structuralism's distinctive features, which will enable us to attack the ideological misinterpretations that this pluralist method of research has generated in current opinion, because of certain fears of fetishizing attachments to cherished metaphysical notions such as subjectivity and meaning ('sens') to which the structural approach was considered harmful.

First let it be said that there is no domain that is structuralism's private property and that like Hermes, the exchanger, the God of the merchants and of crossroads, or the Eros of the Platonic *Symposium*, it is always found in diverse fields of knowledge where its methodology can be put into practice, through bringing to light combinatory arrangements and relationships which constitute configurations and provide the rules for understanding them. Since the structural approach is motivated by the study of the diverse ways in which the parts of any given whole combine among themselves, what really counts, as Jean Pouillon writes, 'is less the objective arrangement than its mode of combination. In addition, to speak of one "mode" presupposes that there are others and structuralism subsequently established itself by drawing the conclusions of this plurality.'[1]

A corollary arises from this. Structuralism is not and cannot be reductionist, as it has been accused of being. It is, on the contrary, the most productive means for delivering us from what may without exaggeration be called the positivist hallucination. 'Form is defined in opposition to a content that is foreign to it; but structure has no content: it is the content itself apprehended in a logical organization conceived of as the property of the real.'[2]

Far from mutilitating and reducing reality, the notion of

structure, because it transgresses the traditional opposition between form and content, enables one to uncode all aspects of the human reality that it analyses. Structuralism's ambition is not, in fact, to reach a point where all meaning has been exhausted, which would mean falling into the substantialist trap once more; on the contrary, a structural approach, whether its object be a literary text, the organization of kinship systems or the arrangements of the signifiers in a dream, remains a strategy that freely admits that its uncoding principle is *local* and not global. This closure or deliberate limitation of its field enables structuralism to undergo modifications as a function of new and open relationships which are brought to light and which can be integrated into the homogeneity of the previously delimited and axiomatized field. If it can thus be conceded to the Sartre of *The Critique of Dialectical Reason* that authentic structuralism is in essence totalizing, it should be immediately added that these totalities are unstable, shifting and relational, i.e. they do not provide the real inner framework of the object under study, but by being a relational strategy they lay themselves open from the outset to being worked upon by a principle of difference, singularity and imbalance that ceaselessly modifies them, suggesting, in a manner more musical than mathematical, as Lévi-Strauss has pointed out, borrowings, readjustments and modes of generation that are continuously remodelled. Structure reveals the principle of dissymmetry and deviance which threatens the equilibrium and harmony of its syntactic arrangements from within, and at the same time enables its types of organization to inscribe themselves in reality. Through the inscription of the dynamic effects of dissymmetry and difference, structuralism, whose methodological gains had been reductively caricatured as nothing more than dry skeletons, enables one to construct models of the real in all its living diversity and to pass from the level of an *Ars combinatoria* to that of an *analysis situs*, thereby covering, thanks to the principle of dissymmetry, the whole field of congruence of the Leibnizian method of which structuralism, contesting the positions of Cartesianism, is the contemporary illustration. As Jean Pouillon says:

By seeing in structure the means of bringing to light different wholes as variants of one another, the question of the relationship between these wholes was left open. It may be a purely conceptual relationship – two societies of the same type providing alternative although independent solutions of the same problem. On the other hand, a real relationship might exist – the groups under consideration being akin, and their respective systems of organization so many dialects of the same ideological language; here the type becomes a family. Finally it may be a matter of successive states of the same whole where structure is the rule of historically real transformations, the explanation of the functioning and future state of the entity. In other words to speak of a combinatory and of variants in no way implies that the former does not conform to a regulated orientation nor that the order of the latter is undetermined or reversible and of no importance. It is therefore of no use abandoning structural analyses so as to describe the dynamism that prevents things from always remaining in the same state.[3]

The dilemma between static structuralism and a dynamics that structuralism has supposedly left to one side is thus a false dilemma. As we have shown in relation to *L'Homme nu*, the inscription of discrepancies and divergencies in structurality is enough to account for the dynamics of variation and changes, without their being any need to postulate any kind of outside force that would rehabilitate a sort of Bergsonian substantialism. Structuralism, to this extent, remains entirely Leibnizian. Similarly, the false charge that has been levied at structuralism for apparently ignoring the diachronic by unduly emphasizing the synchronic does not hold, once it is recognized that structuralism postulates different levels of organization whose interrelations enable one to account for the constitution and composition of the states of a system as well as their disaggregation.

We shall not however follow Jean Pouillon along the road of an ecumenicism that allows him to integrate Marxist contradictions as manipulated by Sartre in the *Critique of Dialectical Reason* into structuralism, for the latter on the contrary has thoroughly exhausted the obsolescent notion of contradiction because it is too bound to a linear notion of negativity the logical relation which goes under the name of contradiction. The logos of contradiction is in fact axiomatized by structuralism to the point of destruction.

But the fact remains that structuralism embraces a problematic of the relations between the interstructural wholes that accounts in clear enough terms for changes and transitions, as Lévi-Strauss has shown, without any need to postulate the existence of a transcendent force obeying the laws of a substantialist dynamics, whether the latter be called infrastructural historical reality or Desire.

'The structural interpretation' writes Lévi-Strauss 'can account both for itself and for others. For inasmuch as it consists in making explicit a system of relationships that other variants only embodied, it integrates them into itself and itself into them on a new level where the definitive fusion of base and form takes place and which is therefore not open to new embodiments. In an act of self-disclosure, the structure of myth puts an end to its own fulfilments.'[4]

It should be noted that in its localized action, structuralism reproduces, but in a combinatory fashion, the aims of what Hegel called absolute knowledge. But to the extent that this self-revelation of structure, comparable to the self-reflection of absolute knowledge, produces structurality as dependent on the ultimate operator or virtual image (which here is the earth-oven, the operator of the structural organization of myths dealing with the origins of fire), then one can say that if on the plane of knowledge structurality gives access to a local syntactic transparency, then on the plane of 'being', on the contrary, structuralism does not arrive at any exhaustive account that would permit one to postulate some profound causality as being obvious. Here we are faced with the Kantian distinction between phenomena and things-in-themselves. Structure is an instrument of elucidation, revealing the fertile relationship between the mind that decodes and the analysed phenomenon. It even presupposes a congruence or profound correlation between these two terms. But to forget that it is a relational and epistemological grid, a heuristic operator, so as to make it an operator of reality that would let itself be reabsorbed back into the solidness of an ontology, achieving the status of a thing-in-itself, would be to re-integrate structuralism into the domain of dogmatic meta-physics. Structuralism's wager is in fact to allow the structural operator to subsist in that 'metastable' state of being the organ-izing principle of a relationship of adequacy between the decoded real and the decoding subject, with no recourse to ontology. Here too, as with Newton, *Hypotheses non fingo*.

A correlative of this mistrust towards everything that might bring it back into the fold of an ontology is the necessary modesty that imprints structural methodology with that fertile stamp of deafness to the solicitations of a causalist dynamism.

Authentic structuralism strives above all to grasp the intrinsic properties of certain types of order. These properties do not express anything that is exterior to them. Or, if one absolutely wishes them to refer to something external, one would have to turn towards cerebral organization conceived as a network whose most diverse ideological systems translate given properties in the terms of a particular structure, with each one in its own way revealing different modes of interconnection.[5]

Biology seems to have understood this lesson, since the research work on the neurophysiology of the brain conducted in particular by Jerry Lettvin of MIT accords to the structure of the Leibnizian *Monadology* more than the scope of an isomorphism between it and the structure of the systems of interconnection in the neurons; here we have the fertility of a model which constitutes a veritable *explanans* for neurophysiology.

But if we want to keep on the path of what Lévi-Strauss has called 'philosophical prudence', enabling one to avoid the trap of reductive interpretations, we should recognize in the ex-clusion of any extrinsic explanatory principle by Lévi-Straussian structuralism, i.e. the expulsion of all substantialisms, a gesture convergent with Lacan's recognition of the *unconscious* as order of the symbolic. Seen as the product of a lack, it dismisses causalist and substantialist interpretations of desire. Jung provides an example of the latter which Freudian structuralism revealing once more its affinity with anthropology, preserves us from. The expulsion of subjectivity thus functions as a necessary methodological prerequisite for the opening of that problematic of relationships and the discontinuous – of the *analysis situs*. Subjectivity, which would encumber the field of the syntactico-semantic arrangements of structurality, constitutes an epistemological obstacle which the structural revolution has enabled us to remove by axiomatization; or by expulsion through effacement in Lévi-Strauss, pulverization in Lacan and elision in Althusser.

With the point of no return reached by the structural episteme in our age has come the necessity of passing from a theologico-existentialist problematic of subjectivity to a problematic of the *trope*, to the deep generative structure whose semantico-syntactic articulation accounts for both the combinations of systems and their functioning in structural 'reality'.

The problem of a point of anchorage seems to have been resolved by Chomsky through rehabilitating the Cartesian *cogito* as a support for the innate ideas constituted by deep structures. We have seen that this entails a kind of fetishism which overcompensates for the absence which structural theory in linguistics had left in the place of the subject. However, we may still pose the question of a site for structurality (metaphorically understood), even though we have accepted the lesson of the diffraction of subjectivity given to us by the Freudian/Lacanian unconscious.

It is with great philosophical prudence that we shall ask this question of the site of structural generation, and of the structural adequation between the heuristic grasp of a cognitive subject upon a phenomenal object. This necessary evacuation of the dogmatic role of a human subject of a substantialist type can be helped by a reading of Kant, by the precautions he takes in positing a formal subject, a juridical 'I think', and not a substantialist one as was the case with Descartes. But as structural anthropology as well as Freudian psychoanalysis show us, this subject is diffracted and caught in the symbolic order, in the structures which pervade, regulate and express themselves through it. The subject then is just a point or stroke upon a mobile and dynamic graph, and so we cannot grant it the epistemological and philosophical supremacy in which the Copernican revolution enthroned it. A Ptolemaic revolution has come about with the advent of the structural episteme, which, far from reinstalling dogmatism and empiricism, has had the effect of causing, as a correlate of structurality, *the deposition of His Majesty the Subject.*

Thus from Kant we shall retain the form of philosophical cautiousness, without abiding by its content, namely, the critique of substantialism (that may be used against Chomskyism) and the phenomenon/noumenon distinction that has the function in Lévi-Strauss of manifesting a necessary epistemological distrust against a dynamics that would cause the structural mechanisms from somewhere 'behind' or 'beyond' structure. J. T. Desanti is asking us to observe a similar epistemological prudence in his fine book *La Philosophie silencieuse* when he suggests that we accept only the propositions of a *weak* and modest materialist epistemology, that is, of an epistemology resigned to being able to 'speak of the apparatus of knowledge only through its own products; and in the domain of the products there is nothing that may give us knowledge of the apparatus itself.'[6] Here too, *Hypotheses non fingo* is the rule when faced with such fearsome questions as: 'What is the mode of relation between the structure that underlies mathematical theory and the system of physical objects themselves?' or 'In what way may the ideal structures that the *mathesis* handles in its explicit systems of notation concern other types of structure to the point of making their regulatory laws explicit (e.g. the group structure invested in the physical structure of crystals)?'

The practice of the structuralist approach in the domain of the human sciences, in which the congruence of the heuristic instrument of the structural figuration and the structures of the object itself are visible, must *a fortiori* remain modest and keep itself from ontologizing structure through forgetting its nature as an operational rule, whose status we are reminded of in Lévi-

Strauss's analysis of the incest taboo or in Freud and Lacan's analysis of Oedipus. It is through refusing to yield to the seductions of a heavy-handed and dogmatic materialist epistemology, à la Engels, that one may avoid the stumbling blocks of a teleological and pre-established harmony. Structuralism, with Serres, puts us on the road to that harmony, but without any recourse to pre-establishment, and indeed we see in the precautions that characterize structural epistemology, as well in the contemporary epistemology of the physico-mathematical sciences, a certain fidelity to the critical intuitions of Kant.

The point of no return, the irreversibility of the structural episteme, in fact consists in dissociating epistemology from the philosophies of consciousness and the subject which continue to occupy and encumber the terrain of knowledge. As Desanti emphasizes in discussing physics and mathematics, only a philosophy of the concept can act as a foundation for a theory of science. We would add that this does not exclude a problematic of the trope, whose semantico-syntactic excess, we have seen, irrevocably confirms a type of fidelity on the part of structuralism to a Kantianism in which the dogmas of a fetishizing positivistic rationality are fortunately threatened.

We may also adopt the programme assigned to the weak materialist epistemology of Desanti, namely, 'bringing to light, within the explicitly constructed corpus of the statements of a science, the contextual relations in accordance with which the objects bound up in the statements are redistributed.'

Then comes a task based on genetics: 'Once having discerned the system of operations and the fields of objects that effectively function in the apparent discourse, the question arises of knowing how they were accomplished and what preconstituted instruments enabled one to deal with them.'

'Finally,' adds Desanti, 'there is the question of the task of criticism.' We may even say that the fidelity of structuralism to the structural dynamics of Leibniz's combinatory networks and to the analyses of the *analysis situs* enable it to fulfil these epistemological tasks, in conjunction with the 'exact' sciences. This is not much perhaps, but inside the limits we have certainly drawn, the tools of structural criticism enable an invaluable intensity to be achieved.

That is why we are surprised to see others using Kant's lesson for different purposes. Instead of recognizing in the fertility of Kantian philosophical cautiousness the origin of the breaks and divisions which constitute structural intelligence in our age and the richness of the applications arising from its methodological rigour, certain thinkers – due to the heartfelt chagrin caused by the expulsion of the human subject, that unbearable Narcissus in the field of contemporary ideology – make the presence of the Kantian terms 'moral faith' or 'practical faith' a pretext for reimporting into the empty site where man once stood a divine subject who comes to light in the light of structurality. The death of man for these theoreticians points to the return of theistic affirmations, which though fideistic are none the less subter- raneously assertoric, even dogmatic. There would be no crime committed here, and one cannot help being seduced by the closeness of the Foucauldian notions of the death of man and the subsequent modifications in the concept of history (which in *L'Archéologie du savoir* would dispense with the double support of a pre-existing meaning) to the Pascalian position of a Jansenist God who does not intervene in history with the nagging vulgarity of a Teilhardian immanentism with which Garaudian Marxists, if there are still any left, and so-called progressive Christians have deafened us in the wake of an ill- digested existentialism and a finalist Marxism. The sensitive God of the *Mémorial* appears to us personally not at all incom- patible with a philosophy of history purged of all finalist meta- physics and of the philosophy of the subject, whether the latter be the Hegelian *Geist*, the proletariat, or the masses labouring in their praxis.

But we would like to register our disagreement with an extrapolation that would lead from the illuminating adoration of this Jansenist God to the banishment of any philosophical problematic. Such an obliterating gesture seems to us to signify undue despair towards philosophy at a time when a firmly established structuralist episteme, purging all metaphysics, finally enables us to restore to *philosophical fiction* both its grasp on the knowledge that it calls into question with Kantian critical modesty and the glittering brilliance of its figurative sources. The latter comes close to the honour rendered by Pascal to the trope, as well as to Kantian schematism, that admirable *speculum in enigmate*. At a time when the absurd rationality/irrationality division is finally relativized thanks to structuralism, and when science admits to owing its conceptual resourcefulness to an archetypal imaginary order, to a basic topological figuration which, now de-ontologized, restores the Baroque metaphor to its rightful position, some have thrown their hands up in despair, and under the pretext that a Pascalian God has visited us when, at a loss, we were faced with the void left by our humanist and anthropotheological idols – now finally spurned – have tried to persuade us that we should gladly sink into an ineffable faith and renounce all philosophy, when we were just on the point of rediscovering its 'part maudite', its figurative sources, the tropological and structural ones of its *Begriffdichtung*.

Let us therefore reread Pascal. His advice that we should not mix up or telescope the different orders together – for then the invaluable fabric of the symbolic on which the figures of speech circulate would, through a reductionist gesture, be abolished – this advice, revealing a generosity towards the symbolic, to the absence and presence of figuration, has never had such urgency. Those who have somewhat hastily been baptized as new Pascals, so eager were they to speak to us once more of God, would do well to meditate upon this. Clear and distinct ideas should not be confused with a rush to smuggle the Holy Face into the meshes and gaps of structure, to see Jesus Christ in the place of the Other of the Lacanian unconscious. And this precipitancy misses its target twice over. First, in asking us to give a guilty conscience to philosophical discourse in its entirety, it cheapens the unprecedented wealth of the structural episteme which has been established in the past ten years, joining up with the *Grammar* of Port Royal, the tropes of Du Marsais, the network of the Leibnizian combinatory, with the Baroque and the figurative wit of the English metaphysical poets, with everything that Cartesianism and its by-product, Lockean empiricism, had repressed in our culture. Some have wanted to shut off the structural episteme's rediscovery of the margins of philosophy as soon as it had been made, whereas it constitutes one of the most important turning points for the philosophy of our era.

The other misfire of this enterprise has more serious consequences for the supporters of that neo-fideistic indiscretion, because it affects the very status of the God they claim to find everywhere in the emptiness and gaps of structure and the symbolic. The Pascalian God, the God of the *Mémorial*, of Abraham, Isaac and Jacob, the God responsive to the heart (that same heart where mathematical truths are inscribed, an intuition which by itself forms one order in the Pascalian poetry composed of difference and meditation, and not of vulgar immediacy), this God is more discrete than you say, for he is a hidden God, a *Deus absconditus*, modest, reserved and not exhibitionist.

You turn him into a meddlesome and obtrusive God who is frantically everywhere at once, even in linguistics and psychoanalysis, a gadfly of the marketplace, who blesses even your most personal trivia and anoints that Narcissism come back onto the ruins of Man, the narcissism of your own contingency. Echoing Nietzsche, we may say that it is time we rung out peals of laughter so as to chase away this interventionist and untutored God.

Deus absconditus; the phrase implies both absence and presence. Pascal has never been of such actuality in structuralism, on condition though that the various orders are not confused, and that a neo-substantialism is not produced through an act of intellectual stroboscopy which at times would re-establish Desire and its Bergsonian energetics, and at others the immediate and exposed God of the oratory.

But as we, personally, do not have the good fortune to receive illuminating visions, we shall modestly continue to remain attentive to the activity of tropes within structure, to that empty space and gap drilled by the semantic order into that of the combinatory articulations of the syntactic, and which implants the tropes and circuits of metaphor and metonymy, not in an anthropomorphic ontology, but in the *silence* of an otherness whose principle, born with Heraclitus and the sophists, still poses to the logos, even in its dialectic form, the pressing problem of a non-mediatizable and non-dialectic negativity.

We have seen that excess of difference and negativity which in an a-topic way both subverts structural syntax and constitutes its pregnancy in the epistemic 'real', in the element of dissymmetry active within the Lévi-Straussian structure. We have also recognized it in Oedipus when the latter reveals, through the incision of castration and the gaps in specular desire, that the subject is missing from its place. We have been able to connect this structure with that of *Verneinung* or denial such as Freud thought it. In it there is also inscribed, as a kind of witness, the radical dissymmetry which articulates Eros and Thanatos together, and which cannot be predicated by a logos of identity or of dialectical contradiction.

It remains for us to bring this structure into relation with a primary operator seen by Lévi-Strauss as having the same status as the prohibition of incest, and this non-formal and non-substantial universal is the archetypal image he proposes in the figure of the earth-oven:

The anticipated image of the earth-oven, offered by the myths of the origin of fire, thus finds itself, in relation to a real object, turned upside down like the image of an object placed outside a camera obscura, and whose light rays form up and cross over so as to penetrate inside by passing through the aperture. In the spatial order this corresponds to that prominent event which, in the time of myth, determines the passage from the state of nature to the state of society.[7]

If we have drawn a parallel between that function of the incest taboo as an exceptional passage from nature to culture, the enigmatic source of an opposition it transgresses, and Lacan's definition of the unconscious as the site of misappreciations and disavowals, it is to see the fecundity of the structural approach inasmuch as it is active in man as a signifying function, as articulating a combinatory syntax of signs (in myths for example), and as a profound semantic which corrupts it and whose effects Chomskyanism, in spite of its self-reproaches, has missed by forgetting the question of the unconscious.

Better still: the schema of the earth-oven as the surface emblem of a concealed universal operator opens up towards a topology which would be the 'truth' of structuralism, as the work of Thom and Petitot on morphogenesis show in the formulation of its problematic, upon the bases of structuralism whose axioms they integrate. This 'truth' henceforth becomes an insistent one, rooted in those two interconnected sites which together press upon the flanks of scientific rationality, threatening it in the name not of a destructive realism but of a structural poetics of tropes, contesting the difference between positivistic statements and an archetypal imaginary order. The reproach of reductionism has to be levelled against those theories that wished to 'go beyond structuralism' by jumping over the Rubicon and accusing it of being an alienating and dehumanizing system of thought. It is the economistic Marxists and their impenitent humanist confreres who have refused to see the episteme of our era evolve towards that enigmatic site where a liberated science rediscovers its roots in the imaginary order, and where a polemical, eristic, and *non-dialectic* thought, i.e. one that is not a slave to any logos, returns in all its splendour. This return, which as we have seen cleaves the syntactic aspect of structuralism in the form of a deep and corrosive semantics, has revealed itself in the empty spaces of the symbolic of the Lacanian unconscious, in that absence/presence borne by the trope. How then, in good faith, can one then accuse structuralism of being a positivistic scientism?

But the enigma of that non-formal and non-substantial universal whose contours Lévi-Straussian structurality has announced in the rediscovery of the mythic invariant of the earth-oven joins up with what in Kant goes beyond rationality and pure Reason, inscribing the trace of a deep semantics whose impact, thanks to repression, the Freudian unconscious has discovered once more. It is in *transcendental schematism* in effect,

to the extent that it outflanks and goes beyond the trans-
cendentality of reason towards the depths of the imagination,
that the enigmatic and Baroque activity of tropes is produced
and the possibility emerges of a general theory of the figurations
of language, one that would also be a structural poetics whose
importance had been felt by Jakobson before the metaphysical
errings of Chomskyanism.

Heidegger was able to take note of this aberrant trajectory of
transcendental schematism in pure Reason and its system. The
schema, which transgresses the difference between the perceptible and the intelligible, does more in fact than merely tie
together intuition and category, a pure concept of the understanding. In spite of that twist which Heidegger persists in giving
to transcendental schematism, making it constitutive of ontological knowledge ('Transcendental schematism is henceforth
the base for any intrinsic possibility of ontological knowledge'[8]),
it always slips away towards an 'originality' that is not part of
being, and from where the *eristic and polemical* spring into
action, even though it was the whole of pure reason's mission to
subdue them, thereby playing into the hands of the logos. But
this function of the schema, once de-ontologized, has priority
over and always exceeds any attempted recuperation by the
rational and transcendental. Not only is the scheme the ancestor
of structure, and the schematism of pure reason the site of
figurative generation for structurality ('On the contrary, the
schema of a pure concept of the understanding is something that
cannot be put into any image'[9]), but schematism, inasmuch as it
gestures towards the abyss of pure imagination, prior to any
empirical intuition, also appears as the absent source, the
Lacanian 'manque à sa place', from where tropes are unfolded
and a topology generated whose functions, detached from their
heraldic and figurative emblematics, consist of invariables of the
movement 'disconnection of the connected, disconnection of the
disconnected, or connection of the disconnected', as Serres has
shown.

These topological and tropological invariants join up with the
most advanced positions of modern mathematics as well as with

the sites of a body with its basic drives that is always caught in the space of the symbolic. At the same time they bear witness to the permanence of the return of a suppressed Heracliteanism, whose principles of separation, as we have said, go beyond the logos and thus the dialectic. Deleuze and Guattari saw this in *L'Anti-Oedipe*, but like Hume, who pulled his boat on to dry land just to let it rot there, they have inserted this polytopy into a materialist ontology, instead of giving a free rein to its symbolic faculty, which is made up of lack and the labour of Thanatos. The ambiguity of Kantian thought thus consists in letting this excess skid off towards something other than metaphysics which, in spite of all the efforts of the critique, still grips Kantian thought in the matrix of identity and presence.

Transcendental schematism as the site of a decentred origin of structurality therefore gestures towards that heterogeneity and heterotopy in which we would not wish to see a theism emerge, confusing and putting a stop to the various orders. What in fact would have been the good of successfully problematizing the notions of contradiction and the dialectic to the point of ruptural dilaceration, and within the structural episteme which marks a point of no return, if it were just to reimport, in the figure of the great Other, the activity of an indiscrete God? Let us here reiterate those reservations which Lévi-Strauss expresses at the end of *L'Homme nu* with respect to this return of the theism of presence, of that God who is more hackneyed than hidden.

There can be no question, therefore, under these new colours, of surreptitiously reintroducing the subject. We would show no indulgence towards that imposture that would swap the left hand for the right, so as to give to philosophy under the table what it claims to have withheld from it on top, and which, by simply replacing the ego by the Other and slipping the metaphysics of desire under the logic of the concept, would take away the latter's foundations. For by replacing the ego by an anonymous Other on the one hand and on the other by an individualized desire (otherwise it would not designate anything), one cannot hide the fact that it would only be necessary to stick them together again and turn them around so as to find on the other side that ego whose abolition had been so noisily proclaimed.[10]

We too are not predisposed to any conjuring trick that would take with the one hand what has been conceded by the other. On the contrary we would rather postulate that the *heterogeneous is not situated in the 'elsewhere' of structure*, but that it is constitutive of structurality itself, in accordance with a certain otherness which, outflanking dialectical contradiction, is conceived of in the apparent bizarreness of Kantian schematism. Kant writes:

This schematism of the pure understanding which is relative to phenomena and their simple form signifies an art hidden in the depths of the human soul, the nature and secrets of which it would indeed be difficult to extract. All that we may say, is that the image is a product of the empirical faculty of the productive imagination, whereas the schema of perceptible concepts (like figures in space) is a product, and in a way a monogram of the pure 'a priori' imagination, by means of which images are first made possible; and that these images can only be bound to the concept by means of the schema they designate, does not mean that they are, in themselves, perfectly adequate to the latter. On the contrary, the schema of a pure concept of the understanding is something that can be reduced to no image.[11]

In our study of Lévi-Strauss we have already said how this text functions in perfect congruence with the analysis of myths, installing the heterogeneous and displaced aspects of structure in the very heart of structurality, and analogous to that extent with the mode of action of the earth-oven, which is an invariant at variance with itself, being both a simple and ubiquitous element as well as a principle of disruption and contestation of the order it establishes: an inaugural displacement which informs a logic whose negativities are no longer mediatizable and exceed the dialectic through the dilacerated polytopy of its structural network. This Kantian challenge, liberated from the suffocating ontology of Heidegger's interpretations, may also serve as a programme for the *schizologic* of the unconscious and for that enigmatic operator which we have recognized in Oedipus, namely, heterotopy.

The heterogeneous is thus at the core of structural thought, as well as of the body which structuralism had been accused of shutting out. 'In reality,' writes Lévi-Strauss, 'the structural analysis which some debase to the level of a decadent and gratuitous game can emerge in the mind only because its model is already in the body.'[12] We shall thus leave as a new frontier for structuralism the study of that unparalleled relationship between the structurality of the symbolic body and biology's recognition of the living as a type of language.

This opening up of structure towards a heterogeneity whose constant effect is to inscribe the corrupting activity of a deep semantics, made up of displacement, lack and dissymmetry, upon syntax and the combinatory, forces one back *to a presocratic dawn* when the logos had not started to pin down the unpredictable heterogeneity of the Discord whose poetics Heraclitus described within the meshes of Parmenidean ontology. It is because we consider that structuralist activity cannot be surpassed, for it is composed equally of an expending element as of a positive combinatory, that the possibility of a return of Heraclitus, that great and repressed other, may be proclaimed by our modernity in the wake of Nietzsche and Freud.

Heraclitus, Kant, Hölderlin, these are the names which mark the road towards the discovery of a structuralism that can be neither surpassed nor bypassed – for it recognizes the activity of lack, of a non-mediatizable negativity at the very heart of the function of the symbolic, as the driving force of its trajectory. It is not a question of stifling the scientific and heuristic progress of localized, fruitful, structuralist activity under the pretensions of a new dogmatic philosophy. Our reading of Pascal has given sufficient warning of the dangers of mixing up the various orders. Nevertheless, it should be noticed that the abrupt rise of this structuralist episteme has brought with it a certain number of ideological and philosophical after-effects which it has seemed opportune to confront with those thinkers who in the singular extremity of their poetics are capable of contesting the logos.

And it is to the very extent that these texts are written into the margins of the philosophy of the logos they corrupt and subvert that they may meet up with structuralism, casting a light upon it so that it reveals still further, through the enigmatic function of the symbolic, its impatience with that logos. These thinkers of heterogeneity open up a new space for philosophy, a new frontier whose challenge, in this presocratic dawn that Western thought has finally reached, is so rich in potential for poetic knowledge. Today, the prophets of a supposed death of philosophy appear ridiculous, as do the pessimists who multiply their raucous warnings against a nihilism that apparently hangs over us all, because we have dared lay our hands on a sacrosanct dialectic, on a moribund and embalmed Marxism. Ridiculous, because these pea-brained thinkers confess to their fear of letting things slip through their fingers. Thrifty with themselves and their concepts, these resentful and straitjacketing 'thinkers' do not wish to see the immensity of the challenge that philosophy has before it, starting from the new bases from which the Parmenidean, Platonic, metaphysical and dialectical logos must absent itself.

'The equilibrium of the universe can only be maintained if change in one direction leads to change in another, that is, if there is incessant *struggle* between the antagonists.' Such fragments from Heraclitus act today as a signal, as that which we must confront beyond the ruins of the dialectical logos. Some have only wished to read in this combat, this strife (the term which Marvell uses in 'To his coy mistress' provides a good image of that savage coition connoted by the Greek *polemos*), a state of *contradiction* upon which the whole genealogy of the dialectical logos has been constructed. Only Freud has produced an opening through which we now glimpse in the enigmatic relation of Eros and Thanatos, interdependent and antagonistic, constituting the symbolic, the force of the Heraclitean *polemos*, of that *Eris* also, that discord which has nothing to do with the dialectic and which upholds the rights of the heterogeneous in the heart of the symbolic. An endless war of contraries clasping each other in an intimate embrace. The thought of Asia is returning, an Asia not yet contaminated by the Hegelian and Marxian dialectic.

In a letter to Johann Georg Hamann, Hölderlin writes of Kant:

Kant is the Moses of our nation; he has dragged it from an Egyptian stupor and led it into the liberating desert of his speculations; he has brought down from the holy mount the abiding law. Doubtlessly they continue to dance around their golden calves and they sorely miss their homely comforts; they should indeed emigrate in the full sense of the word, that is, attain a solitude in order to decide to stop being the slaves of their bodies, to abandon the dead customs and opinions, soulless and empty of meaning, under which, almost inaudible, and deeply incarcerated, groans what is best in their living nature.[13]

Unlike Heidegger, we have not sought in Kant the support of any ontology. It is too early to speak of Being and to be swallowed up by it. Or perhaps too late – who knows? With Hölderlin we are made aware of the profound relationship between the Kantian categorical imperative and the *categorical withdrawal*, as Hölderlin names it, by which the Father has turned his face away from men, 'but continuing to labour uneasily, above our heads, up there, in a completely different world.' And so we may become attentively vigilant through this tragic (*Trauerspiel*) mission fallen to man's lot, which is to remain, as Beaufret says, through his own withdrawal, the guardian of the divine withdrawal: this vigilance, in our reading of structural thought, is exerted against the re-importation of a deified Man, against the indiscrete intrusions of a fideistic God who is a little too close to the phase of 'intuitive representation'. There is no intellectual intuition, Kant tells us, and in his attentiveness to *separation*, a fidelity to the separation inherent in Heraclitean thought may be read.[14] This notion of separation is at work in the distinction between the phenomenon and the thing-in-itself, which we have seen re-emerge in the problematic of structurality, as a 'real' selection out of the possibilities of a combinatory:structure is like the phenomenon, beyond which it would be vain to try and find a kind of Ur-structure, a metastructure of metastructures, a fundamental and primary structure, written into being, *cui nihil majus cogitari possit*. Lévi-Strauss remains the guardian of this Kantian distinction of the phenomenon and of the structure of the thing-in-itself. 'There is no real close to mythical analysis, no secret unity that one may grasp at the end of the work of de-composition. The themes split and divide to infinity . . . Rays with no other source save a virtual one', as Jacques Derrida has written. But as for the supposed blind alleys into which one may be led by according structure, in spite of this virtuality, a heur-istic pertinence, we have seen in our chapter 'The Art of the Fugue' how the reflections contained in *L'Homme nu* enabled them to be resolved, by seeking support in the Kantian dis-tinction between the phenomenon and the thing-in-itself, and by inaugurating through the enigma of the earth-oven as radical operator common to the series of the *Mythologiques*, the thought of the schema. It is Lévi-Straussian structuralism which takes us to the text of 'transcendental schematism' whose enigmatic marginality and profound centrality surpass the economy of the Kantian Critique and open on the one side upon the lack, dissymmetry and displacement that constitute the symbolic (as Lacan says), and on the other upon the problem-atic of that singular, spatial apparatus that the topology and catastrophe theory of René Thom are in the process of inventing.

To conclude, it is thus at this point of Hölderlin's poetry that this unprecedented convergence, borne by the ideology of the structural episteme, takes place between Heraclitean separation, exceeding the logos and the dialectic, and Kantian schematism, opening up for the symbolic the resourcefulness of its arche-typal enigma, to the extent that Hölderlin, ever sensitive to the tragic dimension of Oedipus, foreshadows that of the Freudian Oedipus, and is the first in modern times to pose the problem of the split in the human subject whose scope Lacan rediscovers in his specular analysis:

At this limit, man forgets himself, because he is entirely within that moment; and God because he is nothing more than time; and on both sides there is infidelity : time, because at such a moment it categorically turns aside, and because in it *beginning and end* no longer allow themselves to be coupled together like rhymes; man, because within this moment he must follow that categorical turning aside, and so subsequently, he can in no way consider himself as equal to the initial situation.

Desire, through which the subject is missing from its place, tells of nothing more than this split: 'The presentation of the tragic depends principally on this. That the unendurable (how God and Man join together, how, with all limits abolished, the flustered power of nature and the innermost part of man become passionately One) thought of as the One boundless future purified through a boundless separation.'

Such, in the thinking of Hölderlin, is the emblem of a modernity which, skirting the traps of the substantialisms and totalitarianisms of the logoi, and freely assuming its loss, its spent force and its lack as constitutive, would engage in a new dialogue with the presocratics, in which each phrase would have to be re-invented.

Notes

Notes to Chapter 1

1 See Lévi-Strauss, in *Word, Journal of the Linguistic Circle of New York*, vol. I, no. 2, August 1945, pp. 1–21, and 'Language and the Analysis of Social Laws', *American Anthropologist*, vol. 53, no. 2, April–June 1951, pp. 155–63. Both these articles constitute chapters of Lévi-Strauss's *L'Anthropologie structurale*.

2 Author's translation.

3 Lévi-Strauss, *L'Anthropologie structurale*, p. 74.

4 Cf. my article, 'Le métier de Pénélope or the loom of language', in *Circuit/Cambridge Opinion*, Summer 1969, pp. 39–42.

5 See in particular, *Méthodologie économique* (Paris: P.U.F., 1955); *La mathématique sociale du Marquis de Condorcet* (Paris: P.U.F., 1956); *Pensée formelle et sciences de l'homme* (Paris: Aubier, 1967); *Essai d'une philosophie du style* (Paris: Armand Colin, 1968). The quotation following is from *Pensée formelle et sciences de l'homme*, pp. 3–4.

6 Roland Barthes, *Critique et vérité*, Collection Tel Quel
. (Paris: 1966), p. 50.

7 ibid, pp. 51–2.

8 See *Les Mots et les choses* and *L'Archéologie du savoir*.

9 I develop this thesis in a more extended way in my *Marx est mort* (Paris: Gallimard, 1970).

10   A grievance of this kind, however frequent, always surprises me. It is as if the empiricist failed to understand that the fecundity and relevance of a theory or system lie precisely in the need to discard certain deviant facts at the outset and incorporate them only at a more mature stage. Descartes proclaimed: 'As to Galileo's experiments I deny them all.' More relevant to an English critic is the case of Newton, father of experimental (though not empiricist) physics, who deliberately discarded the 'troubling' planets that were deviant elements in his new-born theory.

11   See my interview with Chomsky in *La Quinzaine littéraire*, no. 74, 1–15 June 1969.

12   'Knowledge of Language', in the *Times Literary Supplement*, 15 May 1969.

13   ibid.

14   Edmund Leach, *Lévi-Strauss* (London: Fontana, 1970), p. 27.

15   ibid, p. 120.

Notes to Chapter 2

1   *L'Idéologie allemande* (Paris: Editions Sociales), pp. 35–6.

2   Editions Galilée.

3   Jean-Marie Benoist, *Marx est mort* (Paris: Gallimard, 1970).

4   Philippe Sollers, *Sur le matérialisme* (Paris: Seuil, 1974), pp. 121–57, 'Sur la contradiction'.

5   What Althusser credits Marx with is having founded a new territory, of having opened up a new continent, the science of the history of social formations. As is known, the opening up of this new epistemological continent is distinguished by a break. Let us return to this notion of the break that is reminiscent of the functioning of the epistemological break that the Copernican revolution represented for Kant. For Althusser the scope of the Marxian revolution is the equivalent of the epistemological break produced

by the foundation of mathematics by the Greeks or of physics by Galileo. The opening up of the historical continent is all the more interesting, as a continent when it opens itself up to knowledge is never empty or virgin, but is already occupied by diverse ideologies or disciplines having one trait in common, that of their ignorance of being in this new continent. The epistemological break that produces this new continent can therefore be compared to a Copernican revolution which instead of basing itself on the subject, *a parte subjecti*, tries to base itself on the object, *a parte objecti*. Let us note in passing the kinship that Althusser's thought bears with that of Spinoza, for whom the idea envelops its own capacity to be affirmed. And the same applies here where the discovery of the new epistemological continent, far from introducing a subject of cognition, bases itself on the object known.

By what ideological formations was the continent recognized by Marx as history, that is historical materialism, occupied? By the philosophy of history, political economy, all formations caught in the field of ideology.

The epistemological break achieved by Marx was to produce the science of history. But it should be noted before examining this recourse of a positivist nature to scientific-ness, that an epistemological break after the fashion of the Copernican revolution is not an isolated moment but a continual process of theoretical elaboration which is at the same time that of a liberation.

Althusser is therefore attentive to the philosophical product of any great scientific transformation. Any great scientific transformation produces in effect a corresponding transformation in the field of philosophy. Let us note here the introduction of a generative schema that poses the scientific as deep structure in contrast to a surface structure that would have either a philosophical or ideological nature. In this particular case one would speak of a philosophy, since in some way it is a question of a true ideology. But unlike the theoreticians of the automatic and mechanistic reflection, Althusser introduces the effectivity of a generative process which is none other than a productive process of transformation comparable to that which opens new scientific continents.

Curiously, and without according much importance to the axiomatic revolution which he doubtless includes in the field of each of the continents or regional ontologies that he announces, Althusser posits the three principal continents as being:

(1) mathematics, which was reflected in philosophy by Platonic thought;

(2) physics, which gave birth to the Cartesian transformation in philosophy;

(3) history, which with the historical materialism of Marx brought about a philosophical revolution that has to be appreciated in the light of the *XIth Thesis on Feuerbach*: 'Philosophers have only interpreted the world in various ways. The point is to change it.' Chomsky used these theses in his *Russell Lectures*, perhaps confirming the possibility of thinking together the theory of change in its theoretical practice and in Marx. We shall return to this point, but it seems to us that the major obstacle here is the presence of those social sciences that occupy the field of the historical continent: it can be compared to the survival of Aristotelian physics fifty years after the epistemological break of Galileo.

The state of denial in which bourgeois philosophy has kept Marx and Lenin works for Althusser as an occultation or denial of the scientificness of historical materialism which he hopes will be lifted to the profit both of political truth and of dialectical materialism.

6 In effect, with Marx a *different* dialectic is produced. The production of this other theatre of the dialectic tool is twice subordinated to a logic of truth: first, by the scientific truth accorded to the end product, historical materialism, and

secondly by the presupposition that within the mystical husk of Hegelian dialectical idealism there would be a kernel of truth or a sort of rational base. These two concessions to a logic of truth perhaps reintegrate Althusserian dogmas into the field of Western metaphysics which thereby seems scarcely to have budged an inch since Parmenides, Plato and Aristotle.

But what our attention is drawn to here is the *dual effect* of this transformation by which the instrument of transformation is transformed through its own labour. The importance accorded by Lenin to Hegel can then be understood to the extent that he grasped the essential moment of transformation. But we would like to assimilate it to the workings of psychoanalytical desire which, not content with changing objects in a process which could be that, for example, of sublimation, itself undergoes a transformation in its nature. In any case this would be the level of the second effect of Freudianism in the Althusserian problematic, and the importance that Althusser gives to the following confession of Marx would have been impossible without the Lacanian return to Freud: 'When I was writing the first volume of *Capital*, the mediocre and pretentious epigones who dictate their laws to Germany referred to Hegel in the same way that Mendelssohn did to Spinoza, as a filthy cur. That is why, 'adds Marx with a provocative smile, 'I shall *flirt* with Hegel and declare myself his great disciple; I am going to "Kokettieren" with his ways'.

This transformation of the dialectic in the performance of its own labour is reminiscent of the change brought about by Rousseau in the *Social Contract*, which is nothing less than a change of *modus essendi* as well as a radical transformation of problematic through an unprecedented contract that has the property of generating one of its terms – the political body as association not existing before the contractual act. . . . A change in the *modus essendi* of the human aggregation which through that extraordinary moment of the contract becomes an association, and a change in problematic, for a new continent has been conquered for political science. Neither Hobbes nor Locke, for whom the contract consisted in an abdication or a delegation, were able to generate this radical change.

7   Louis Althusser, 'Contradiction and Overdetermination' in *For Marx* (London: Allen Lane, 1969), p. 99.

8   ibid, pp. 97–8.

9   Jean-Marie Benoist, *Tyrannie du logos* (Paris: Minuit, 1975).

10 L. Althusser, *Eléments d'autocritique* (Paris: Hachette, 1974), p. 61.

11 Althusser, *For Marx*, op. cit., p. 127.

It should be noted in passing that the Althusserian concern not to let structure be besieged by forces of a substantialist type that would act in the wings and give it a sort of extrinsic causalist dynamism is structuralist through and through, whatever he might say.

12 ibid, p. 113.

Notes to Chapter 4

1   Jacques Monod, *Le Hasard et la nécessité, essai sur la philosophie naturelle de la Biologie moderne* (Paris: Seuil, 1970), p. 26. (English trans: *Chance and Necessity*.)

2   ibid., p. 27.

3   ibid., p. 135.

4   ibid.

5   ibid., p. 150.

6   ibid., p. 22.

7   ibid., p. 27.

8   ibid., p. 32.

9   Surprising because it accords nothing to the transcendental already conceived by Kant as a non-substantial and formal subject, nor to scientific practice as labour.

10 Monod, op. cit., p. 191.

11 Michel Foucault, *L'Archéologie du savoir*, Bibliothèque des sciences humaines (Paris: Gallimard, 1969).

Notes to Chapter 5

1 Gaston Bachelard, *La Philosophie du non*, 4th edition (Paris: P.U.F., 1966), p. 135.
2 Jean-Marie Benoist, *Marx est mort* (Paris: Gallimard, 1970), chapter 6, p. 21, pp. 215, 234, 242 *et seq.*
3 Bachelard, op. cit., pp. 136–7.
4 Author's italics.
5 Bachelard, op. cit., p. 138.
6 ibid.
7 ibid., p. 145.
8 Michel Serres, *Hermès ou la communication* (Paris: Minuit, 1969).
9 Jean Piaget, *Structuralism* (London: Routledge and Kegan Paul, 1971).
10 ibid., p. 5.
11 ibid., p. 124.
12 Jacques Derrida, *passim.*
13 Cf. *Tyrannie du logos* (Paris: Minuit, 1975).
14 Cf. André Green, *Un Oeil en trop* (Paris: Minuit, 1969).
15 Jean-Marie Benoist, 'La Glande et le rêve', an essay on the fictional procedures of Descartes, in preparation.
16 *Histoire de la folie à l'age classique* (Paris: Plon, 1964), p. 57.
17 See the chapter 'The Art of the Fugue'.
18 *Tyrannie du logos*, op. cit.
19 Lacan, *Ecrits* (Paris: Seuil, 1966), p. 99.
20 Deleuze-Guattari, *Capitalisme et schizophrénie*, *L'Anti-Oedipe* (Paris: Minuit, 1972).
21 ibid., pp. 63–4.
22 ibid.
23 ibid., p. 65.
24 ibid., p. 66.

25 ibid., p. 71.
26 ibid., p. 161.
27 ibid., p. 203.
28 ibid., p. 204.
29 ibid., p. 205.
30 ibid., p. 218.
31 Serres, op. cit.
32 Jean Pouillon, *Fétiches sans fétichisme* (Paris: Maspero, 1975), p. 16.
33 Editions de Minuit, 1975.
34 Moustapha Safouan, *Etudes sur l'Oedipe* (Paris: Seuil, 1974).
35 *L'Anti-Oedipe*, op. cit., pp. 98–9.
36 ibid., p. 130.
37 In Lacan, op. cit., pp. 531–83.
38 'Le Sujet en procès: le langage poétique', *Tel Quel*, no 62, summer 1975.
39 Lacan, op. cit., 'Séminaire sur la lettre volée'.
40 ibid., p. 116.
41 ibid., p. 117.
42 Daniel Sibony, *Le Nom et le corps* (Paris: Seuil, 1974), p. 17.
43 *Tyrannie du logos*.

Notes to Chapter 6

1 C. Lévi-Strauss: discussion with R. Bellour, 'Réconcilier le sensible et l'intelligible', in *Le Monde des Livres* (5 November 1971), p. 17.
2 ibid., p. 17.
3 ibid., p. 20.
4 ibid.
5 *L'Homme nu*, p. 32.
6 ibid.
7 ibid., p. 33.
8 ibid., p. 545.

9 J. M. Benoist, 'Structuralism, a new frontier', *Cambridge Review* (22 October 1971).

10 Piaget, *Le Structuralisme* (Paris: P.U.F., 1970). English translation, *Structuralism* (London: Routledge, 1971), pp. 106–19.

11 *L'Homme nu*, p. 561.

12 ibid., p. 555.

13 ibid., p. 539.

14 Lévi-Strauss, *La Pensée sauvage* (Paris: Plon, 1962). English translation, *The Savage Mind* (London: Weidenfeld and Nicolson.

15 *L'Homme nu*, p. 539.

16 ibid.

17 ibid., p. 107.

18 ibid., pp. 589ff.

19 ibid., p. 86.

20 ibid., p. 87.

21 ibid., p. 13.

22 ibid., p. 14.

23 ibid., p. 554.

24 ibid., p. 539.

25 ibid., p. 112.

26 ibid., p. 118.

27 ibid., p. 110.

28 ibid., p. 109.

29 ibid., p. 38, footnote.

30 ibid., p. 577.

31 Cf. Gérard Granel, *L'Equivoque ontologique de la pensée kantienne* (Paris: Gallimard, 1970).

32 Lévi-Strauss, 'Race et histoire', in *Médiations* (Paris: Gonthier, 1968).

33 *The Savage Mind*, p. 232.

34 ibid., p. 234.

35 ibid., pp. 243, 244.

36 ibid., pp. 245–69.

37 ibid., p. 250.

38 ibid., p. 256.

39   ibid.
40   ibid., p. 268.
41   ibid., p. 247.
42   ibid., p. 247f.
43   ibid., p. 249.
44   *L'Homme nu*, p. 542.
45   ibid., p. 543.
46   ibid.
47   ibid., p. 542.
48   ibid., p. 543.
49   ibid., p. 542.
50   J. L. Borges, *Fictions*, new edition (Paris: 1968).
51   Michel Serres, *Hermès ou la communication*, and *Hermès II: l'interférence* (Paris: Minuit, 1972).
52   Bernaud Pautrat, *Versions du soleil* (Paris: Seuil, 1972).
53   Kant, *Critique of Pure Reason*, 'Of the Schematism of the Pure Conception of the Understanding', Meiklejohn's translation, p. 109ff.
54   *L'Homme nu*, p. 576.

Notes to Chapter 7

1   Jean Pouillon, *Fétiches sans fétichisme* (Paris: Maspero, 1975), p. 20 in 'Structure, un essai de définition'.
2   Cl. Levi-Strauss, 'L'analyse morphologique des contes russes', 1960, quoted by Pouillon, op. cit., p. 22.
3   ibid., p. 23.
4   *L'Homme nu*, op. cit., 'finale', p. 561.
5   ibid., p. 561.
6   See the chapter 'Matérialisme et épistémologie, in *La Philosophie silencieuse* (Paris: Seuil, 1975).
7   *L'Homme nu*, p. 556.
8   *Kant et le problème de la métaphysique* (Paris: Gallimard, 1953), p. 166.
9   ibid., p. 160.
10 *L'Homme nu*, p. 563.